HEINEMANN SCHOOL MANAGEMENT

Using Assessment for School Improvement

by
Mary James

Heinemann Educational Publishers
Halley Court, Jordan Hill, Oxford OX2 8EJ
a division of Reed Educational & Professional Publishing Ltd

OXFORD   FLORENCE   PRAGUE   MADRID
ATHENS   MELBOURNE   AUCKLAND
KUALA LUMPUR   SINGAPORE   TOKYO
IBADAN   NAIROBI   KAMPALA   JOHANNESBURG
GABORONE   PORTSMOUTH NH (US)   CHICAGO
MEXICO CITY   SÃO PAULO

Heinemann is a registered trademark of Reed Educational & Professional Publishing Ltd

© Mary James 1998

First published 1998

02 01 00 99 98
10 9 8 7 6 5 4 3 2 1

British Library Cataloguing in Publication Data

ISBN 0 435 80046 9

Typeset and illustrated by ⁊ Tek-Art, Croydon, Surrey
Printed and bound in Great Britain by Biddles Ltd, Guildford

Acknowledgements
The publishers would like to thank the following for permission to reproduce copyright material: The American Educational Research Association for the extract from 'Meaning and values in test validation', by Samuel Messick, in *Educational Researcher* 18 (2), 1989, pp.5–11, copyright 1989 by the American Educational Research Association, reprinted by permission of the publisher on pp.155–6; The Association of Assessment Inspectors and Advisers (AAIA) for the extracts from the AAIA's *Members' Handbook*, 1996–7, on p.37, and from *Teacher Assessment in Action*, 1996, p.103; Carfax Publishing Limited (PO Box 25, Abingdon, Oxfordshire, OX14 3UE) for the extract from 'Assessment and Classroom Learning', by Black and Wiliams, in *Assessment in Education* 5 (1), 1988, on pp.101–2; Cassell Plc for the extract on p.195, reproduced from 'Personal-social education and the whole curriculum', by Chris Watkins, in R. Best et al. (eds) *Pastoral Care and Personal-social Education*, 1995, by permission of Cassell Plc, Wellington House, 125 Strand, London, England; Paul Chapman Publishing Ltd for the data from *Enhancing Quality in Assessment*, by Wynne Harlen, 1994, p.143, on p.167; David Higham Associates for the extracts from *Matilda*, by Roald Dahl, on p.222; HMSO for extracts from its publications on pp.29, 60, 70, 225: Crown copyright is reproduced with the permission of the Controller of Her Majesty's Stationery Office; The Institute of Directors for the extract from their press release of 14/8/97, on p.146; extracts from 'Formative assessment and the design of instructional systems', by D. Royce Sadler, in *Instructional Science* vol. 18, 1989, pp.119–44 is reproduced on pp.172 and 173 with the kind permission of Kluwer Academic Publishers; The National Council for Educational Technology for the extracts from *Using IT for assessment: key issues*, 1995, on pp.232–3; The National Foundation for Educational Research (NFER) for the extract from *Hitting the Targets*, by I. Schagen and P. Weston (et al.), 1997, on p.259; The Open University Press for the extracts from *Competence-Based Assessment*, by Alison Wolf, 1995, on pp.147–8; Richard Pring for the extract from his article 'Personal Development', on p.33; The Qualifications and Curriculum Authority (QCA) for the extracts on pp. 57, 63, 72–3, 77, 188; Suffolk Local Education Authority for the extracts from their 1997 report on pp.51 and 52; Routledge Journals for the extracts from 'Why criterion-referenced assessment is unlikely to improve learning', by Mary Simpson, in *The Curriculum Journal*, 1990, pp.171–83, on p.182; Dylan Wiliam, for the extract from his article 'Some technical issues in assessment' on p.158.

The publishers have made every effort to contact copyright holders. However, if any material has been incorrectly acknowledged, the publishers would be pleased to correct this at the earliest opportunity.

Contents

	Introduction	1
	Who this book is for and its aims	1
	How to use this book	2
1	**Whole school assessment policy**	**5**
	A backwards glance	5
	Evidence from OFSTED reports: the nineties	9
	What constitutes assessment, recording and reporting?	14
	Policy development as a process of change	16
	Further reading	21
	Activities	21
2	**First principles**	**23**
	Policy as more than the sum of practices	23
	Developing a rationale	23
	Purposes of assessment, recording and reporting	24
	Principles for policy	31
	Principles into practice	35
	Principles as criteria for evaluation	39
	Activities	40
3	**External expectations, with special reference to Key Stage 3**	**43**
	Constraints and possibilities	43
	Sources of information on external expectations	45
	Transfer from Key Stage 2	48
	Statutory assessment	54
	Other requirements related to Key Stage 3 assessment, recording and reporting	65
	Matters of professional judgement	66
	Further reading	68
	Activity	68
4	**The 14–19 scenario**	**70**
	A new and distinct phase of education?	70
	Mapping the pathways	71
	Key Stage 3 meets Key Stage 4	72
	Vocational meets academic	76

Contents

Route planning	81
Further reading	83
Activity	84

5 *Types of assessment 1:* Assessments made in the course of teaching — 85
Introduction — 85
Assessment as part of classroom process — 86
Routine marking of classwork and homework — 94
Further reading — 103
Activities — 104

6 *Types of assessment 2:* Periodic tests and assessment tasks — 106
Introduction — 106
The limitations of end-of-unit assessment — 107
What form of test or task? — 108
Authentic assessment tasks: an important alternative — 115
Are special assessments for summative purposes really necessary? — 122
Activity — 123

7 *Types of assessment 3:* Standardised tests and examinations — 125
Introduction — 125
Standardised tests — 126
Test construction — 132
Test administration — 134
Interpretation of test results — 135
Explaining and drawing implications from test results — 138
Examinations — 142
Norm-referencing and traditional examinations — 143
Criterion-referencing and vocational qualifications — 146
Further reading — 149
Activity — 150

8 Creating confidence in assessments — 151
What makes a 'good' assessment? — 151
Validity — 151
Reliability — 157
The relationship between reliability and validity — 158
Implications for schools — 160
Further reading — 167
Activity — 168

Contents

9	**Assessment, learning and the involvement of students**	**171**
	Assessment *of* learning or assessment *for* learning?	171
	Formative assessment	172
	The involvement of students in assessment	173
	Formative assessment and theories of learning	179
	Distinguishing formative from summative assessment	183
	Using evidence appropriately to improve performance	185
	Linking formative and summative assessment	186
	Developing this new approach	189
	Further reading	189
	Activities	190
10	**Doing justice to all the educational achievements of all students**	**192**
	Justice as fairness	192
	Beyond subjects: assessing the 'whole child'	192
	Ensuring that assessments provide equality of opportunity	200
	Further reading	209
	Activities	210
11	**Manageable recording and meaningful reporting**	**212**
	Process and product	212
	Teachers' everyday records	214
	Reports to parents	219
	Discussions with parents	223
	Lessons to be learned from SEN reviews and IEPs	226
	The National Record of Achievement	227
	The use of information technology	230
	Activities	233
12	**Using assessment data for monitoring and target setting**	**236**
	Archery across the curriculum	236
	National targets	237
	Measures of school effectiveness	238
	Performance indicators	238
	Ways of analysing assessment data	244
	Target setting in schools	252
	From the 'What' to the 'How'	257
	Further reading	260
	Activities	260
	Index	**263**

This book is dedicated to the memory of Professor Desmond Nuttall who was one of the country's finest researchers in the field of assessment. His foremost concern was that assessments should be fair to students and enhance, rather than diminish, the quality of their lives. In my last conversation with him, one month before his early death, he suggested that I should write this book for teachers. I have tried to follow his lead.

Mary James
Cambridge, October 1997

Introduction

Who this book is for and its aims

This book has a very specific aim. It has been written to help those who have responsibility for school policy on assessment, recording and reporting – and those who advise and support them – to develop and implement effective systems at school level which promote good practice at classroom level. The principal idea is that assessment processes should be put to work for school improvement by assisting schools and teachers in helping students to learn, thereby increasing their achievements.

In particular, the book has the needs and circumstances of secondary schools in England and Wales in mind, although many of the ideas and much of the advice will have relevance in other places and to other phases of education. Depending on the way in which responsibilities are allocated in particular schools, it is likely to be of special interest to headteachers, deputies, assessment co-ordinators, key stage co-ordinators and heads of faculties or departments. Local authority advisers, consultants and lecturers from higher education who support schools in the development of policy and practice will also find this a source of ideas.

Developing assessment strategies and methods

The motivation to write a book on ways of developing assessment policy and practice came from a perception that, despite a burgeoning literature on assessment, and new national and local expectations concerning assessment, recording and reporting, teachers and school managers still lack confidence, experience and expertise in this area. This seems surprising since marking pupils' work, providing feedback, creating internal tests and examinations, using standardised tests, administering national tests and examinations and writing reports on pupils' achievements, is a substantial proportion of the job of every secondary school teacher. However, until recently, few teachers received much in the way of initial training in assessment strategies and methods. This situation is changing but for older generations of teachers, and notably those who now hold senior positions in schools, the foundations of their assessment practice may be somewhat shaky.

Why something so fundamental to teachers' practice should have been so neglected is difficult to explain but it may be because of the way that teacher training courses were structured in the past. It may also have had something to do with an assumption, supported and maintained by commercial interests, that 'real' assessment was the job of test development agencies and examinations boards. The job of teachers was therefore confined to administering these tests and examinations. What assessment they did in the privacy of their own classrooms was largely their own affair and technical issues such as validity and reliability were of little account as long as assessments *seemed* to serve the purposes for which they were used.

This state of affairs is, of course, no longer tenable. New forms of certification at 16 and 18, National Curriculum assessment and OFSTED inspection, all require that teachers think more deeply about what they do in terms of assessment, and that schools co-ordinate assessment practice in coherent and manageable ways.

■ Assessment practice and whole school policy

Given this background, this book is written to help teachers understand and make decisions about the important questions in assessment practice at classroom level, but it is framed with regard to a need to develop whole school policy. It looks at ways in which ideas can be developed in practice in the social culture of schools. For this reason it has two parallel foci: assessment issues and development issues. This dual emphasis has given the book its particular structure which combines general discussion and illustration of issues with practical activities that can be used for staff development.

■ How to use this book

I have chosen to begin with two chapters that tackle directly the need for schools to develop whole school policy in order to provide a coherent framework within which departments and teachers can locate their own practice. Ostensibly this looks a bit 'top down' but it is premised on an assumption that no school will start with a clean slate.

All schools already have a lot of assessment going on and the most urgent question is about bringing different practices together in a way that makes sense and is purposeful. What is needed is a set of criteria to decide which practices need to change, which need to be retained and what more needs to be introduced. These criteria need to be developed at school level, so this book starts there, although managers need to recognise that they will really be working at the point where 'top down' meets 'bottom up'. This is likely to entail a great deal of talking, listening, discussion, persuasion, negotiation and, probably, a certain amount of compromise.

Creating a general framework

The first two chapters provide schools with a way of creating a general framework for policy and practice. Inevitably any policy for assessment, recording and reporting will have to encompass a great deal of the work of any school. A second assumption therefore is that it is unrealistic to expect any school, however advanced in its thinking and existing practice, to have every aspect in place and working effectively in a short space of time. The hurried production of a seemingly detailed and comprehensive policy document, perhaps in preparation for an OFSTED inspection, is no guarantee that policy will be implemented rapidly.

More effective in my view is the development of a framework of principles, or criteria, from which the details of policy in particular areas can be worked out in a phased manner. This allows a certain amount of trialing of procedures which is a necessary part of any development process. It is also infinitely more manageable than an all-or-nothing approach and is less demanding of already busy staff. The fragmentation of policy can, however, be avoided because development in particular areas, such as marking policy, reports to parents or the utilisation of assessment results, should be in line with the policy framework.

I suggest therefore that the reader begins with Chapters 1 and 2 because these set the scene and propose strategies for establishing a policy framework. Thereafter, chapters may be chosen according to the school's priorities for development. They are ordered in a way to provide a logical sequence and some readers may prefer to follow the development of ideas that this represents. However, this is not essential; each chapter has a coherent theme of its own and links across chapters are provided through cross-referencing.

Staff development activities

At the end of each chapter there are suggestions for practical staff development activities. Many of these could be incorporated into the five professional development days that every school is currently obliged to plan each year. Indeed, if the school has chosen to make assessment policy and practice the focus of its school development plan, these activities might provide the foundation for a coherent programme of development. For this reason, senior managers might chose to look at the activities first in order to decide which themes and issues should be tackled as a priority in their school. This will then provide them with a strategy for using the book.

In addition to practical activities, most chapters are concluded by annotated references to further reading. These may be of particular interest to teachers who are engaged in courses of further professional development and academic study. Taken together the collection constitutes a small but fairly comprehensive library of reference material on the range of issues in educational assessment.

1 Whole school assessment policy

■ A backwards glance

The development of assessment, recording and reporting policy is not an area where we can expect to start from scratch. Taken-for-granted assumptions need to be tackled in order to make progress. Not everything will need to be discarded but familiar practices will need to be examined afresh to see whether they stand up to the claims made for them. Are assessments really used to plan next steps in students' learning? Do marks and grades mean anything to the learners who receive them? What kinds of achievement are really valued? Are professional judgements consistent across a group of colleagues? Do reports really tell parents what they want or need to know? And so on. The list of questions is potentially enormous.

■ An anecdote: assessment in the seventies

In 1974 I took up my third teaching post in secondary schools. In my first week, I was presented with a staff handbook. It contained a short section entitled 'School assessment policy' which baldly stated that, 'it is school policy to mark students' work using a five-point A–E scale'. There was nothing more. At the time I saw no problem with this and I duly started to grade classwork and homework according to whether I judged that a student's work was very good (A), good (B), average (C), below average (D), or very poor (E). In my head I had some image of the bell-curve of normal distribution, gleaned no doubt from some psychology lecture in my initial training, so I determined that the majority of my students (about 40 per cent) should be awarded Cs, smaller proportions should get Bs (20 per cent) and Ds (20 per cent), and the remainder would probably have As and Es. I was quite confident about this way of marking students' work because I thought it was a 'scientific' thing to do.

However, when I handed back to students my first set of marking I found myself facing a rebellion. I discovered that their previous teacher had used marks primarily to 'motivate' students! She had therefore chosen to ignore the bottom three grades in the school's agreed five-point scale but extended the top two to create her own ten-point scale: A++, A+, A, A−, A− −, B++, B+, B, B−, B− −. She had used marks to reward rather than to grade students; so my mark of C for what I considered to be an 'average' piece of work was interpreted as a punishment and therefore hurtful.

What this trivial example illustrates is that I and my colleagues had no *explicit and shared understanding* about *why* we were assessing students. Had we been asked about purposes, a majority of us might have said that assessment provided us with a means of checking what students had assimilated of our teaching, which helped us to identify gaps to be filled. It also provided us with a mark book full of grades that we could scan for an overall achievement grade to transfer to twice-yearly reports for parents. And, for older students, it provided us with a means of predicting approximate grade levels in 16+ examinations so that we could satisfy ourselves and others that we had entered students for an appropriate examination. If I am honest, I would probably also admit that assessment was sometimes used effectively as a control mechanism: a class test, for example, was a useful way of ensuring a peaceful lesson!

If it is true that we thought little about *why* we were assessing, we thought only fractionally more deeply about *what* and *how* we were assessing. The predominant emphasis in the courses that I taught was on the acquisition of knowledge and most of the assessment, both internal and through external examination, involved information recall. However, by the mid-1970s, the influence of CSE and early proposals for a common system of examining at 16+ were encouraging assessment of understanding through the application of knowledge. Process skills of data-handling were also being given more prominence in a number of traditionally content-heavy subjects, such as science, history and geography.

At the time, much of this debate passed me by and most of my classroom assessments remained directed towards finding out what factual knowledge students had acquired in my lessons. The 'marking' of written work was the dominant mode and I assessed through setting exercises, essays, notes and short-answer tests. I always considered group and class discussion to be an important context for teaching and learning but it never occurred to me at the time that oral skills or collaborative learning should be formally assessed in what was then my subject area (social studies/sociology), although I knew that oral assessment was carried out in English and modern languages, and other forms of 'outcome' were assessed in the 'practical' subjects.

In accordance with my school's 'policy', I used the A–E grades for an overall judgement of the quality of a piece of work, although I usually added some narrative comment to this as well as correcting major errors. For the most part, staff at my school combined 'impression marking' for essays with the use of more formal marking schemes for structured tasks. Students' work could therefore acquire an A–E grade by the scaling of numerical marks, for example, out of ten or twenty. Occasionally, students were asked to mark their own work but always using a strict marking scheme of 'correct' answers that the teacher had devised. Marking was mostly done by teachers away from the students, in the staff room, in 'non-contact' periods, or at home, and handed back to students in the next lesson.

Most teachers supplemented this routine assessment with periodic class tests, half-termly or at the end of a syllabus theme. Formal internal examinations were also conducted once or twice a year when results were invariably given in the form of percentages. All these assessment activities were entirely teacher-controlled.

Although these *marking practices* were widespread across the school in which I worked, and they were mostly in line with what had been stated as school policy, they did not add up to a *whole school policy for assessment, recording and reporting*. Assessment, recording and reporting involve a much broader range of activities than marking, although this is one element. More importantly, the concept of *whole school policy* implies that agreed practices are promulgated on the basis of an articulated *rationale* which encompasses clearly-stated *purposes, principles and procedures* derived from shared educational *aims and values*.

An early NFER study: assessment in the eighties

An apparent confusion of *policy* with *practice* presented a major difficulty for researchers at the National Foundation for Educational Research (NFER) who, in 1984, published what is still probably the only empirical study of school assessment policies *per se*[1].

The study was based on a survey of assessment of eleven to fourteen year olds in 97 middle and secondary schools, supplemented by three case studies. Findings indicated that two-thirds of headteachers claimed to have written policies or were embarked on developing one. This claim was supported by classroom teachers although a high proportion said

---

[1] Engel-Cough, E., Davis, P. with Sumner, R. (1984) *Assessing Pupils: a study of policy and practice*. Windsor: NFER/Nelson.

that they had not actually read the document! Moreover, when invited, only fourteen schools sent copies of their policies to the researchers. Scrutiny of these revealed them to be very simple and limited to specifying the use of five-point scales for grading ability, attainment or effort, based on an assumption of 'normal distribution' and a perceived need to compare the performances of individuals within a year group or set. In other words these policies were little different from the 'policy' I was presented with in 1974. If school policies existed at all:

- they were not clearly articulated in terms of purposes and principles;
- if written down, they merely encompassed formulae for marking students' work and synthesising continuous and periodic assessments;
- they focused principally on a perceived need for comparative data for grading and comparing the performance of students;
- they fulfilled a need to maintain an internal record-keeping system although the purpose of this was not altogether clear.

An interesting issue is whether a school policy, by definition, has to be written down. The NFER researchers referred to some schools having 'implicit' policies and it is possible to imagine a school whose way of working reveals that a particular policy is consistently implemented even if it has not been formalised in documentation. Conversely, as this study revealed, schools can possess policy documents without much evidence that they are read by staff or put into practice.

More recent developments in assessment

Of course, a great deal has happened since the early 1980s to change the situation that the NFER researchers observed. New forms of 16+ examination and certification have been introduced: GCSE in England and Wales and Standard Grade in Scotland, together with NVQs and GNVQs and their Scottish equivalents.

Many schools were involved in a large pilot of records of achievement in the late 1980s which was followed by the introduction of the National Record of Achievement for all school leavers. At the same time many schools, local authorities and examining boards developed graded assessment schemes although these were somewhat overtaken by the introduction of National Curriculum assessment throughout the 5–16 age range in England and Wales. Scotland and Northern Ireland now have their own arrangements. A Code of Practice on assessment and provision for children with special educational needs has been introduced nationally. Within England, the introduction of OFSTED inspections has also had a powerful impact.

Collectively, all these developments have forced or encouraged schools to give more attention to the development of school-level policies and to make them more explicit, more comprehensive and more coherent. In other words there has been increased recognition that whole-school assessment policy needs to:

- clarify and make explicit the purpose of various assessment procedures;
- bring about some rationalisation of all forms of assessment and recording that exist in schools, with reference to a set of coherent principles;
- define the scope and nature of assessment practice.

Have assessment policies progressed?

It would be easy to conclude that, given the current level of interest in assessment, most schools are now well on the way to achieving their goals of policy development. It would be interesting therefore to repeat the study that the NFER carried out in order to see what has changed. Obviously this would require both time and funds to do the job properly but some limited investigation is possible by scrutinising the evidence presented in OFSTED reports on individual schools. In preparation for writing this chapter I carried out my own small-scale investigation.

Evidence from OFSTED reports: the nineties

In the first four-yearly cycle of OFSTED inspections (1992–6), inspection teams were asked to report specifically on the quality of assessment, recording and reporting in schools (section 7.2 in Part 2 of the 1995 *Framework for the inspection of schools*). Soon after publication, reports are made available from OFSTED via the Internet. This made it possible to select a sample of the most recent reports and extract the sections on assessment, recording and reporting. I chose twenty reports from nineteen secondary schools and one middle school in twenty different local authorities. The inspections to which they referred were all carried out between April 1994 and October 1995, although most were carried out in 1995.

In 1995 the OFSTED Framework required that all reports should include evaluation of:

- the accuracy and consistency of assessment, including the marking of students' work, and a judgement of the extent to which assessment of the work of individual students is used to promote higher standards;
- arrangements for assessing and recording students' achievements and progress;
- whether the school complies with the requirements for recording National Curriculum assessments and with requirements for students with statements of special educational needs;
- the extent to which the school analyses any data in order to improve students' performance.

Recurrent themes and issues regarding assessment policy

The sections of the reports generally made interesting reading. Apart from the requirement to cover the areas specified, there was no fixed format for reporting within sections, so it was not possible to compare OFSTED reports in precise quantitative ways – for instance, by stating a proportion of schools with written policy documents. However, even a provisional content analysis revealed some clear, recurrent themes and issues:

1 The majority of schools had assessment policies of some description although these were sometimes restricted to 'marking' policies.

2 There was evidence that many of these policies were recently written and were more in the nature of 'statements of intent' than operational guidelines. Probably this was an indication of the flurry of policy-writing activity that has characterised many schools' preparations for OFSTED inspection.

3 Some policies were clearly based on a consideration of rationale and principles but others were simply guidance or prescriptions for practice. They indicated what should be done but not why.

4 In *all* schools, inspectors noted inconsistency in the implementation of assessment policies across subject departments, and often within departments as well. The most frequent criticism in all reports concerned the variability in teachers' assessment practice, particularly regarding marking.

5 Inconsistency in policy and practice between key stages was also noted. Assessment, recording and reporting in sixth forms was generally detailed, thorough and helpful to students. Also assessment practice in Key Stage 4 was more consistent because planning of work, mark schemes and the checking of standards between teachers was guided by GCSE syllabuses and criteria. But assessment in Key Stage 3 was often underdeveloped.

6 As an element of policy, many schools recommended or required departments to use either a five-point (A–E) grading scale or a seven-point (A–G) grading scale. This encouraged departments to create norm-referenced systems (see Chapter 7 page 132). Rarely was it clear how these grades related to National Curriculum levels and criteria. This meant that students had little understanding of the standards that were expected of them or the progress they were making with regard to the National Curriculum.

7 Comments on students' work, and in reports to parents, were generally very variable in content and quality. Too often, according to the inspectors, narrative comments related to attitude, effort and behaviour but neglected to evaluate learning in terms of knowledge, skills and understanding.

8 There was little evidence of arrangements to ensure consistency of assessment judgements between teachers within departments or across schools, except in relation to the formal arrangements for GCSE. A very small number of schools had made some attempt at moderation and others had begun to collect portfolios of exemplar material but this was not widespread and there was a lack of clarity about how this might be used.

9 Perhaps the most serious criticism was that there was very little evidence that assessment, recording and reporting was being used to monitor students' progress and to inform planning of teaching and learning. This undermined the suggestion that the formative purpose of assessment should be paramount.

10 There was little evidence that records received from primary schools were systematically used for planning progression in students' learning, even where extensive information was received, including samples of students' work and information on National Curriculum attainment levels.

11 In a few schools, student self-assessment, review and action-planning had been introduced, often as a development associated with records

of achievement. Where it occurred, this was generally valued by students although it was still not clear whether it contributed formatively to their learning.

12 Most schools issued a well presented National Record of Achievement to school leavers to which they had contributed. This was valued highly. Some schools also maintained records of achievement or student portfolios lower down the school although these varied in their quality and usefulness.

13 Most schools fulfilled statutory requirements regarding National Curriculum assessments and reports to parents, although the separate reporting of Religious Education was frequently neglected. However reporting formats varied considerably, even within a school, and were sometimes confusing.

14 Most schools had begun to analyse test and examination data but there was still little evidence that such analyses were used to identify areas for improvement. Where such data had proved useful, the analysis usually involved value-added measures using some form of baseline data. In these cases the help of an external agency had sometimes been sought to carry out the analysis, the results of which were then used by headteachers in discussion with department or faculty heads.

15 The schools which attracted the highest praise for their efforts tended to be those where assessment, recording and reporting had been a priority in the school's development plan; where responsibility for development and monitoring had been delegated to a member of senior management, often a deputy head, and where this individual was supported by a cross-faculty or cross-department working group.

A mixed picture

The overall picture that emerges from these OFSTED reports is still very mixed. There is undoubtedly greater awareness of the need for coherent school policy in this area of their work. Clearly many schools have moved a long way from the situation that the NFER study reported (see page 7), although there are still major problems concerning variable practice and lack of the all-important formative dimension. However, there is still evidence that too many schools muddle along with systems that appear to weld practices generated to meet new external demands with older practices that owe more to habit than to any clear rationale. The result is inevitably a Heath Robinson affair.

Implications for school development: support for change

The OFSTED reports were expected to identify key points for action but OFSTED itself concentrated on inspection and distanced itself from the advisory role. Although OFSTED requires schools to develop action plans in response to its reports, it is beyond its remit to support schools in their efforts to improve their practice. Schools have to seek help from elsewhere: from other schools, local advisory services, independent consultants and other in-service providers such as HE institutions. Books and other publications are another source of help.

As indicated in the Introduction on page 2, in the past, very few teacher training programmes have paid much attention to this aspect of professional education. Similarly, advice to secondary school teachers, as they attempt to implement new systems of testing and examination, has not always been supported by practical help from local authorities (because of funding constraints) or from national agencies such as SCAA (because of political and logistical constraints) to the extent that would make a wide and deep impact on secondary teachers' assessment practice.

The contrast with the practical support that was given to teachers of five to seven year olds in the early 1990s is marked. These were in the front-line when the National Curriculum was introduced and the implementation of the assessment and testing arrangements depended entirely on their good will and expertise. As a consequence, infants' teachers may now be the 'experts' in the system: a reversal of the situation when teachers involved in 16+ examinations were regarded as the most knowledgeable on assessment issues.

A thorough rethink

Whilst not wishing to imply that there is little good practice in secondary schools, which is clearly not the case, the evidence from OFSTED reports and elsewhere suggests that there can be no place for complacency. There is much development work still to be done.

The brief analysis of just twenty OFSTED reports provides an agenda of priorities for development and the list of points outlined above is broadly reflected in the chapter headings of this book. However, what is most obviously revealed by these reports is a need, not simply for piecemeal development of separate practices, but to think through, in terms of first principles, the whole of what a school does under the rubric of assessment, recording and reporting. The development of policy on the basis of principles will be the focus of Chapter 2.

What constitutes assessment, recording and reporting?

Often the three words, assessment, recording and reporting, are lumped together with little effort to distinguish between them. This is understandable because some of the familiar language of assessment conflates these separate concepts. For example, when teachers are asked about assessment they often speak about 'marking'. This conflates the processes of gathering evidence about students' learning, evaluating the quality of that learning and identifying achievements and weaknesses, making a record of that evaluation through 'marks' and comments in teachers' mark books or on students' work, and communicating the evaluation to students using marks as the medium.

The need for conceptual clarity

Ordinarily this shorthand for a range of activities is helpful but if we wish to improve practice we may have to be more precise because development may need to focus on particular activities. In the case of 'marking', the kind of evidence used as a basis of assessment judgements may be the issue; or we may be more concerned with the message that the 'marks' communicate to students. In other words we need to 'unpack' the ideas that we sum up by the word 'marking'.

Similarly, without a degree of conceptual clarity, we could put all our eggs into one basket when thinking about what we need to develop in terms of assessment, recording and reporting policy. For example, perceptions of what is involved sometimes focus on the use of tests or the need to create efficient record-keeping systems and neglect equally important areas. At the present time, the scope of assessment, recording and reporting policy can be very wide. In secondary schools it might be expected to provide guidelines to cover all of the following systems, and perhaps more:

What constitutes assessment, recording and reporting? 15

- for marking classwork and homework;
- for formative teacher assessment and student self-assessment and target setting, and for incorporating this into teaching and learning;
- for linking assessment processes and outcomes into curriculum planning;
- for the administration of statutory assessment arrangements and external examinations;
- for continuous assessment, including internal periodic tests and examinations;
- for the use of standardised tests for the purposes of monitoring, diagnosis and as a basis for student grouping;
- for diagnosis, review and the development of individual education plans for children with special educational needs;
- for developing and assuring consistency in teachers' assessment judgements through intra- and inter-school moderation;
- for the development of subject portfolios, or other exemplar materials, to illustrate the standards applied in the assessment of students' work;
- for recording students' performance, including the selection, retention and up-dating of evidence of significant achievements, possibly in the form of teachers' or students' logbooks or individual portfolios of work samples;
- for recording personal experiences, interests and achievements by students towards the creation of a record of achievement;
- for reporting to parents and involving parents in consultation;
- for arranging appropriate access to records by outside agencies with a legitimate interest in students' performance, e.g. education support services, careers officers;
- for the production of transfer documents and records from teacher to teacher and from school to school;
- for the production of the National Record of Achievement;
- for using individual performance data for comparative purposes to determine relative levels of achievement for individuals, groups or the whole school, and for publishing results;

- for using student outcome data for evaluative purposes, e.g. to judge the appropriateness of curriculum provision or the effectiveness of teaching in ways that are valid, fair and helpful;
- for evaluating the effectiveness of all the above.

Assessment as process, not product

Of the eighteen systems identified above, most involve the production of some form of documentation. For this reason, it is easy to equate assessment with record-keeping and reporting and to concentrate most effort on tangible products. This is especially understandable when schools are expected to have documents to show inspectors. But assessment is first and foremost a *process*: it involves seeking data that might shed light on students' achievement, then analysing and interpreting those data and, finally, making judgements about the quality of learning by evaluating the evidence in the light of standards.

Recording and reporting involve processes too, but they are different from assessment in important ways: record-keeping primarily involves the organisation and management of data (marks, grades, comments, examples of work etc.), whereas reporting is about communication.

It is sometimes helpful to think about these distinctions between assessment, recording and reporting. We can then avoid losing sight of the different processes that each of these elements entails even if, in practice, they run together.

This conceptual clarity is important when it comes to developing policy on the basis of principles. If a school decides, for example, that assessment, recording and reporting 'should involve students in order to motivate their learning', staff will need to work out what this principle might mean in the different and separate contexts of (i) assessment, (ii) recording and (iii) reporting. If they take account of only one area, such as reporting, important opportunities might be missed.

Policy development as a process of change

If it is important to recognise that the essence of assessment, recording and reporting lies in processes rather than products, the same is equally true of the concept of policy. It is a mistake to think of policy as documentation, although the question 'Has your school an assessment, recording and reporting policy?' often invites the presentation of a written document. Policy may be enshrined in a document but if it is to warrant the label, it should be evident in the ways of doing things that staff espouse *and* in their practice. The documentation aspect is perhaps better described as 'guidelines' and some schools choose this title for policy documents.

▆▆▆ Documentation: a 'statement of intent'

Realistically, the formulation of a rationale, principles and procedures to guide practice often precedes implementation, which takes considerable time. Evidence that espoused-policy is often ahead of policy-in-practice was indicated in the OFSTED reports that were reviewed. This is not something of which to be ashamed, unless documents are being used as a smoke-screen to disguise the fact that nothing is happening. The OFSTED inspectors perceived this to be the case in some schools, but in others they recognised that the policy documentation constituted a 'statement of intent' which was being worked on and would bear fruit in a reasonable space of time. One school, which was heavily criticised for some of its existing practices, was nevertheless commended because:

> *The school has identified assessment as a priority in its development plan and the recently appointed deputy headteacher has responsibility for leading this. A small working group has met frequently since November 1994 to develop a policy and this has now reached the draft stage. The policy is very much a statement of intent. It raises a number of important principles which are intended to inform practice as it develops across the whole school.*

This extract demonstrates the extent to which the development of whole school policy must be considered as part of school development planning and how important it is to put in place a structure of support to develop policy through the stages of formulation to implementation. However well intentioned, it is never satisfactory for a headteacher, or someone to whom the task has been delegated, to write a policy over the weekend and deliver it in a staff meeting on Monday morning with the expectation that it will be put into practice on Tuesday.

This caricature is, of course, now rarely manifest in schools but it reminds us of the importance of recognising that development of this area, as in other forms of school improvement, is about stimulating change in human systems. For this reason, it is worth revisiting what we know about the nature of educational change and the conditions that favour it, then identifying the implications for the development of school assessment policy.

The nature of educational change

Michael Fullan, a professor in Canada, has drawn our attention to the fact that educational change is not an event but a process. This simple statement reminds us that it takes place over time and is rooted in its own history. The need for change does not arrive 'out of the blue' but arises from former experience. Neither is there any point when we can confidently declare that change is complete; mostly there will be further changes and modifications.

In the modern (or post-modern) world we are learning to accept change as a constant feature in our lives. We also recognise that we really have only two choices: either we adapt to changes that are pressed upon us or we pro-actively initiate or shape changes to our own aims and purposes.

A second major contribution that Michael Fullan has made to our thinking about educational change is to focus attention on *implementation*. This he sees to be the crucial stage in bringing about any change, because a change that is not implemented can hardly be said to have happened at all.

Characteristics of successful implementation

At the beginning of a chapter on implementation in his book, *The New Meaning of Educational Change* (see page 21 for full reference), Michael Fullan quotes, with irony, what an outgoing deputy minister of education said to a colleague:

> Well, the hard work is done. We have the policy passed; now all you have to do is implement it.

But implementation is not a straightforward matter. As Fullan points out, innovations have become more holistic in scope, involving many aspects of the work of a school. They have also become more organic and multi-level and it is no longer possible to treat individual roles or factors as if they operated separately from one another. The relationship between roles or features of an innovation are usually highly dynamic. This is certainly true of the development and implementation of assessment, recording and reporting policy which is likely to reach into every aspect of the work of the school. It will affect teaching and learning in classrooms, school culture and management systems, relations with parents and other schools, the standing of the school in the community, and so on.

In analysing what it is that contributes to successful implementation and, hence, improvement, Fullan identifies six important themes which inter-relate:

Fullan's factors affecting educational change

Vision-building
This gives values, purpose and integrity to the change. It has two dimensions: a shared vision of what the *school* could look like, which provides direction and driving power for change; a shared vision of the *change process* itself, which provides a general strategy for getting there.

Evolutionary planning
Successful schools adapt their plans as they go along to improve the fit between the change and condition in the school so that advantage can be taken of new developments and opportunities. Top-down initiative is also blended with bottom-up participation.

Initiative-taking and empowerment
Power-sharing is crucial. Leaders in successful schools support and stimulate initiative-taking by others. They will set up cross-hierarchical steering groups (often involving parents and students as well as staff) and authority and resources will be devolved to these. In other words, leaders will give up power without losing control in order to promote the development of collaborative work cultures. Continuous pressure to get things done needs to be balanced by support and this is achieved through constant communication, which underlines the fact that change is very much a social process.

Staff development and resource assistance
Staff development is central to successful implementation but intensive pre-implementation training or one-shot workshops are not very helpful. The need is for ongoing, interactive in-service training *during implementation* so that learning of new conceptions, skills and behaviour can be cumulative. Getting over the critical initial hump is important but so is follow-through. Again the chief requirement is 'social energy' because this requires sustained interaction.

Monitoring/problem-coping
This serves two functions: it provides access to good ideas and it helps to weed out mistakes and deal with problems before they get too deeply embedded. Successful schools redesign, create new roles, provide additional assistance and time as problems come to light. This demands a commitment to monitoring which in turn requires openness and trust and a desire to get better results.

Restructuring
This refers to the way the school is organised as a workplace. It might involve making more time for individual and team planning, new teaching arrangements and the creation of new roles.

Implementation of change in the context of assessment

All of Fullan's themes have relevance for a school that is developing assessment, recording and reporting policy because it is likely to involve major change. The way these themes are interpreted in relation to this particular development will vary according to a school's circumstances, but it is possible to translate Fullan's general observation into more specific advice to suit this context. Thus it is probable that the successful development and implementation of whole school assessment policy will require:

- a clear vision of the goals of a school assessment policy;
- a general, strategic plan for development;
- general direction and constant encouragement from the headteacher to get things done;
- delegation of the principal role for orchestrating development to someone, such as a deputy head or senior teacher, who has the authority and who can be given the time and resources to engage in the sustained social interaction that the task will require over a considerable period;
- the setting up of an assessment, recording and reporting working group to be the engine for development and change;
- a commitment to develop an ongoing programme of staff development to support various aspects of policy implementation; this may involve outsiders but an ongoing association with the school would be preferable to one-off in-service sessions;
- a monitoring system to aid problem-detection and problem-solving (or 'problem-coping' which is Fullan's perhaps more realistic term);
- flexibility within the school organisation to alter roles, patterns of working or the distribution of resources.

The chapters that follow deal mainly with issues concerning the substance of assessment, recording and reporting policy, but development is premised on the creation of an institutional structure for development. Thus the activities which conclude each chapter provide ideas for assessment co-ordinators or working groups to work on, or ideas for staff development sessions.

Further reading

If you have not already come across Michael Fullan's seminal book *The New Meaning of Educational Change,* published by Cassell in 1991, you may be interested in reading it as you plan your development strategy. The book synthesises a great deal of research but helpful practical advice can be extrapolated from it. It is also reassuring in that it does not portray successful change as proceeding in tidy, rational sequences but as essentially messy processes that are often quite limited in their achievements.

ACTIVITIES

1 Updating on OFSTED issues

You might like to check whether the analysis of issues arising from OFSTED inspections carried out in 1994–5 (see page 10) still holds good when you come to read this book. This may be important if current concerns have changed because they provide a useful agenda to work on. You can replicate my investigation by using a computer to call up OFSTED reports on the Internet and printing off the relevant section. Until April 1996, reports had a discrete section (7.2) on assessment, recording and reporting. After this date the OFSTED Handbook changed and references to assessment may be found embedded in the following sections: 3.2 Key Indicators; 4.1 Attainment and Progress; 5.1 Teaching; 5.2 Curriculum and Assessment (the main section); 5.4 Support, Guidance and Pupils' Welfare; 5.5 Partnership with Parents and the Community.

Schools in Wales are not inspected by OFSTED; this remains the responsibility of Her Majesty's Chief Inspector of Schools in Wales and HMI. Wales also has its own framework for inspection. The 1996 version retains a discrete section (section 9) on assessment, recording and reporting.

2 Audit of current practice

On the assumption that all schools have existing practices, a useful activity at this point, and a basis for future work, would be to carry out an audit of current assessment, recording and reporting procedures. This could be a task either for the assessment co-ordinator or for members of the working group. It can be carried out at three levels: school-wide procedures; departmental procedures; classroom procedures. In investigating *what* is going on, try to find out *why* because this will give you a clue to the principles that individuals and groups value. As a guide to what to find out about, the following list might be helpful:

▶

- planning for assessment;
- ongoing assessment;
- marking and feedback to students;
- end-of-key-stage assessment;
- recording and evidence;
- reporting to parents and guardians;
- transferring assessment information;
- using assessment results for evaluation;
- how systems are managed.

When you have collected the information, analyse it for similarities, differences and patterns within and across departments (and possibly teachers). Create a priority list of the issues that you think require the most urgent attention. This analytical task can be done by one individual but the exercise would be more powerful if done by a group and shared with all staff, who could be asked to comment upon it and refine it. You will need to be aware of the understandable sensitivities of some staff who may feel they are in danger of being exposed and criticised. A code of practice, negotiated with colleagues, about the ways in which data will be collected and used – e.g. to ensure that the practices of individuals are not identified – may be important.

2 First principles

■ Policy as more than the sum of practices

It is quite common for people to infer that assessment practices that are shared across a school are evidence for the existence of a whole school policy. But it is relatively easy for superficially similar practices to disguise different intentions or uses.

In Chapter 1, I described how a teaching colleague and I interpreted our school's requirement to use an A–E grading scale in quite different ways (see page 5). If a school has an agreed assessment *policy* (as distinct from instructions about what is to be done) this would be less likely to happen because procedures and practices would be underpinned by a shared understanding of purposes and principles. This provides the rationale or justification for the development of specific procedures.

The development of such a rationale should come first. If procedures are already in place which were developed at some earlier point in a school's history without reference to such a rationale, a decision about their continuation should rest on an evaluation of whether they really serve the purposes that are now sought. A rationale gives practices meaning and coherence and therefore defines the sum of the parts.

■ Developing a rationale

At its simplest level, a rationale is a statement of reasons for doing something. In relation to assessment in schools this has two dimensions. The first is concerned with the question of what assessment is for: what *purposes* it is expected to serve. The second is concerned with *principles* that will inform the pursuit of purposes. Both derive from the *values* that individuals or groups of people hold. These determine the goals that are thought to be most worthwhile and ways of achieving them that are considered to be most acceptable or appropriate.

In reality, purposes and principles are often closely linked: statements of purpose often imply certain principles and vice versa. For example, one principle that appears in many school assessment policies is that 'assessment should be integrated with teaching and learning and not regarded as a "bolt-on" activity'. This statement of principle values the contribution that assessment can and should make to the improvement of teaching and learning. By acknowledging the importance of the formative role it is also a statement about purpose. Purposes and principles are not, therefore, entirely discrete although it is sometimes helpful to deal with them separately in order to sort out some confusions. This is what I have chosen to do in what follows.

■ Purposes of assessment, recording and reporting

Most of the key texts on assessment that have been written since the 1970s begin by reviewing the purposes of assessment. This is appropriate because all subsequent decisions about choice of assessment methods should be made on the basis of judgements about 'fitness for purpose'. In order to decide what to assess, how to assess, and who is in the best position to carry it out, it is necessary to be clear about why assessment is thought to be important and what it is supposed to achieve. Most textbook authors offer a list of possible purposes although these usually differ slightly. One of the reasons why each writer seems to come up with a slightly different list of purposes is that the categories overlap. For example, prediction based on grading often leads to specific forms of guidance or selection. The categories can therefore be clustered.

■ Balancing internal and external purposes

One helpful way to view the list is to identify those purposes related primarily to policies *internal* to the school and another cluster relating to those policies that are *external* to the school. For example, diagnosis, feedback to students and teachers, student grouping, curriculum improvement and individual target setting are purposes internal to the school, whilst certification and accountability are purposes largely external to the school.

This is a useful distinction because it can be used to evaluate the balance of assessment activities carried out within a school. In recent years there has been increased external pressure to make schools accountable through the publication of performance tables etc. Thus,

Composite list of commonly quoted purposes

- diagnosis;
- screening;
- allocating resources;
- feedback to students;
- aid to learning;
- target setting;
- feedback to teacher;
- improvement of curriculum planning and teaching;
- grading;
- student grouping;
- transfer information;
- prediction;
- guidance;
- selection;
- certification and accreditation;
- monitoring standards within and across schools and across the educational system as a whole;
- evaluation of programmes of study or the performance of teachers and schools;
- accountability.

there has been new emphasis on assessment data collection for monitoring, evaluation, marketing and accountability purposes. Statutory requirements cannot be avoided and there is a natural tendency to give them priority – to put what *has* to be done first. This can create an imbalance in a school's assessment procedures with internal purposes either sacrificed or made secondary to external purposes. Schools should be watchful of this because their aims for the education of their students are unlikely to be well served if they only pay regard to external demands. Schools' assessment policies require a balance of assessment purposes.

Another way of viewing assessment purposes is to cluster them according to whether they have a developmental/learning function or a public accountability function. (To some degree this clustering aligns with the internal/external distinction because internal purposes tend to be developmental whereas external purposes tend to focus on accountability.) This distinction between developmental and accountability purposes has become a major source of tension over National Curriculum assessment in England and Wales.

TGAT's formulation of assessment purposes

After the Government announced, in 1987, its intention to introduce a National Curriculum, it first set up a Task Group on Assessment and Testing (TGAT) to advise on an associated assessment framework. TGAT's remit was to propose a system for National Curriculum assessment (NCA) that would be capable of serving formative, diagnostic, summative and evaluative purposes. The TGAT Report distinguished these purposes in the following way:

- **formative** so that the positive achievements of a student may be recognised and discussed and the appropriate next steps planned;
- **diagnostic** through which learning difficulties may be scrutinised and classified so that appropriate remedial help and guidance can be provided;
- **summative** for the recording of the overall achievement of a student in a systematic way;
- **evaluative** by means of which some aspects of the work of a school, an LEA or other discrete part of the education service can be assessed and/or reported upon.

This established two new terms – formative and summative – in the lexicon of assessment purposes. The formative/summative distinction was first used by Michael Scriven in 1967 in an American Educational Research Association monograph on *The Methodology of Evaluation*, which was primarily concerned with the evaluation of educational programmes. It proved to be a helpful distinction and it was increasingly used in a variety of contexts. TGAT used the distinction in the context of assessment of students' learning. In this context, the formative purpose is served if evidence and judgements about students' present learning are used to decide what teachers and learners need to do so that further progress in learning may be made.

Summative assessment has a rather different function. As the word implies, summative assessment is concerned with 'summing up' the achievements of a student at a given point in their educational career, often by means of allocating a grade, score or level. This information is useful for reporting purposes and may subsequently be used for many of the 'purposes' in the composite list on page 25, such as selection, certification, guidance, and monitoring system effectiveness. These may best be clustered under the two main categories: formative assessment and summative assessment.

Many schools have found TGAT's formulation of assessment purposes to be helpful and have chosen to reproduce them in their assessment policies. However, in some ways the four purposes are a curious combination and need further scrutiny before being adopted. For example, one could argue that the formative purpose subsumes the diagnostic. If assessment information is to be used to plan next steps in teaching and learning then it is surely important that both achievements and difficulties are examined. Similarly, the evaluative purpose is of a rather different order from both formative and summative purposes. The two latter purposes relate directly to the assessment of individual students, or groups of students, but the evaluative purpose is served by the *use of assessment results* as evidence of school, LEA and system effectiveness. There may therefore be a further distinction to be made between *direct* and *indirect* assessment purposes or, perhaps, between the *purposes* of assessment *per se* and the *uses* of assessment information.

■ Determining priorities of purpose

These are subtle distinctions but they can have profound implications for schools if the relative importance of, and balance between, certain purposes is not considered. Schools need to determine where their priorities lie and what proportion of their effort and resources they are prepared to give to different purposes. Simply making a list of purposes in a policy document disguises the kinds of decisions that have to be taken in practice. It is therefore worth giving thought to the following:

- **Choice**   what range of purposes will the school pursue?

- **Balance**   what will be the balance between internal and external purposes, developmental and accountability purposes, and direct and indirect purposes?

- **Priority**   what purposes should be considered most important and therefore attract the largest share of the available resource?

If schools consider these criteria carefully at an early stage, they will be encouraged to weigh up the relative costs and benefits of pursuing different purposes. This could have important consequences both educationally and in terms of school finance. For example, if priorities are not considered fully, schools can be persuaded by advertising or hearsay to purchase expensive off-the-shelf standardised tests or external services for value-added analysis, which may prove to have only limited usefulness. They might then realise, when the money is already spent, that the provision of time or in-service support to develop formative classroom assessment might have been a better use of their resources. Careful choice and prioritising of purposes is therefore likely to be prudent as well as educationally sound. There is little point in an impressive list of purposes for assessment, recording and reporting that a school cannot practically deliver.

The relationship between formative and summative purposes

One of the issues, over which there has been much debate, concerns the relationship between assessment for formative purposes and assessment for summative purposes. Since these are possibly the two most important categories of purposes, any tension between the two is likely to be significant.

TGAT argued that, at least before the age of sixteen, summative purposes could be met through a system primarily developed for formative purposes: information generated to plan next steps in teaching and learning could provide the basis of summative judgements of what a student had achieved at a given point. TGAT did not, however, feel that the reverse was equally true: that summative assessments could provide adequate information for formative decisions. Summative assessments, because they are generalised and reductive, have very limited formative value although the *evidence* from which summative assessments are derived can also be used formatively. However, this use can be lost if the need to make decisions about overall grades or levels comes to dominate practice. Being aware of this difficulty, TGAT gave priority to formative purposes because they interpreted their remit as requiring them to propose a workable system that would enhance *teaching and learning*.

Teachers' assessment and national tests combined

One aspect of TGAT's proposals was that the system should combine teachers' own assessment results (TA) with the results they obtained with standard tests or tasks (SATs). Nowhere did TGAT associate teacher assessment specifically with the formative function and the standard tests with the summative function: indeed this would have contradicted their view that a system designed for formative purposes could meet all the needs of national assessment before sixteen. However, as the system TGAT initially proposed was implemented and adapted, it became clear that formative assessment was increasingly associated with TA, which was itself becoming distinct from the national tests (SATs).

Expressions of this developing view can be found in early publications from the School Examinations and Assessment Council (SEAC), the quango originally set up by the 1988 Act to operationalise the National Curriculum assessment system. The perceived distinction between the formative function of TA and the summative function of SATs/tests, and their relationship to each other, was made even more overt in the reports of the 1993 Dearing Review of National Curriculum and Assessment. In the 1993 Interim Report, Dearing wrote:

> It is particularly important that we are clear about the purposes of national tests as distinct from those of assessment. Teacher assessment lies at the heart of the learning progress (sic) in that new learning must be matched to what a pupil already knows and can do. It is the teacher in his/her classroom who, day in day out, undertakes this vitally important task of formative assessment. (. . .) the purpose of national tests is primarily to provide a summative contribution to the assessment of performance.

Dearing nevertheless strove to give the formative and summative roles parity of esteem by recommending that TA and national test results should be reported to parents alongside each other. Subsequent government circulars on reporting students' achievements have sought to implement this recommendation.

Problems associated with numerical scoring

The Dearing proposals, however, contain a logical problem. The requirement to report a TA score, in terms of a numerical level attained by the end of the key stage, still demands that teachers should 'sum up' their teacher assessments by aggregating and reducing their supposedly formative judgements, on criteria expressed in words, to the numerical form used in the tests. Thus, whatever had been claimed for teacher assessment, under the new arrangements, teachers are still expected to convert qualitative, formative assessments into quantitative, summative 'results'.

There is also a psychological problem with the National Curriculum assessment system as it stands post-Dearing. Whatever the rhetoric about the formative role of teacher assessment, if teachers know that they have to produce a numerical 'level' to describe a student's attainment, that concern tends to dominate and block their attention to detail that might have more formative value.

This was brought home forcibly for me in some research I carried out with a colleague, Colin Conner, in 1994. As part of this, I observed Key Stage 1 moderators from three LEAs carry out a cross-moderation exercise using sixteen samples of the work of five to seven year olds, which had all been teacher assessed (part of TA). To my surprise, none of the samples carried any evidence of diagnostic or formative comment, either on the work itself or on the teacher's annotation sheets that accompanied each sample. Moreover, few of the samples presented any evidence that the children had been set challenging tasks that could have revealed their particular strengths and weaknesses. The usefulness of the tasks for formative purposes was therefore minimal. All the evidence suggested that teachers 'played safe' and gave children tasks that enabled them to perform adequately on the National Curriculum criteria which, in turn, enabled teachers to identify the appropriate National Curriculum level. Key Stage 1 teachers had become skilful in this, but there was very little evidence that their skills of formative assessment had been enhanced through their involvement with statutory teacher assessment.

It is hoped that the post-Dearing change to the use of 'level descriptions' applied to the *range* of a student's work in the core subjects at the end of the key stage will go some way to ameliorate this situation. However, the *Exemplification of Standards* material that was published by the School Curriculum and Assessment Authority (SCAA) in 1995, still focuses solely upon the allocation of National Curriculum criteria and levels to samples, and misses the opportunity to show teachers how evidence of particular strengths and weakness in students' work can be used formatively.

On the basis of the above, one could argue that the national assessment system, which originally underscored the importance of assessment to support teaching and learning (the diagnostic and formative purposes) has, through successive reinterpretation and redefinition, been transformed into a system primarily designed to monitor standards in schools (summative and evaluative purposes). If this is the case, it will be up to schools to reclaim the formative role for assessment. As I pointed out in Chapter 1, schools have received encouragement in this direction from OFSTED inspections, which have criticised schools that have not been able to demonstrate how assessment has informed teaching and learning. (Chapter 9 gives detailed advice on ways of implementing formative assessment.)

Principles for policy

After clarity about purposes, the second, and related, element in a policy rationale needs to be clarity about the principles that will guide the development of assessment, recording and reporting procedures. A principle can be interpreted in at least two slightly different ways. In a fairly neutral way, a principle can be understood as a general guide to action, but more usually it possesses an ethical connotation concerning codes of *right* conduct. Most people who are involved in educating the young recognise that they are involved in something that is in essence a moral activity underpinned by *values*. For this reason, at least some principles for assessment are likely to have a moral dimension; they will be about what *ought* to happen for reasons of justice and fairness etc. So how should they be derived?

Identifying educational aims

There would be very little sense in having a set of principles to guide assessment practice that are unconnected with the educational aims of the school as a whole. If assessment is supposed to support the school in promoting high standards of learning and high quality teaching, assessment principles must be consistent with the school's broader educational aims. For this reason, it is worth using any articulated school aims as the starting point for developing more specific principles for assessment.

Most secondary schools now have statements of aims which they publish in their school prospectuses. The following page shows an example. This particular school has a general 'mission statement' and a more specific list of 'aims'; other schools might articulate something similar as educational purposes, key objectives or goals (the label does not matter much).

Reflecting aims in assessment principles

From this particular set of aims, two features emerge strongly as needing to be reflected in assessment principles. The first has to do with the emphasis on equal opportunities and support for students who experience learning difficulties. To be consistent with school aims, I would expect that this school's assessment policy would contain some principles that state (i) that assessment procedures should enable the school to monitor its equal opportunities policy and (ii) that the procedures used should themselves actively promote the achievement

Mission statement

To provide an education that gives all students an equal opportunity to achieve their fullest development intellectually, socially, emotionally, spiritually and physically and to equip them with skills and the confidence and maturity to meet the demands of a career, as caring and responsible members of a family and a community.

Aims

(i) to help students develop lively, enquiring minds and physical skills; giving them the ability to question and to argue rationally, and to apply themselves to tasks;

(ii) to instil respect for moral values, for other people and for oneself, and tolerance of other races, religions, and ways of life;

(iii) to help students understand the world in which we live, and the interdependence of nations;

(iv) to help students use language effectively and imaginatively in reading, writing and speaking;

(v) to help students appreciate how a nation earns and maintains its standard of living and properly to esteem the essential role of industry and commerce in this process;

(vi) to provide a basis of mathematical, scientific and technical knowledge, enabling boys and girls to learn the essential skills needed in a fast-changing world of work;

(vii) to teach children about human achievement and aspirations in the arts and sciences, in religion, and in the search for a more just social order;

(viii) to encourage and foster individual creativity among children whose disadvantages inhibit their capacity to learn, if necessary by making additional resources available to them.

Swavesey Village College, Cambridge, *Prospectus,* 1997

by *all* students of the best of which they are capable. (Equal opportunities in the context of assessment are discussed in Chapter 10.)

The second feature concerns the breadth of the curriculum and the emphasis on the school having an important role in the development of the 'whole person'. It would be inappropriate therefore if the school's assessment, recording and reporting systems were concerned only with assessing the cognitive achievements of students in a limited number of academic areas. As Richard Pring, Professor of Education at

Oxford University, pointed out in 1985 when writing about personal development in schools[1]:

> Any kind of development that is important enough to promote is important enough to be assessed in some broad sense of that term. If one knows what personal development means, then one must have some rough idea of what counts as having achieved it in some respect. (. . .) But that is not to say that personal development should be assessed through tests or examinations. It does mean that one has to make judgements, and that to make judgements one needs to think by what criteria and on what evidence one is to make them.

Bearing this in mind, another set of principles consistent with Swavesey Village College's aims would have to do with the need to develop appropriate assessment systems that would embrace the social, emotional, spiritual and physical development of the individual, as well as the academic and vocational.

Alternative ways to develop policy principles

My argument so far has been that the development of assessment, recording and reporting principles should first have reference to the more general educational aims of the school and be consistent with them. In this sense then, they can be derived 'top-down'. But teachers within the school will already be carrying out assessments and many will be guided by personal principles for practice. These may not be clearly articulated but they may be deeply held. They may also be a considerable source of tension among teachers, and confusion among students, if different teachers hold rigidly to different principles. (For example, heated debated can be generated in staffrooms over the question of whether or not marking should be done in red pen because of the messages it conveys to students!)

Another way of deriving principles for whole school assessment policy is, therefore, to elicit teachers' individual principles and to discuss them in departmental meetings with a view to achieving argeement as far as possible. The process can then be repeated at whole staff meetings. There would be a research and support role here for the school assessment co-ordinator and the process would, essentially, be 'bottom-up'.

A somewhat easier third option is to make a collection of assessment, recording and reporting principles from other sources. These are then used as the basis of a staff development activity designed to encourage discussion and agreement about a set of principles to guide practice in a

---

[1] Pring, R. 'Personal Development'. In P. Lang and M. Marland (eds) (1985) *New Directions in Pastoral Care.* Stanley Thornes.

particular school and in accordance with the school's general aims. (An activity that I have led in schools is set out at the end of this chapter on pages 40–42.) The following is a list of 24 principles collated from various sources. I have harmonised them so that they all begin with the word 'should' which expresses obligation. I have also tried to ensure that each statement embraces a single idea because multiple statements are difficult to operationalise, which is the next stage in policy development. Thirdly I have tried to eliminate overlaps. There are gaps, I am sure, but this list is only intended as a starting point.

Assessment, recording and reporting:

- should be integrated into teaching and learning;
- should motivate students;
- should be ongoing;
- should embrace the intellectual, social, emotional, spiritual, moral and physical development of the student;
- should be fair to all students whatever their race, gender, culture or religion;
- should actively involve students;
- should reflect partnership with parents and the wider community;
- should be manageable;
- should provide useful information in an accessible and intelligible form;
- should meet statutory requirements;
- should identify strengths, weaknesses and targets for development;
- should provide diagnostic information about special educational needs and guidance about how to cope with them;
- should be criterion-referenced;
- should provide summative information on students' attainments (compared with norms for the age group) and achievements (in relation to their capabilities);
- should provide information to evaluate the curriculum, teaching and the performance of the school;
- should provide a basis for dialogue between teachers, students and parents;
- should assist the development of differentiated teaching;
- should link judgements about achievement to evidence;

▶

- should incorporate procedures for ensuring consistency in standards;
- should communicate assessment information in a constructive fashion;
- should provide information in jargon-free natural language, not simply marks, grades or numerical levels;
- should make explicit the links with learning aims or objectives and success criteria;
- should respect differences between subjects;
- should encourage mutual respect and peer support.

Selecting the most important principles

Some people might argue that *all* these principles should be incorporated into schools' assessment policies although some principles might be interpreted as mutually exclusive. However, policies should not be idealised statements, but statements of practical intent. Therefore, initially, schools need to select priorities. In my experience this is not as difficult as one might imagine and teachers are usually able to agree a list of ten or twelve principles that they consider most important and most urgent. For example, after a two-hour session around Activity 1 (see page 40), a staff of 60+ were able to agree the priority list of assessment principles for their school shown on the next page.

Another set of principles is shown on page 37. These were produced by the Association of Assessment Inspectors and Advisers (AAIA) to help schools review what they are currently doing with assessment, recording and reporting. A list of the AAIA's assessment policy principles list is given here because schools may find it helpful to know the principles endorsed by LEA inspectors and advisers nationwide.

Principles into practice

A question that has interested me is whether, in large secondary schools, whole school policy needs to be much more than an agreed set of purposes and principles. 'Small is beautiful' and a short statement is more likely to be carried in people's heads and used as a regular reference for practice. Moreover, whilst it is one thing to agree statements of general principle across a diverse staff group, trying to come to agreement about a plethora of details of practice is a very different enterprise, and probably unnecessary.

First principles

> **Emerging Assessment, Recording and Reporting Policy Principles**
>
> Assessment, recording and reporting should:
>
> - be manageable;
> - be integrated into teaching and learning in an ongoing way;
> - identify strengths and weaknesses and indicate targets for progress;
> - motivate students by actively involving them;
> - be fair to students;
> - provide accessible information in an intelligible form;
> - form the basis of a dialogue between teachers, students and parents;
> - embrace academic, social, emotional and moral learning;
> - meet statutory requirements;
> - make explicit links with learning aims and success criteria;
> - provide information to evaluate the curriculum, teaching and learning;
> - incorporate procedures for ensuring consistency in standards.

Copland Community School, Wembley, Middlesex, October 1995

There are likely to be some areas where common practice may be vital, for example, in the style of reporting to parents, but it may not be a good idea to start from an assumption that identical practice has to be the necessary corollary of shared principles. In most secondary schools, departments will advance forcible reasons why they should be allowed to do things differently from others. This may have a lot to with 'balkanised attitudes' and professional territorialism but the arguments cannot simply be pushed aside.

A more productive approach, in my view, is to invite departments to take the school's agreed list of assessment, recording and reporting principles and ask them to work out how they would wish to operationalise them in their own particular context and in relation to their curricular domains. (See Activity 2 on page 41.) The object would be to develop a set of departmental procedures consistent with the broad whole school policy. In this sense, departments would then have their own departmental guidelines but whole school coherence would derive from shared principles. Reports of OFSTED inspections indicate that this is what inspectors were expecting to see but were often disappointed.

Assessment Policy: Principles

CLASSROOM PRACTICE: Good assessment practice:

- is based upon clear curriculum intentions;
- plays an integral part in classroom activities;
- is appropriate to the task;
- focuses on learning processes as well as learning outcomes;
- allows for unexpected as well as intended outcomes;
- draws upon a wide range of evidence;
- places achievement in context;
- indicates strengths and identifies weaknesses;
- involves pupils in reflection and review;
- informs about individual progress.

RECORDS: Teachers' records should:

- be ongoing and cumulative;
- be accessible and useful;
- identify and describe the progress and achievements of the pupil;
- show the attainment of each pupil as required in the National Curriculum;
- be based upon evidence, using different teaching styles and approaches, from: observing; listening and asking questions; setting tasks/tests; selecting examples of pupils' work.

REPORTS: Pupils' reports should:

- include descriptive assessment;
- refer to supportive evidence;
- use positive statements;
- place achievements in context;
- discriminate between attainment and achievement;
- report against specific criteria;
- avoid speculation and jargon;
- identify targets for future learning;
- target audience: pupil, parent, teacher.

AAIA – Members' Handbook, 1996–7

Developing practical departmental guidelines

In many ways the development of practical departmental guidelines is likely to be the most difficult part of policy development and departments will need considerable time and support to complete the task. This might involve in-service training sessions on specific assessment issues (such as those focused on by later chapters). They would also be helped by the support of the assessment co-ordinator acting as a 'critical friend'. He or she might be expected to feed in ideas, perhaps those that other departments have found helpful, and to challenge taken-for-granted assumptions rooted in traditional practices.

A cross-department working group would also be a support to the development of guidelines within departments. This would enable teachers to exchange ideas and experience but it could also be a forum for monitoring the extent to which emerging departmental policies are coherent and consistent with one another. It could also identify areas in which school principles are not likely to be upheld unless all departments adopt a common procedure or practice. The question of whether all departments adopt a common grading scale to make reporting intelligible to students and parents, may be a case in point.

Assessment, recording and reporting

133. The school has given a high priority to the development of policy and effective practice in assessment, recording and reporting. The school assessment co-ordinator is a member of the senior management team. School assessment policy was rewritten in June 1995 as an outcome of a cross-school working party on which all faculties were represented. The policy document, which deals with all the important aspects of assessment, marking and recording and includes guidelines on the various roles of all staff involved, is of high quality. The co-ordinator is currently engaged in mediating with heads of faculties to ensure policy becomes embedded within subject departments.

134. All subject departments have assessment policies except PSHE. In English, science, modern foreign languages, and design and technology, policies are clearly in line with those of the school but in others, e.g. geography, history and mathematics, policies need revision and further development to incorporate school requirements. Assessment practice across, and to some extent within departments is variable. In most cases it does not yet comply fully with school guidelines but the school recognises that this is a developing situation.

Copland Community School, OFSTED Inspection Report, 1995

This realistic view of departmental practice developing, over time and with adequate support, from the basis of agreed purposes and principles, was recognised and valued in the report that Copland Community School received from OFSTED inspectors in the autumn term of 1995 (see page 38).

In terms of school policy documents, it may suffice to have a fairly brief whole school document consisting of statements of purposes and principles. This may be followed by a section outlining how departments are expected to develop their own guidelines based on the principles, how this will be managed and supported, how roles and responsibilities will be allocated, and how departmental practice will be monitored and evaluated to ensure whole school consistency. Departmental guidelines can then be produced as appendices to this whole school document. This flexibility should facilitate regular revision as circumstances dictate.

Principles as criteria for evaluation

In addition to providing the basis for the development of practical procedures, principles perform another important function. If they are seriously held, they should become the criteria for evaluating the effectiveness of assessment, recording and reporting practice. For example, if the principle that 'Assessment, recording and reporting should be integrated into teaching and learning in an ongoing way' is an espoused principle, practice should be developed on this basis and any evaluation of a school's policy-in-practice would seek evidence that this principle was manifest. This important relationship between principles, procedures, practices and evaluative criteria is represented below:

Figure 2.1 **The relationship between principles, procedures, practice and evaluative criteria**

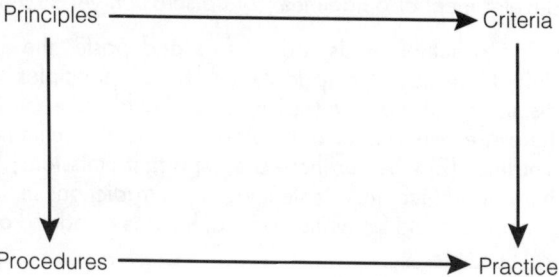

ACTIVITIES

1 Making a priority list of principles

The objective of this exercise is to allow democratic participation in the development of a consensus list of principles i.e. empowering the most naturally reticent and preventing any particularly vociferous members of staff from dominating and controlling decision-making. If the 'rules' are strictly adhered to, every individual's opinion should be equally valued.

This activity is suitable for a whole school professional development day. With an appropriate introduction it will take about 90 minutes. It could be orchestrated by the school assessment co-ordinator or equivalent. In preparation, all staff should be allocated to cross-department or cross-faculty groups of six to eight. Each group should be arranged around a table. On the table should be lists of principles such as the 24 that I have itemised on pages 35–6. (You may wish to use these, adapt them, or substitute your own from other sources.) Each member of the group will need a list. There should also be a separate envelope on each table in which one list of principles, on card, has been cut up so that they can be easily sorted. Plain paper and glue will enable the construction of a group list. The following instructions could also be printed and a copy placed on each table, or they could be displayed by an overhead projector.

(i)   In cross-departmental groups, elect a chair, a scribe and a timekeeper.

(ii) Each individual to choose the *ten* principles they think are most important and rank them from 10 (highest) to 1 (lowest). *No discussion* at this point. (10 minutes)

(iii) The scribe to make a composite list by eliminating the principles with no votes then noting the rankings given for each of the principles. Total the numbers against each of the principles: the principle with the *highest* score is the first principle. Compile a priority list in this way. (A list of the top ten or a dozen principles is probably all that can be managed as a first stage in the development of guidelines.) *No discussion* yet. (10 minutes)

(iv) Using a set of cards, or scissors and paste, the group chair should display the priority order of principles and invite *discussion at this point*. Discussion should focus on (1) whether there are overlaps in principles that might be eliminated by re-wording; (2) whether there are important omissions; (3) whether there are logical inconsistencies or contradictions in the list. New principles could be written on blank cards or added at this point.

NB The strong preferences of some individuals should not be allowed to overrule the votes already expressed unless there is clear agreement. (15 minutes)

(v) Scribe to write final agreed list and hand to the school's assessment co-ordinator who can then repeat stage (iii) and construct a definitive list of principles for the school as a whole.

2 Drafting departmental guidelines for assessment, recording and reporting procedures

This activity can be begun during a whole staff professional development day, perhaps following on from Activity 1. However, it involves faculty or departmental groups and can be conducted in departmental bases. It would benefit from the support of the school assessment co-ordinator or member of the school working group acting as critical friend. For this reason the timing of the activity might be better if it were not synchronous with the activity in other departments.

In preparation, departments will need large sheets of paper (A3?) with the school's agreed principles numbered down the left-hand side and three columns headed (1) Assessment (evidence and judgements), (2) Recording and (3) Reporting, along the top. This will provide a matrix. Departments should also be provided with the following written instructions:

(i) Take each principle in turn, starting with the first, and outline a procedure or practice for (1) assessment; (2) recording; (3) reporting, which would be consistent with the principle but appropriate to your subject area. (Try to make a distinction between assessment, recording and reporting but do not feel that you have to fill all three columns for all principles.)

(ii) When you have finished, look at the guidelines you have created as a whole. Look for inconsistencies and gaps, and check that statutory requirements have been met. Discuss ways to eliminate inconsistencies, fill gaps and incorporate statutory requirements. Then revise your guidelines.

(iii) Hand your draft guidelines to the assessment co-ordinator who will photocopy them for other departments and act as critical friend. When you have seen the ideas of other departments, and when the assessment co-ordinator has made suggestions for improvement, the guidelines should be revised again. At this point, some decisions may be taken about the need for some common practices across the school.

(Note: In my experience, teachers find it difficult to distinguish assessment procedures from recording procedures. They often assume that making a mark or grade *is* assessment. They therefore need to be helped to see that this is *preceded* by the act of collecting observations and making judgements about them. They need to consider how they will collect data and what criteria they will use to judge achievement.)

3 Drawing up a timetable and plan for development of assessment, recording and reporting

Once principles and preliminary departmental guidelines have been established it is important to plan a programme for development and implementation. This might best be done by the school assessment co-ordinator in discussion with members of a cross-faculty working party. Senior management will also need to be involved because, ideally, development of assessment, recording and reporting should be part of the school's development plan. Questions that need to be addressed will be:

- What needs to be given priority attention in each department?
- When should/can this happen?
- Who should be involved?
- What will be the process?
- Who should take responsibility, for what?
- What resources are needed: materials, time, training etc?
- What outcomes are expected?
- How will each development be evaluated?

This list of questions could be turned into a planning matrix with dates down the left-hand side and headings (Priority; Staff; Process; Leader(s); Resources; Expected outcomes; Evaluation) along the top.

3 External expectations, with special reference to Key Stage 3

Constraints and possibilities

In formulating school assessment, recording and reporting policy, it is important to take into account statutory requirements, which must be fulfilled by law, and other expectations which represent the reasonable demands of different groups of educational stakeholders. This does not mean, however, that such expectations should become the *framework* for school policy. This would make school policy almost entirely reactive.

Of course, in times of rapid and sometimes confusing educational change, it is tempting for schools to ask, 'Just tell us what we have to do', and to use minimal requirements as the basis for policy and practice. Even 'minimal' requirements are complex enough when all the procedures related to National Curriculum assessment, special needs assessment, GCSE, A– and AS–level, GNVQ and NVQ are taken into account. What energy can teachers be expected to have to think beyond this? However, to create a system based only on what *has* to be done is likely to be fragmented and biased towards certain purposes (mainly summative and reporting). It is also likely to encourage a focus on the mechanical aspects of assessment, such as assigning grades and levels and form-filling, rather than on the acts of observation and judgement of learning that are at the heart of the assessment process.

Incorporating external requirements

External requirements and expectations certainly need to be *incorporated* into school policy but they do not need to *determine* it. As I have said in Chapter 2, a coherent school policy needs to be founded first on careful deliberation of the principles that are valued by a particular school in its particular context. There will be times when internal aims and purposes and external requirements seem to be in conflict but it is possible to view these points of tension positively, as moments for critical and creative thinking, rather than negatively, as demanding inevitable compromise or capitulation.

In other words there is often no need for schools to shrug their collective shoulders and to give in to what they regard as a bureaucratic burden only marginally related to what they consider to be their central aims and tasks. Experience suggests that when they do this they often create for themselves an unnecessarily heavy workload, sometimes far beyond the requirements of legislation.

Lessons from the past

Examples of this phenomenon abounded in the early days of National Curriculum implementation. For example, at Key Stage 1, where National Curriculum assessment was first introduced, many schools created elaborate and even bizarre recording systems for teacher assessment. Teachers walked around infants' classrooms carrying clipboards and filling in complex tick-lists of hundreds of statements of attainment. Sometimes they even wore (literally) an 'assessment hat' which signalled to children that they were working in assessment mode and should not be asked questions!

Their cupboards were often stuffed with portfolios of all the work that the children had produced during the key stage so that they could produce the 'evidence' for their assessments should a moderator or inspector make a visit. Some equally curious interpretations of National Curriculum assessment requirements were also evident at Key Stage 3 in the early days, so this phenomenon was by no means unique to primary schools.

In both primary and secondary schools, teachers would probably have been saved a good deal of unnecessary work if they had not simply *reacted* to what they perceived to be demanded of them by government. If schools had previously thought through policies for routine classroom assessment and recording, it is likely that they would possess the evidence to fulfil statutory requirements for assessment information without having to create something additional, specifically for this purpose. It is often possible to meet official requirements by using adaptations of more everyday practices, although well-established practices will need to be evaluated and sometimes changed or discarded.

The worst possible scenarios usually arise when new requirements and practices are simply 'bolted on', which often leads to meaningless activity and work overload. The art is to separate what is negotiable from what is not negotiable, and to try to build those things that are not negotiable into a coherent system based on principles whilst taking positive advantage of those things that can be treated more flexibly according to the school's declared values.

Sources of information on external expectations

Agencies and their relationships

In this section, and those that immediately follow, I will describe some of the statutory arrangements as they apply to schools in England. Much the same things are required of schools in Wales, except that the relevant government department is the Welsh Office and Wales has its own curriculum and assessment authority (ACAC: Awdurdod Cwricwlwm ac Asescu Cymru). One notable difference is the expectation that Welsh should be taught and assessed as a core subject in Welsh-medium schools. The provisions of the 1988 Education Reform Act do not apply in Scotland which has different curriculum and assessment arrangements; Northern Ireland has arrangements which are similar to England under the 1989 Education Reform (Northern Ireland) Order. Unfortunately I do not have space to deal with these here but teachers in Scotland and Northern Ireland will have other sources of information.

One of the problems for schools in England is that information on all the different assessment requirements that pertain to students from age eleven to nineteen comes from a variety of different agencies. There is no transparent overall co-ordination although this problem has been recognised and has led to a number of agency mergers in the 1990s. For example, the 1988 Education Reform Act created separate bodies to oversee the implementation of the National Curriculum (the National Curriculum Council) and assessment and examinations (the School Examinations and Assessment Council). It soon became clear that to separate curriculum and assessment was a nonsense, so in 1993 these bodies were merged into the School Curriculum and Assessment Authority (SCAA).

Subsequently the division of responsibility for academic and vocational courses became equally untenable so, on 1 October 1997, SCAA and the National Council for Vocational Qualifications (NCVQ) merged to become the Qualifications and Curriculum Authority (QCA). This agency is directly accountable to the central goverment department responsible for education. This has also changed its name twice since the 1988 Act: from the Department of Education and Science (DES) to the

Department for Education (DoE) and then to the Department for Education and Employment (DfEE).

■ The co-ordinating role of QCA

As did its forebears, QCA exerts some control over other agencies such as those responsible for the development of National Curriculum tests, the examining boards and the awarding bodies for vocational qualifications. For example, the QCA commissions the production and evaluation of the Key Stage tests and has to approve courses leading to external qualifications before they can be offered in schools. Thus there is a kind of hierarchy of accountability linking many of the agencies that schools deal with in respect of external assessment and examination as this diagram shows:

Figure 3.1 **Accountability of agencies with responsibility for external assessment and examinations**

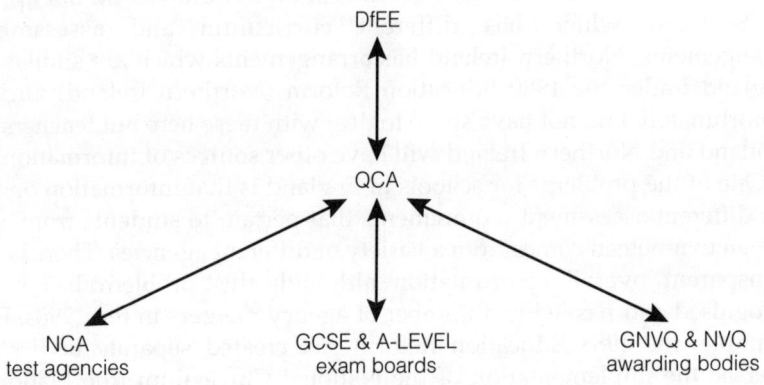

■ Co-ordination of information within the school

All of these bodies produce volumes of material which are either sent direct to schools or can be requested. Simply keeping abreast of developments is a major task and argues strongly for the appointment of a school assessment co-ordinator, as a member of the senior management team, who will be expected to keep up to date and develop an overview. Sensibly, this co-ordinator would also be the school's examinations officer although, if the assessment co-ordinator is supported by a working group, this task might be delegated. Whether the role is taken by an individual or group, the tasks of co-ordination with respect to information gathering involve: (1) collecting all the information that is relevant to the school; (2) sorting priorities for action (some information is essential, some is helpful and some is merely interesting!); (3) piecing together the jigsaw of the different bits of information so that some meaningful picture emerges.

Collecting information

The first task is helped somewhat by the fact that both the DfEE and QCA (as SCAA did previously) produce and distribute, free to all schools, regular newsletters which summarise recent developments and provide lists of recent publications.

Sorting priorities for action

With respect to the second task, it is helpful to bear in mind the distinction between statutory requirements and non-statutory guidance. The former are mandatory and schools are bound by law to comply with them, whilst the latter are advisory. The *framework* of law is set out in relevant *Education Acts*. In 1996, two new Acts of Parliament were passed: the Education Act 1996 and the Schools Inspections Act 1996. These two Acts brought together, consolidated and restated the content of a number of previous laws to make access more convenient. In 1997, another Education Act was passed. This has relevance to assessment because in Section 19 it contains provisions for legislation to require target setting in schools (see Chapter 12 page 252). Rarely, however, do schools need to refer to the Acts themselves.

Of more immediate concern to schools are the *regulations* which set out the *detail* of what is required by law. These regulations are to be found in statutory instruments, called *Education Orders*, which are issued from time to time. In the case of end of Key Stage assessment, a new order is issued every year, e.g. *The Education (National Curriculum) (Key Stage 3 Assessment Arrangements) (England) Order 1996 SI 2116*. Titles are not exactly snappy! Legal requirements are also set out in official *Circulars* which carry a number indicating the year of issue and the number in the series issued that year, e.g. *Circular 2/97 – Reports on Pupils' Achievements in Secondary Schools in 1996/97*. Both Orders and Circulars are issued by the DfEE. The DfEE in association with QCA (previously SCAA) usually publishes more user-friendly versions of these regulations for use in schools by particular groups of teachers, e.g. SCAA leaflet KS3/96/567 *Key Stage 3 Assessment Arrangements: Non-core Subjects*. Other information from these and other bodies is usually in the nature of guidance and there is normally an element of discretion about whether and how schools choose to use it.

Piecing together the jigsaw

The third task for assessment co-ordinators, i.e. putting the jigsaw together, is possibly the most difficult but it is also the one where schools receive least help from central agencies. This is for the simple reason that the circumstances of each school are different and a single formula is unlikely to work in all contexts. However, in the past, SCAA produced useful booklets on managing the curriculum and assessment at the various key stages which drew on examples of practice suited to a range of contexts. A number of Local Education Authorities also offer materials and in-service training to support their schools in the interpretation and implementation of legal requirements.

▮ Issues in transfer across the key stages

In the sections that follow, I shall attempt to summarise the key external expectations that schools need to take into account when planning assessment at Key Stage 3. (Key Stages 4 and what schools often refer to as Key Stage 5 will be dealt with in the next chapter.) Many schools now have key stage co-ordinators and it is sensible to deal with their concerns, but, for the sake of progression, continuity and overall coherence, it will also be important to recognise issues that have relevance across key stages. It is at these points of transfer that confusion for students and parents so often occurs. I begin, therefore, with issues of transfer from Key Stage 2.

Inevitably, this chapter can only take account of information that is available at the time of writing, so there are parts that may become quite rapidly out of date. Its chief value therefore is likely to be as a framework for identifying those aspects of mandatory assessment, recording and reporting that school policy should encompass, and as a basis for checking later pronouncements from official sources. For some readers it might also be useful as a snapshot in time, i.e. 1997.

▮ Transfer from Key Stage 2

▮ Continuity in curriculum experience and learning

By the time that children transfer to the secondary phase of their education at the age of eleven, they have completed more than half of their compulsory schooling. For all its early faults, the National

Curriculum was designed with the laudable aim of providing a structure for continuity and progression in children's learning from age five to sixteen in a range of subjects deemed worthy of study. The reasonable expectation was that teaching and learning at each key stage would build on the teaching and learning at the previous key stage.

The reality, especially between Key Stage 2 and Key Stage 3, when most children change schools, is that continuity in curriculum experience and learning is largely *assumed* to be achieved through the device of constructing schemes of work on the basis of the published programmes of study in the subject orders. In other words, continuity in learning is largely constructed as a feature of curriculum planning (in relation to the paper blueprint) rather than as a feature of learners, who may or may not have learned in the ways intended by the curriculum designers.

Rarely, it seems, has information about what teachers have *actually* taught and what children have *actually* learned at the previous key stage been used extensively in planning next steps in learning for individuals and groups. A leaflet from SCAA in 1997 on *Managing end of Key Stage 2 assessment* expressed disquiet that: 'There continues to be much evidence that, despite all Year 6 children being assessed under the same arrangements, potential information from Year 6 teachers is greatly under-used'.

Some evidence of the current transfer situation

Evidence of this kind has been provided by Suffolk LEA which, in 1996, undertook an investigation of what happens when students transfer to their next schools at ages of nine, eleven and thirteen. (Suffolk has first, middle and upper schools as well as primary and high schools.) This involved county advisers in tracking the progress of 360 students in 32 schools. The extract on the following two pages is from the executive summary of the report.

I am grateful to Suffolk LEA for allowing me to reproduce this very candid and direct extract from their report because it could be read as a particular criticism of Suffolk schools. I include it here because I am sure that a similar picture would emerge from a national study. Indeed, when discussing these findings, inspectors and advisers from five other local authorities thought the picture was much the same in their county schools. Similarly, my analysis of OFSTED reports in Chapter 1 indicated that lack of use of transfer information was a common criticism.

Summary of the findings of an investigation into transfer in Suffolk

- In the overwhelming majority of cases schools are very good at ensuring that pupils are well prepared for transfer and that they settle into the new routines with the minimum of disturbance.

- The degree to which schools build on the standards already achieved by pupils in previous schools varies from school to school and subject to subject. In general this is not done well and much of the work of pupils and teachers in previous schools is undervalued.

- The standards which are ignored most are those achieved by higher attaining pupils. Continuing provision for pupils who have some learning difficulties tends to be much better.

- The dip in progress indicated by reading test progress data, which takes place in many schools when pupils transfer, is often the result of a reading curriculum in the receiving school which is too narrow. In all phases, and particularly in schools where standards are lower than might be expected, the full range of reading skills is not being systematically taught. This raises issues about the teaching of reading in successive phases in addition to those concerning quantity and challenge. Progress in speaking and listening is uneven. Progress in writing is usually better.

- In some schools, failure to build on previous attainment in mathematics means that pupils' progress is set back by a year, or more.

- Most schools are only partially successful in building on pupils' previous attainment in science. More able pupils are most disadvantaged and this is particularly the case in investigational work.

- Some teachers have suitably high expectations of pupils on entry to their schools. Many do not and often fail to recognise the sophistication of some of the work which has been done previously. Where staff in the new school use the documentation on pupils' attainment which they receive, expectations overall are usually higher.

- Discussion about the curriculum and pupils' standards tends to be best between middle and upper schools, variable between first and middle schools and worst between primary and high schools. 'Liaison' at present focuses mostly on curriculum plans, materials, SEN and pastoral matters. Very little time is spent discussing pupils' attainment and standards. This needs to change, for whilst ▶

> curriculum planning is a prerequisite to ensuring appropriate progression and standards of attainment, it is not sufficient on its own. Liaison should focus specifically on standards of work and expectations of pupils. All teachers need a common understanding of what constitutes high attainment in a subject at a given age.
>
> **In summary, although some schools are much better than others, 'receiving' schools tend to underestimate what their new pupils, particularly above average pupils, know, understand and are able to do.**
>
> **Teachers too often unknowingly set limits on the standards which their youngest pupils are capable of achieving.**
>
> **Improving teachers' knowledge of what has already been achieved by their new intake and ensuring that teachers use that knowledge in planning their course and preparing their lessons is a crucial element in raising achievement throughout Suffolk schools. All contributing schools need to send simple and accessible information to receiving schools and all receiving schools need to use it.**

Suffolk Education Department, Inspection and Advice Division (1997)

■ Doubtful validity of the 'clean slate' approach

The weight of evidence would appear to undermine any argument for the 'clean slate' or 'fresh start' that has frequently been pleaded on the basis that some students needed to escape low expectations. On the contrary, it would seem that the fresh start approach is more likely to allow low expectations to be established and remain unchallenged! I have always suspected that the 'fresh start' approach has often been adopted on the grounds of convenience rather than the principle claimed for it. There is no doubting that it is enormously difficult to devise an effective system for collecting and using transfer information.

■ Legal requirements

At the time of writing, the current legal requirements for the content of reports to receiving schools are contained in DfEE Circulars 1/97 (primary schools) and 2/97 (secondary schools). According to Circular 1/97, transfer reports for individual students at the end of Key Stage 2 must contain the results of statutory National Curriculum assessments (both TA and test levels) by subject and, where available, attainment target, at all previous key stages (i.e. both Key Stage 1 and Key Stage 2).

This means that primary schools must include information for key stages assessed by previous schools. Schools are also asked to provide teacher assessments of progress against applicable attainment targets in the core subjects since the last statutory assessment or since the student arrived at the reporting school. This can take the form of narrative commentary rather than a numerical level and is mainly relevant to students transferring at times other than the end of the key stage, for example at the end of Year 8 between some middle and upper schools. Nothing else is required by *law* and no particular reporting format is prescribed.

Information not required by law

However, there is a quantity of other information that schools might wish, and might be expected to pass on. This includes those things additionally mentioned by SCAA:

- Age-related standardised scores for Key Stage 2 tests which will be made available from 1997 to schools that request them. These will allow finer discrimination between students than the allocation of broad National Curriculum levels and will take more account of date of birth. This may be helpful for monitoring purposes.
- Information, in narrative form, about students' strengths, weaknesses and interests.
- Information about students' behaviour and attendance.
- Details of students with special educational needs.
- Details of students for whom English is an additional language.
- The last annual report to parents.

Some primary schools also like to send portfolios of students' work at Key Stage 2, although the Suffolk LEA report on transfer arrangements, mentioned above, is worth quoting on this issue:

The principle of parsimony needs to apply. Feeder schools should only send what is necessary and what will be used. It is probably unnecessary in most cases to send large portfolios of work with each pupil. These may never be read. It is probably more helpful for National Curriculum levels and test data where available to be accompanied by a sample of work which shows the range of attainment across the pupils who are transferring, with an emphasis on that achieved by the best.

Problems to be overcome

The underlying concern here is with practicability. A balance needs to be achieved between, on the one hand, passing on sufficient information to enable sound judgements to be made by teachers about appropriate curriculum provision matched to the needs of individual students, and to enable future monitoring of the receiving school's effectiveness, and, on the other hand, creating a system for collecting, analysing and disseminating information that is manageable. There are a number of very specific problems to be overcome:

1 Most secondary schools receive students from a considerable number of feeder primary schools. This may average four or five main schools in rural areas but can be more than forty in urban areas. Moreover, the open enrolment provisions of the 1988 Act, enabling more parental choice, have increased the likelihood that students will come from a wider spread of primary schools. Receiving schools would be helped if information transferred to them came in a common format at an agreed time but this is difficult to achieve, especially if students arrive from different counties or from grant maintained and independent as well as LEA schools.

2 Much of the information required to be passed on by primary schools only becomes available late in the summer term. In the document already referred to, SCAA suggested that anticipated TA levels might be passed on in mid-May, followed by final TA and test levels in the first week of July and the full school record at the end of the summer term. The prospect of some secondary schools receiving three tranches of information from upwards of forty feeder schools in the summer term is too much to contemplate! More sensible, in my view, would be agreement between feeder schools to ensure that all their information is sent to the receiving school, in one tranche, by 1 September. Secondary schools might then be able to allocate and plan time to use this information at the beginning of the new school year.

3 In most primary schools, students are taught by a class teacher or a small team who will be familiar with writing a single report on each child. However, information on progress in different subjects will need to be distributed across departments in most secondary schools. The reporting format needs to take into account this need for information to be portioned out. Schools, LEAs and commercial organisations are tackling this issue in various ways, ranging from the

creation of sophisticated computer programs to the 'lavatory paper' or perforated forms solution.

Statutory assessment

In Key Stage 3, the weight of statutory requirement relates to National Curriculum assessment *at the end of the key stage*. I will deal with this first because it looms so large, but I shall return later to other matters that have relevance throughout the key stage. National Curriculum assessment in England and Wales has two main aspects: national tests and statutory teacher assessment (TA).

National Curriculum tests: scope

In 1997 tests in the 'core' subjects (English, mathematics and science) were mandatory for all Year 9 students, in state schools, who were expected to achieve above level 3 in English and above level 2 in maths and science. For those students working below these levels there were *optional* classroom-based tasks. For each of these subjects, there were two papers to assess attainment up to level 7, in English and science, and up to level 8 in maths. There were also extension papers for students who were thought to be able to achieve above these levels (i.e. level 8 or exceptional performance). In English, all students sat the same papers but students were entered for tiered papers in maths (4 tiers) and science (2 tiers).

In 1997, national pilots of additional papers testing grammar, spelling and punctuation in English, and mental arithmetic in maths, were intended to pave the way for the incorporation of these tests into statutory assessment in 1998. Mental tests in mathematics will go ahead in 1998 but English grammar tests have been delayed for further piloting. There were no tests for non-core subjects.

Marking of test papers

National test papers are marked by external marking agencies but, in contrast to GCSE examinations, marked scripts are returned to schools. The purpose of this is to give value to the notion that tests can have a diagnostic, formative function. It is expected (though not required) that teachers will use them to feed back into teaching, learning and curriculum planning.

However, the national evaluation of Key Stage 3 assessment arrangements in 1995 and 1996, conducted by a team of researchers under the direction of Hilary Radnor at Exeter University, found little evidence of this. Only 15 per cent of departments of the schools sampled in 1996 used scripts diagnostically and half of all departments said that they would not be making any use of them. The main problem lay in the lack of annotation on the scripts. Often there were only ticks to indicate that the examiner had read the script. English teachers, in particular, claimed that they would have to remark the scripts themselves if they were to make any use of them for formative purposes. One English teacher, quoted in the evaluation report, reacted strongly:

There is a contradiction in returning scripts – it is done in the interest of good educational practice within a system of assessment established in complete contradiction to these principles!

The evaluation report for 1995 had recommended that scripts should be annotated but this had not been put into practice for 1996. No doubt this would have been too costly and would have exposed markers' judgements to even greater challenges than they experienced in 1995, when considerable disquiet was expressed about the marking of English in particular. Moreover, the purpose of tests is primarily a summative one and the allocation of marks, from which National Curriculum levels are derived, is the clear priority for external marking agencies.

Interpreting test results in relation to National Curriculum levels

Test results are expressed as National Curriculum levels, although the levels are calculated on the basis of numerical marks awarded to questions. Marks are allocated in relation to performance defined in the level descriptions for each attainment target, but this process of mark allocation is done by the agencies who construct the tests and devise the mark scheme. They also determine the level boundaries by reference to the standards defined by the level descriptions, the results of pre-testing, and a level confirmation exercise carried out on a national sample of scripts before results are finalised and returned to schools.

This process has moved National Curriculum testing into the realm of measurement and, although a relationship between marks and level criteria still exists, this is no longer transparent to teachers who might wish to use scripts for formative feedback. Test papers indicate that a question carries, say, 18 marks, but teachers need to study the marking schemes if they are to understand how marks are related to National Curriculum levels.

Questioning the content validity of the tests

As in all time-constrained assessments, National Curriculum tests only lightly sample the subject domain. This inevitably raises issues about content validity: the extent to which the test validly reflects the scope of the curriculum in a given area.

In the 1996 national evaluation, concerns about content (also construct and consequential) validity were raised especially in relation to the assessment of Shakespeare in English. For example, teachers criticised the test for giving too much attention to Shakespeare at the expense of other forms of literature dealt with in the programme of study. (This example and issues of validity are dealt with more fully in Chapter 8 on page 161.) Similarly, none of the tests in the core subjects assesses the 'process' attainment targets (AT1s): speaking and listening in English; using and applying mathematics; experimental and investigative science. There is some reason, therefore, to question the extent to which the tests are tests of English, mathematics and science *as defined in the National Curriculum.* In this sense the other element of statutory assessment, teacher assessment (TA), can be regarded as more complete because it is intended to provide an assessment of attainment across the whole subject programme and across the whole of the key stage.

Statutory teacher assessment (TA)

From 1997, teachers of core subjects (English, mathematics, science) and foundation subjects (history, geography, design and technology, information technology, modern foreign languages, art, music and physical education) were required by law to summarise their assessment for each student in Year 9. In the core subjects and in all foundation subjects *except art, music and PE,* teachers were required to give a level for each attainment target and an overall subject level by averaging attainment target levels. In some subjects (history, geography and IT) there is only one attainment target so this level carries over; in other subjects (English, science, modern foreign languages) attainment targets are equally weighted; in others (mathematics, design and technology) some attainment targets have differential weightings.

'Best fit' judgements on level descriptions

In all these subjects, teachers were expected to consider *evidence* of students' achievements in relation to the programme of study across the key stage and to make a *judgement* about the level descriptions that 'best fit' their attainment by the end of the key stage. According to 1997 DfEE/SCAA guidance:

> *In reaching a judgement, teachers should use their knowledge of a pupil's work over time, including written, practical and oral work in the classroom, homework and results of other school examinations or tests. The aim is for a rounded judgement which:*
>
> - *is based on knowledge of how the pupil performs across a range of contexts;*
>
> - *takes into account strengths and weaknesses of that pupil's performance;*
>
> - *is checked against adjacent level descriptions to ensure that the level awarded is the closest match to the pupil's performance in each attainment target.*

What is wanted is a *qualitative* judgement expressed as a *numerical* level. Teachers were encouraged to weigh up relative strengths and weaknesses in the composite level descriptions, allowing strengths in one area to compensate for weaknesses in others if this was necessary to meet the 'best fit' criterion.

The evidence collected by the national evaluation of Key Stage 3 assessment in 1996 indicated that teachers were still coming to terms with level descriptions. Only assessment in the core subjects was investigated but there appeared to be clear differences that might be associated with the cultures of different subjects. For example, English departments expressed a general liking for best-fit level descriptions; mathematics departments were not very enthusiastic, perceiving them as 'rather vague'; whilst the attitudes expressed by science departments were mixed.

The basis of these different attitudes may have been the somewhat uneasy alliance between the qualitative and quantitative aspects of teacher assessment, with English teachers feeling more confident with the former because qualitative judgements in relation to the study of English are their stock in trade.

The preferences of teachers with different subject backgrounds was also reflected in the kinds of evidence departments used to support their judgements. Of the suggestions made by DfEE/SCAA (see above), it was notable that the sources used with the greatest frequency by English departments were regular written and oral classroom assignments, whereas mathematics and science departments used periodic tests and examinations. In part this may reflect English departments' greater familiarity and liking for continuous assessment based on assignments (associated with GCSE), whilst maths and science departments feel more comfortable with aggregating results (often expressed as numerical scores) of end of unit/module tests.

These kinds of differences may also be reflected in non-core subjects. One of the tasks for school assessment co-ordinators or Key Stage 3 co-ordinators, therefore, might be to bring departments together to share their different practices with a view to examining the different assumptions behind them and expanding teachers' perspectives on what is possible and extending the range of their practice.

End of key stage descriptions for art, music and physical education

Within the non-core subjects, the picture of statutory teacher assessment is further complicated by the fact that art, music and PE do not have have *level* descriptions but *end of key stage* descriptions which are meant to represent the expected attainment of the average Year 9 student. The attainment of students is not therefore differentiated by level, but teachers are expected to make a judgement about the extent to which students have met the end of key stage description. The judgement should relate to the subject as a whole, but, in art and music, which have two attainment targets each, the judgement should make reference to both.

To date, there has been no prescription about the way in which teachers should record and report their judgements in relation to end of key stage statements in these subjects. A *narrative* statement would probably communicate best to students and their parents and was implied in the reporting regulations for 1997. However, in 1997, some schools were evidently confused by the DfEE's proposal that an A–D category system should be used for reporting summary data in art, music and PE for *national data collection* purposes. This was *optional* for schools and there was *no suggestion* that this system should be used for reporting to students and parents. Indeed, it could be very confusing if schools were to adopt such a category system for more general purposes because the letters attached to categories are in the reverse order to what one would expect from common grading systems used in schools. Thus, 'A' describes students working towards the expectation for the end of the key stage, whilst 'D' describes students demonstrating exceptional performance!

Materials to assist teacher assessment

In order to assist teachers in making TA judgements, SCAA produced *Exemplification of Standards* material in all National Curriculum subjects and optional task and test materials in the non-core subjects. These constitute non-statutory guidance but their production was motivated particularly by a concern to promote consistency in teachers' judgements across schools. They were therefore accompanied by more general guidance on *Consistency in Teacher Assessment*. (The issue of consistency will be dealt with more fully in Chapter 8 on page 157.)

The 1996 national evaluation from Exeter University reported that 80 per cent of English departments had made some use of the exemplification material, with 50 per cent claiming to have made good use of it, but there was no mention of its use in maths or science. In 1996, SCAA commissioned from Bath University an evaluation specifically of the use of exemplification materials for the core subjects, although the findings were not available when I wrote this chapter.

Finalising TA results

Teachers are required to finalise their teacher assessment results two weeks before the end of the summer term. (A precise date is given in the annual instructions from DfEE/QCA.) This is a date after the results of the national tests have been returned to schools. The report of the Dearing Review in 1993 reiterated the belief that tests and teacher assessment should be regarded as separate but complementary measures and that they should continue to be reported alongside one another. However, it was considered that teachers might wish to take account of test results when finalising their TA.

The national evaluation of assessment arrangements in 1995 and 1996 found two distinct perspectives among teachers towards the relationship of TA to test results. A *leveller perspective* was characterised by a belief in the importance of comparable levels. Teachers holding this view strove to create a close match between the two sets of results because they saw the tests and TA as validating one another.

In contrast, a *differentialist perspective* was characterised by a belief that differences in levels might be expected because TA takes a wider view in terms of time, assessment contexts and forms of expression (practical and oral as well as written) and creates different assessment conditions for students.

In 1995 the differentialist perspective predominated among English teachers and the leveller perspective predominated among mathematics and science teachers, although more of the latter were becoming differentialist by 1996. Teachers acknowledged that there were reasons other than educational ones that were affecting their professional behaviour. The authors of the report pointed out that:

The 'market forces' context within which their schools were now operating, were (sic) pressuring departments to seriously question anything greater than a one level difference between the two assessments. Hence, those who believed that it was reasonable for the test and teacher assessment levels to be different perceived their professional practice was compromised in the 'bigger issue' of the school's public image.

Once the results are finalised, bearing in mind that there is an appeals procedure for test results, and before the end of the summer term in Year 9, schools are required to report results to parents and to the National Data Collection.

Reporting to parents

Statutory requirements

In 1997, the requirements for reporting National Curriculum assessment results to parents were set out in Circular 2/97. This circular is updated annually although contents usually change in only small, but sometimes significant, details. It is always important to refer to the current circular, not least because it contains the previous year's tables of national results which are needed for comparative reporting in the core subjects.

For the core subjects, the regulations required that parents should be given:

- each student's National Curriculum test result (where applicable, because there was no requirement for results of tasks for students working below the test levels) and teacher assessment subject level, and a statement saying that the levels have been arrived at by statutory assessment;
- a brief commentary on these results indicating what they show about a student's progress;
- comparative information showing how the student has performed in comparison with other students of the same age in the school, and nationally using DfEE data of the previous year's results.

For non-core subjects, requirements were that parents should be informed of:

- teacher assessment subject levels in history, geography, design and technology, information technology and a modern foreign language, and a brief commentary on what these results show about a student's progress;

- a commentary on the student's attainment in relation to end of key stage statements in art, music and PE;
- for subjects with level outcomes, comparative information showing how the student has performed in comparison with others of the same age in the school (in 1997 no comparative information was required for art, music and PE, nor in relation to national standards).

In an important footnote, Circular 2/97 set out what was required in the 'brief commentary' on progress in all subjects. As a minimum, schools were expected to comment on progress with reference to *a student's own* previous attainment and also in relation to *other students* in the same year, drawing attention to any particular strengths and weaknesses.

In addition to this information which related specifically to National Curriculum assessment, annual reports to parents in Year 9 are also expected to contain:

- comments on other subjects (e.g. RE) and activities (e.g. extra-curricular activities);
- a statement about general progress;
- a record of attendance;
- information on arrangements for discussion.

Integrating requirements into a reporting system

The question for schools is how to integrate these statutory reporting requirements into their pattern of reporting in Year 9. The national evaluation of Key Stage 3 assessment in 1996 reported that about one third of schools in their sample reported to parents fully and formally once a year in the spring term around the time when option choices are made and a parents' evening is held. For these schools, sending out test results at the end of July became a supplementary form of reporting, generally accompanied by an explanatory letter from the headteacher.

The other two-thirds of schools reported at least twice a year with over 60 per cent reporting fully in July with interim reports at Christmas or during the spring term. The National Curriculum results were therefore either integrated into the July report or attached to it as an appendix.

In both the integrated and the separated versions, there was evidence that many parents were receiving reports on subjects that included information in a confusing mix of reporting modes: National Curriculum levels for statutory tests and TA, predicted GCSE grades, percentages for internal examination results, letter grades for effort, rating scales for other aspects, and narrative statements and commentary from teachers and students. Moreover, within schools there was little evidence of consistency across subjects. Little wonder then that the national evaluation quotes one parent as saying:

> In his school report I could not understand the scoring levels. Tiers, levels, marks? I am a bus driver but schooling is over my head. Is Level 3 high or low?

In the light of this evidence, one has to wonder whether many schools have really thought about how parents will 'read' all this information. Without doubt National Curriculum assessment requirements have added another layer to complicate matters but the parts will not be understood unless there is some attention to the whole. Without some rationalisation in the light of first principles, reports will not inform but only mystify. (Reporting is dealt with more fully in Chapter 11.)

National data collection

In 1997, one week after NC teacher assessment results were finalised and a week before the end of the summer term, schools were required to submit both test and TA results to the national database, ostensibly, 'to facilitate the earlier publication of 1997 national results, in response to requests from LEAs and school'!

In 1996 data could be sent to the National Data Collection manually or electronically, using a software disk provided by SCAA or software available from a commercial company, SIMS. 60 per cent of co-ordinators who responded to the relevant question in the national evaluation's survey, said that they had used the software for this purpose. Some said that they found it user-friendly. However, the fact that the proportion of use was not higher was thought to relate to the time-consuming nature of inputting the data.

At this time both test results and TA results had to be transferred manually on to the SCAA software. Some teachers requested that test results should be sent to them electronically for easy transfer and that Optical Mark Reader (OMR) sheets should be provided to make input of TA results easier. In the so-called electronic age, I would expect some changes to be made in line with these recommedations but readers will need to check this.

Organisation of statutory Key Stage 3 assessment

One whole section of Exeter University's 1996 evaluation report, on organisation and administration of the tests, was left out of the version that was made publicly available by SCAA, the sponsor of the work. In this section the evaluation team reported the following:

> Whilst the vast majority of KS3 assessment co-ordinators in England and Wales found the overall administrative procedures associated with KS3 acceptable, it has to be reported that only 60 per cent regarded the amount of time *taken up with the administration of KS3 assessment as being acceptable* (my emphasis).

In the light of this comment, I decided to try to think through the administrative tasks associated with statutory assessment, in sequence. Though many, I am sure I have left some out!

Administrative tasks associated with statutory assessment

- Read, and inwardly digest, DfEE/QCA leaflets on Key Stage 3 assessment arrangements, external marking, the reporting circular, and all other relevant communications from the DfEE, QCA, External Marking Agencies, and LEAs – and distribute subject specific booklets to departments.

- Discuss and support use of exemplification and optional test and task material for the purposes of statutory teacher assessment.

- Establish which students, if any, will be disapplied from all or part of the National Curriculum Assessment requirements and which will do classroom-based tasks; arrange for the latter to be conducted between January and July.

- Seek permissions for special arrangements for students with special educational needs or English as an additional language and make requests for supply cover for the administration of tasks to students working at the lowest levels.

- Get information from departments about the numbers of papers to be ordered in the relevant tiers and send off test order forms.

- Check receipt of the correct quantity of test papers in the correct tiers, and the mark sheets and instructions, then place in a secure storage place.

- Arrange accommodation for the students taking the tests. (In 1996, the national evaluation found that 91 per cent of schools in England used one large space such as a hall or gym; only 13 per cent used separate classrooms.)

- Inform parents about the tests prior to the students sitting them.

▶

- Organise test invigilation and ensure that teachers are prepared by having read the notes for teachers.
- Oversee the opening of test papers and the conduct of the tests on the designated days.
- Package completed scripts and dispatch to markers using the designated national carrier.
- Check results and scripts when they are returned to school; establish whether teachers are content with the results or whether they wish to invoke the appeals procedure in particular cases.
- Ensure arrangements are in place for the finalising of teacher assessments.
- Prepare statistics of the results of students across the year group and collate with national statistics for the previous year, for comparative purposes, both for reporting to parents and for internal monitoring.
- Co-ordinate reports to parents and prepare explanatory letter if necessary.
- Organise input of test and TA results on to software or stationery for national data collection.

By any definition this list amounts to a high administrative workload and even if teachers describe the procedures as acceptable, one has to question the sense in which they are using this term. They may be acceptable in that they are 'doable' but whether it is worthwhile tying up so much of an educator's time in this amount of bureaucratic detail is highly questionable. Moreover, one would understand if, having completed these tasks, co-ordinators had very little energy left for guiding and supporting the development of internal assessment policy across the key stage. Yet I would consider this to be the more important role for an assessment leader.

■ Other requirements related to Key Stage 3 assessment, recording and reporting

In comparison with the amount of work associated with end of key stage assessment and reporting, government requirements with respect to the rest of Key Stage 3 appear rather light. However, there are a number of areas that should be mentioned.

Assessment of students with special educational needs

Assessment and reporting in relation to those students identified as having special educational needs is usually taken to be the separate responsibility of the Special Educational Needs Co-ordinator (SENCO). However, the issues that arise overlap with general issues in assessment, recording and reporting for all students and it makes good sense for SEN co-ordinators, school assessment co-ordinators and key stage co-ordinators to work closely together.

Since the introduction of the SEN Code of Practice, the assessment and diagnosis of special needs, and the planning and monitoring of educational provision in the light of this evidence, has been exemplary in many schools. It is a matter of some regret, therefore, that the resources are not available for the system of diagnostic assessment, individual educational plans and annual review to be extended to all students. After all, it has become a truism to say that all learners have some special education needs; in an ideal world this kind of provision would be made for all.

For those children with statements of special educational needs, official requirements, found in the SEN Code of Practice, focus on (1) procedures for ascertaining needs, (2) the annual review, which must involve consultation with parents, and (3) the development of individual education plans (IEPs). According to the more general 1997 Circular on reporting students' achievements: 'Reports for the annual review of a student's statement of SEN may, if the schools wish, serve as the annual report to parents. If so, headteachers must ensure that the minimum information required by the regulations is included.'

Record keeping and annual reporting to parents

Schools are required to keep records on every student and these must be updated at least once a year. These are expected to include information on academic achievements, other skills and abilities, and progess in the school. However, there are no requirements about how, or in what form, these records should be kept. These are considered to be matters that schools should decide for themselves. Schools also have an obligation to report annually to parents on their child's progress. There are no regulations about when this should be and most schools choose to 'stagger' their schedule of report writing so that the load is spread across the year and so that parents receive the information at an appropriate time. Many also introduce 'interim' reports into this schedule (termly or half-yearly). However, this is not a legal requirement. What *is* required is that at some point in both Year 7 and Year 8, parents receive information on the following:

- comments on progress in National Curriculum subjects (reference to levels is not required);
- comments on progress in other subjects and activities;
- a comment on general progress;
- a record of attendance;
- details about arrangements for discussion.

There is no prescription about the form that these reports should take nor on the way that progress should be reported. These are also considered to be professional matters that individual schools should decide. (Chapter 11 examines the professional considerations that should inform these decisions.)

The new National Record of Achievement

In Feburary 1997, the government announced its intention to relaunch the National Record of Achievement (NRA) as a new record, possibly to be called Progress File (or PROFIL). In contrast to its predecessor, this is intended for all students to use from the age of fourteen, i.e. from Year 9. The new NRA is intended to be a working file, probably loose-leaf, containing information to help young people make decisions and prepare for further and higher education, training and jobs. There are to be sections for records and evidence of achievements, interests and employment experience and a detachable section to be used to present information to employers.

The main idea behind the relaunched record is to provide a support for the *process* of career planning, rather than just providing a prestige document for presentation to employers, who, according to evaluations, were slow to take them up. The idea of introducing them in Year 9 is to encourage and enable teachers and students to begin the process of career planning at this point when youngsters are given their first opportunities to make subject choices. It is unlikely that anything will be laid down in regulations about how the new NRA should be used in Key Stage 3 but readers will need to 'watch this space'.

Matters of professional judgement

Developing policy beyond the scope of the regulations

In this chapter, I have tried to set out those things that the government requires with respect to assessment, recording and reporting in Key

Stage 3. What is striking about these regulations is that they all relate to *summative* features of assessment. Despite the early rhetoric about the formative purpose of, for example, teacher assessment, the emphasis is indubitably on summing up attainment and reporting academic outcomes. There are one or two nods in the direction of the formative purpose, as in the reporting Circular's footnote that asks for brief commentary on strengths and weaknesses, but there is little more.

Teachers and schools should therefore be alert to the possibility that if they were to fulfil the letter of the law, but not develop policy that goes beyond it, they would only meet one of two key purposes of assessment. They would be emphasising summative assessment for external accountability, rather than formative assessment for internal development and learning. Moreover, they would be concentrating only on academic outcomes in defined areas and neglecting other aspects of achievement that most schools and parents also value. I have in mind personal, social, practical and moral qualities and skills.

There is no intention that what the government sets out in regulations should define the limit of what schools do. Indeed there is an informal expectation that schools will develop their own policies to encompass a broader definition of assessment and recording. These decisions, however, are left entirely to the professional judgement of teachers and schools. These are not inconsiderable matters for deliberation because observing learning, marking work, providing and acting on feedback, recording evidence and recognising achievement in its broadest sense play a large part in the daily lives of teachers and students. Indeed, if Key Stage 3 is considered as a whole, what teachers do in assessment terms on a day-to-day basis should receive equivalent, if not more, attention than statutory assessment because it permeates teaching and learning throughout the key stages, and has the greater potential to contribute to the formative purpose.

It is easy to forget this if we allow ourselves to be weighed down by requirements for statutory end of key stage assessment. We need to remind ourselves that Key Stage 3 results will not have quite the 'high stakes' value of GCSE results as long as they remain unpublished and as long as they are not used as the sole basis for important decisions such as selection. Therefore their importance needs to be put into perspective and each school needs to consider ways to balance external requirements with internal priorities in order to promote its educational purposes. Much of the rest of this book will be an attempt to help schools to come to professional decisions about these matters.

Further reading

If you are interested in reading about the development of National Curriculum assessment policy at national level, a readable account has been written by Richard Daugherty who, as former Chair of the Curriculum Council for Wales, was close to the action. His book is entitled *National Curriculum Assessment: a Review of Policy 1987 to 1994*, and was published by The Falmer Press in 1995.

ACTIVITY

Mapping exercise

This activity is designed to help key stage co-ordinators and assessment co-ordinators map those things that they are required to do and also to find space for new development. The idea is to protect some staff time for the development of aspects of assessment not covered by regulations.

(i) First it will be important to update information about current regulations. It may be helpful to annotate the framework given in this chapter, which will inevitably become out of date with respect to some details.

(ii) Secondly, using a calendar of the school year, list the various activities that need to be accomplished, in time sequence, noting who will be responsible.

(iii) Thirdly, plot this in the form of a graph of the school year so that you have a representation of the peaks and troughs of 'required' assessment and recording activities. In a different colour, map on to this the peaks and troughs of other activities that have a major impact on the school, e.g. school visits.

(iv) Finally, identify a few troughs in activity (relatively speaking of course!) which might be used to implement some professional planning and development with colleagues in relation to internal, formative, developmental assessment.

From the example graph opposite, it is immediately apparent that a great deal of activity related to assessment, recording and reporting takes place *throughout* the year. This leaves very little time for new development. Even in the summer term, when Year 11 are often on 'study leave' around the time of their examinations, there is so much 'other activity' that planning staff development at this time would be difficult. Realistically, in this particular school, the beginning of the autumn term provides the best opportunity for in-service education and training, possibly with some follow-up around Easter.

Activity 69

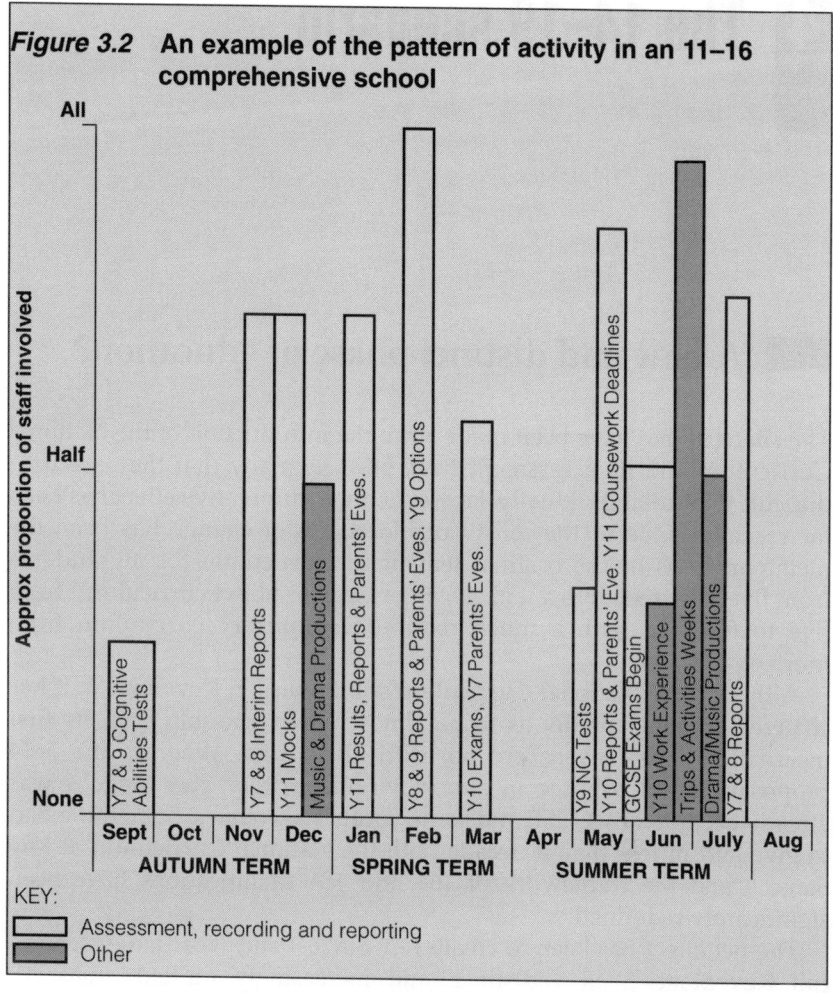

Figure 3.2 An example of the pattern of activity in an 11–16 comprehensive school

4 The 14–19 scenario

■ A new and distinct phase of education?

The changes that have been made since the introduction of the National Curriculum and its assessment have been so many that they are now difficult to recall individually. However, their cumulative effect has been far reaching. One of the most notable effects of change has been the metamorphosis of the original ten-subject curriculum for all students from five to sixteen into a ten, eleven or twelve subject curriculum[1] from five to fourteen with a much reduced compulsory curriculum from fourteen to sixteen.

Although the National Curriculum still applies in Key Stage 4, it has changed so substantially as to be almost unrecognisable from its first incarnation. The reasons are not difficult to find. Whereas the 5–14 proposals found a home in almost virgin territory, Key Stage 4 was already occupied by GCSE and some vocational courses. Something had to give and in less than a decade both the National Curriculum at Key Stage 4 and the framework of 16+ and 18+ qualifications have been significantly redefined.

The net effect has been to create Key Stage 4 and what many schools call Key Stage 5 as a distinct, and increasingly unified, phase of education. That this is a desirable development was a key message from the Dearing Review of the National Curriculum in 1993:

> . . . the age of 14 should be seen as the beginning of a distinct phase which runs through to 19, and allows young people to follow courses which lead progressively through from Key Stage 4 to education and training post 16.

---

[1] Information technology has emerged as a separate subject; modern foreign languages are not taught in Key Stages 1 and 2; and Welsh is an additional subject in Wales.

The Dearing Review also argued that as a nation we had for too long taken a narrow view of achievement and we should provide and recognise three pathways: the general (often, perhaps wrongly, described as academic) pathway, the vocational pathway and the occupational pathway. Although always easier said than done, these three pathways should be esteemed alike.

Dearing's subsequent review of 16–19 qualifications, published by SCAA in 1996, included proposals for 'a coherent national framework, covering all the main qualifications and the achievements of young people at every level of ability' (see Figure 4.1 on page 77). This framework attempted to incorporate all three pathways and demonstrate how they might relate to one another. The emerging character of 14–19 education and training broadly follows the pattern and direction that he proposed.

Dearing's full report of his review of 16–19 qualifications ran to some 700 pages so a detailed description of all the courses available to fourteen to nineteen year olds would not be possible or appropriate here. All I intend to do in this chapter is map the main features of the territory and to draw attention to some of the issues for assessment that require consideration by teachers in schools. This will be a basis for some of the more detailed discussion in subsequent chapters.

■ Mapping the pathways

The use of metaphor is familiar in education and 14–19 education is especially replete with it. Metaphors to do with travel are particularly common: pathways, destinations, routes (U-turns!). Perhaps this is not surprising because schooling in these years is increasingly focused on the acquisition of the qualifications that are regarded as the 'passports' to the next stage of education, training or employment. The choice of pathways to particular destinations therefore becomes critical. However, the topography and culture of the place the young person is coming from is often very different from that of the destination; to make the journey requires the learning of a new language, new expectations and conventions and even a new set of assumptions about what is valued in 'the other country'.

One of the most interesting things about assessment in relation to the 14–19 curriculum is the extent to which the assumptions underpinning policy and practice in one key stage or in relation to a particular pathway have accommodated, or been accommodated by, the assumptions underpinning policy and practice in an adjacent key stage or pathway. However, this can be the source of considerable difficulty for teachers as they try to make sense of a complex system. It is somewhat akin to negotiating Spaghetti Junction!

In the sections that follow I examine the issues at a number of points where different assessment systems meet.

Key Stage 3 meets Key Stage 4

Transition from Key Stage 3

Although most students in the secondary phase will not physically change schools at the end of Year 9, the transition from Key Stage 3 to Key Stage 4 can be as crucial as the transition from Key Stage 2 for many of the same reasons (described in Chapter 3). Issues of progression, curriculum continuity and coherence are important because it is the students who experience the transition and can easily become confused. If they simply give up trying to understand, they may go through the motions required in different courses for the sake of the qualification but they may not actually learn very much of lasting value to them.

The problem of mixed messages may not be so evident to teachers who do not have exactly the same experience as their students. Neither do agencies – which are involved with the development of different curricula, courses and qualifications – always seem sufficiently aware of the tensions created with the pronouncements of others in the field.

This issue was picked up by the national evaluation of Key Stage 3 assessment in 1996. The following is from section 4.7 of the version of the report from Exeter University that SCAA published:

> Curriculum coherence and complementary forms of assessment to honestly reflect genuine attainment and achievements of pupils progressing from KS3 to 14–16 then through to 19 is also an important consideration. At present, there is a different emphasis between messages about knowledge and learning that emanate from the different government agencies involved in education and training about the purpose of schooling 5–14 and the approaches to knowledge, learning and assessment that are encouraged by linking education to economic development for young people beyond the age of 14. For example:
>
> - the language of 'the pupil should be taught to' in the National Curriculum documentation turns into the language of learning 'opportunities' in the 14 –19 literature;
> - acquiring content knowledge and instrumental mechanistic learning of mathematical and English skills is replaced with an important

> emphasis on flexible, social and employability skills and practical knowledge relevant to a working life;
>
> - *the emphasis on marks and scores comparing one child with another is replaced by the recognition of the need for each individual to be able to articulate through the assessment process what they know.*

Recognising that the end of Key Stage 3 now marked the conclusion of an important phase in youngsters' education, and, for some, the last time they would study arts and humanities subjects, which are no longer compulsory in Key Stage 4, the national evaluation made the following suggestion.

> *The establishment of a comprehensive knowledge base about individual pupil achievements at the end of KS3 could act as a bridge between these different phases of learning, 5–14 and 14–19, and at the same time improve the effectiveness of the KS3 assessment arrangements as an educational tool that gives value for money.*

To this end the evaluators recommended reducing the current testing programme by half, to one externally marked test per core subject, and reporting test results in the context of broader summative statutory teacher assessment within the relaunched National Record of Achievement. This would give status to the new NRA for fourteen year olds as the record of achievement 5–14 and as the basis for planning 'first steps in the pathway of each child's lifelong learning journey'.

The National Curriculum in Key Stage 4 and contrasts with Key Stage 3

From autumn 1996, the National Curriculum for Key Stage 4 in English maintained schools was reduced to a compulsory extended core expected to occupy 60 per cent of curriculum time, allowing space for a wider choice of academic and vocational options:

- English;
- mathematics;
- science;
- design and technology;
- information technology;
- a modern foreign language;
- physical education.

This list is remarkable for the way in which it underwrites an 'employers' curriculum' with clear emphasis on subjects deemed to be necessary for economic activity in global markets. The disappearance of the humanities and arts from this compulsory list indicates that arguments for a 'liberal humanist education for all' or 'education of the whole child' have currently lost out in national debates. Of course, most schools will continue to offer history, geography, art and music as options but these no longer have a protected place or a prescribed programme of study for this key stage.

All maintained schools continue to have an obligation (defined in the 1944 Education Act) to provide religious education throughout Key Stages 4 *and* 5. The provision of sex education is also a requirement and careers education is likely to be made statutory.

The curriculum taught as courses

One of the important differences between Key Stage 4 and those that precede it, is that the curriculum is taught and assessed as *courses*. It is expected that the National Curriculum at Key Stage 4 will be provided through courses leading to approved qualifications such as GCSE (full courses are required in core subjects but short courses may be taken in design and technology, a modern foreign language, information technology and physical education), GNVQ (Part One in seven vocational areas or individual units in foreign languages and information technology), or new Entry Level qualifications in literacy, numeracy and information technology. All the relevant qualifications are therefore expected to incorporate National Curriculum requirements into their syllabuses.

Syllabuses and clarity about assessment

The GCSE *Regulations and Criteria*, published by SCAA/ACAC in 1995, contained a useful definition of what a syllabus is:

> *The complete description of what may be assessed and how assessment will be made in relation to a particular qualification.*

A syllabus is therefore quite different from the National Curriculum Programmes of Study which set out only what teachers are expected to teach, or even the National Curriculum Attainment Targets which are simply descriptions of standards. In relation to statutory teacher assessment at Key Stages 1, 2 and 3 there is no prescription about 'what may be assessed and how assessment will be made' and teachers are expected to devise their own assessments in order to meet statutory obligations.

In contrast, at Key Stage 4, the qualifications-awarding bodies take much of this responsibility from teachers by providing detailed assessment schemes. For example, according to the general regulations, all GCSE syllabuses must include a scheme of assessment which specifies:

- the relationships between assessment objectives and examination components;
- the assessment methods and techniques to be used and the weightings allocated to each examination component;
- the weightings allocated to coursework, terminal examination and end-of-module tests;
- the time allocated to question papers and other timed assessments;
- the means by which differentiation is to be achieved;
- descriptions for grades F, C and A (the high stakes grades);
- the method of moderation to be applied to any coursework.

Syllabuses are also required to set out regulations for the setting, assessment, conduct and moderation of coursework in accordance with the Mandatory Code of Practice for the GCSE.

The structure of GNVQ qualifications is similar in this respect with assessment even more thoroughly prescribed and integrated into the curriculum and learning process. The GNVQ is a *unit-based* qualification at Foundation, Intermediate and Advanced Levels. Each unit is broken down into *elements* which lists *performance criteria* specifying the standards that candidates must achieve. The depth and breadth of coverage expected is provided in *range statements*, whilst *evidence indicators* describe the evidence that candidates must produce and the activities from which such evidence will be derived. Examples *(amplification)* and *guidance* on teaching and learning are also provided.

What all this amounts to, in the case of both GCSE and GNVQ, is a fairly tight specification that indicates to teachers not only what they should teach but what coursework they should set, how this should be collated, marked and moderated or verified, and how they should prepare students for tests and examination. In other words they know precisely what they have to do.

None of this detail and clarity about assessment arrangements is provided at Key Stage 3, and whilst some teachers welcome the freedom this gives them to devise appropriate Key Stage 3 assessments according their judgements of fitness to purpose and context, others flounder and are tempted to fall back on familiar practices without much thought to their validity.

Their experience with GCSE or GNVQ does not always help them because so many assessment decisions are made for them by the awarding bodies that, without fully understanding the principles behind them, they cannot always use this experience in the construction of their own assessment schemes at Key Stage 3. This may explain why the confidence of teachers with 16+ assessment and examinations does not always filter down to assessment at Key Stage 3 and why they often need a lot of support to develop appropriate assessment systems for students in years 7–9.

Vocational meets academic

The proposed framework of national qualifications

As mentioned earlier, Sir Ron Dearing's 1996 review of qualifications was set up to 'consider and advise the Secretaries of State for Education and Employment and for Wales on ways to strengthen, consolidate and improve the framework for 16–19 qualifications'.

To some extent Dearing's hands were tied because, before embarking on his review, he was told that the government wanted (a) to retain the integrity of GCE A–levels as the 'gold standard', and (b) to build on current developments in GNVQs and NVQs. In other words he was not able to put all existing qualifications into the melting pot in order to come up with something entirely new that would satisfy the evident need for a more coherent and simplified system of post–16 qualifications. All he could do was to create a framework incorporating the different pathways and stating which level in one pathway should be deemed to be equivalent to a specified level in another pathway (see Figure 4.1 on page 77).

For at least forty years there has been debate about the negative effects of early specialisation in the English system and the higher status accorded to academic qualifications which undermines the value of vocational skills and knowledge that are so important to a country's economic health. Many people have argued for broader qualifications in Key Stage 5 which incorporate and value both academic and vocational achievements.

As one step in this direction, but mainly away from too early specialisation, some schools have successfully implemented the International

Figure 4.1 Proposed framework of national qualifications

National Award: Advanced Level

| AS and A Level | GNVQ Advanced Level | NVQ Level 3 |

National Award: Intermediate Level

| GCSE Grades A*–C | GNVQ Intermediate Level | NVQ Level 2 |

National Award: Foundation Level

| GCSE Grades D–G | GNVQ Foundation Level | NVQ Level 1 |

National Award: Entry Level

Common to all pathways:
Three grades A/B/C
(equivalent in demand to National Curriculum Level 3, 2 and 1 but contextualised for the post–16 age group)

Dearing, R. (1996), *Review of Qualifications for 16–19 year olds: summary report*, London, SCAA, p.8.

Baccalaureate. This has proved popular with parents and students and has not noticeably disadvantaged students applying to universities or for jobs. If Sir Ron had not been told that he should preserve the A–level he might have proposed the creation of a British Baccalaureate. In the circumstances, all he could do was to recommend the creation of National Certificates and National Diplomas that would recognise achievement in breadth and depth of study across a range of qualifications.

The change of government in May 1997 raised the possibility that a British Baccalaureate could be put back on the agenda – one Minister was known to favour it. This seems unlikely, however, as proposals being discussed at the time of writing (October 1997) appear to favour a single national certificate for eighteen year olds based on whole qualifications, not a mix-and-match. However, it is proposed that A–levels and AS–levels should be reformed and relaunched (possibly in 1999) and GNVQs upgraded to the 'gold standard' so that they are genuinely 'applied A–Levels'.

In this sense, QCA, on behalf of government in England, may follow the example of Scotland, where the Scottish Qualifications Authority (the equivalent of the QCA in England) is proposing to oversee a wholesale reform of the Scottish Highers (the equivalent of A–levels) in order to create a properly unified system of vocational and academic qualifications.

This is a rapidly changing area of education and readers will need to keep up to date. Hopefully, this account has cleared some of the ground.

Tensions between the NVQ/GNVQ and the GCSE/GCE models of learning and assessment

In addition to problems associated with the legacy of a system in which academic and vocational qualifications have been perceived to have different cultural value and economic currency, there are other substantial differences between GCSE/GCE and NVQ/GNVQ which pose a challenge to claims for equivalence – in any intrinsic sense. These differences have to do with the very different conceptions of learning and assessment that they embody.

When I contrasted Key Stage 4 assessment issues with Key Stage 3, I mentioned that there are similarities between the various pathways available in Key Stage 4 and 5 because students generally follow *courses* defined by *syllabuses*. For example, the development of GCSEs, GCE A–levels and GNVQs all follow a broadly similar pattern:

- the creation of content – syllabus or specification;
- the specification of assessment instruments – examination papers, tests, marking schemes, assignments, portfolios etc
- an awarding process – marking, standardisation, verification, determining grades, certification.

However, there are also substantial differences between general and academic courses (GCSEs and GCE A–levels) and vocational and occupational courses (NVQs and GNVQs).

The GCSE/GCE model

Although there are differences between GCSE and GCE A–level, not only in the depth and breadth of syllabuses but also in their modes of assessment, both are premised on a conception of learning and assessment that values the acquisition of subject content knowledge, understanding of concepts and processes and ability in executing key skills especially literacy, numeracy and IT competence. The emphasis that is placed on assessment through terminal or end of module examination in both GCSE and GCE indicates that candidates are expected to learn material in such a way that they can 'produce' evidence of their knowledge, skills and understanding in time-constrained situations without much reference to sources of information. Although *application* of knowledge is tested in these circumstances, a certain amount of learning as memorisation still features in these examinations.

Timed examinations and set coursework can only *sample* the learning that may have taken place within a two-year course. GCSE and GCE awards are therefore made on the basis of an assumption of generalisability: that the level of performance a candidate demonstrates on a limited number of assessment tasks and test items would be the same had the assessments sampled the curriculum and learning differently.

Within the 1995 GCSE mandatory Code of Practice, for example, Chief Examiners are only expected to sample *half* of the relevant statements within attainment targets and programmes of study when devising GCSE question papers for National Curriculum subjects. In order to prepare students for the questions that might arise, teachers usually attempt to cover the entire syllabus (although, as a teacher, I can recall attempting some judicious selection of content, based on a careful analysis of past papers!). In the interests of coverage, teachers usually engage in a good deal of direct instruction and generally provide notes and learning activities that students will be able to draw on in assessed assignments and examinations. Although terminal examinations and tests are externally marked, teachers are expected to mark coursework according to carefully prescribed criteria and with the help of exemplar material. Their judgements are standardised and moderated but most teachers acquire reasonable confidence in marking coursework because they are assessing knowledge and understanding in their own subject, i.e. one in which they qualified at a high level.

The NVQ/GNVQ model

The assumptions underpinning NVQ and GNVQ are often quite different. GNVQ is more commonly adopted in schools than NVQ because it offers general preparation for work or further study in a broad vocational area, rather than training for a specific occupation. Nevertheless, some schools do offer NVQs, for example in Business Administration, and they work closely with employers to the extent that students are on work placement for two days a week and in school for the remaining three days. At national level, NVQs were established first and GNVQs were very much moulded in their image. This had strengths but it has also created a number of problems that were investigated in 1996 by a review group chaired by John Capey.

At the heart of the NVQ model is a conception of valued learning as *competence* to perform a particular job. Competence is further defined as *mastery* of identified performance skills. This definition has two important implications for assessment. First, the level of competence is measured on the basis of *outcomes* which may be in the form of the performance of processes (e.g. planning, information handling) or the production of artefacts.

The outcomes approach is central to the NVQ model and was expounded by Gordon Jessup, in his 1991 book, *Outcomes: NVQs and the Emerging Model of Education and Training*, published by Falmer Press. Jessup argues that outcomes should not be understood in a narrow behavioural sense because worthwhile performance outcomes involve the application of knowledge as well as skill. However, the focus was designed to shift attention to learning that can be observed in the doing. In consequence, it places less emphasis on the importance of teaching. This provides scope for the Accreditation of Prior Learning (APL) which might be demonstrable but which would not necessarily arise from participation in formal courses.

The second implication for assessment which arises from the concept of mastery is the requirement for an assessment regime designed to measure an individual's performance in *every* element of the occupational role. The concept of 'sampling' performance has little credibility with employers: for example, a building firm is unlikely to accept that a joiner can make mortice and tenon joints if (s)he has only demonstrated dovetails – they will want to know that (s)he can do both. The exhaustive approach to assessment that is required to satisfy the concept of mastery assumes that the learner is self-pacing and will take the time that adequate demonstration of performance demands. This kind of assessment cannot be accomplished through time-constrained external examination so the responsibility falls on trained internal assessors to carry out continuous assessment, moderated by accredited internal and external verifiers.

This model was used as the basis for the development of GNVQs but it rapidly became evident that application to two-year courses in general vocational areas run by teachers in schools was encountering huge problems. These problems were almost entirely focused on assessment and were the reason why the National Council for Vocational Qualifications commissioned an independent review. The resulting Capey Report of 1996 praised the GNVQ model in its outcomes approach and the centrality it gave to the production of a portfolio as evidence of a student's learning.

The review group perceived students to be highly motivated by the clear specification of what was required of them and the recognition that they should be able to 'know' when they had achieved particular targets. There was little anxiety about 'getting it right on the night', as there was with GCE A–level, although the external tests that were introduced as a 'low hurdle' to confirm broad coverage had become a major obstacle preventing students from completing their courses. The problems with GNVQ assessment were sizeable, however, and contributed to a judgement that it had become virtually unmanageable for the following reasons, among others:

- The NVQ mastery model was not appropriate to the study of broad vocational areas and assessment needed to be based on key knowledge and skills in units, rather than detailed and exhaustive demonstration of competence in elements. The latter had led to students becoming expert filers rather than competent learners.

- Having been borrowed from occupational training, the language of GNVQs was not familiar in schools. It shared none of the language of the National Curriculum or GCSE/GCE which made it confusing or inaccessible to both teachers and students.

- Unlike work-based assessors and verifiers for NVQs, teachers rarely had recent experience of working in the vocational area of the courses they were teaching. Their competence to assess or to verify assessments was therefore often in doubt and the Capey Report recommended that prompt attention should be given to training.

At the time of writing, these issues are under consideration and vocational qualifications are to be relaunched. Hopefully some of these problems, which are undoubtedly causing some schools to hang back from involvement, will be resolved.

In Figure 4.2 on page 82 I have attempted to represent diagrammatically some of the differences in emphasis between academic and vocational assessment. As an ideal-type classification it runs the risk of caricature but it may help to unravel some of the mysteries.

■ Route planning

In what must surely be an understatement, the document *Progression 14–19*, published by SCAA in 1996, said:

Figure 4.2 **Models of learning and assessment underpinning academic and vocational qualifications**

	Academic qualifications	Vocational qualifications
Concept of learning	acquiring knowledge and understanding	developing competence
Focus of assessment	subject content and application of knowledge	outcomes: process skills and products
Role of teacher	to cover syllabus	to provide opportunities for students to demonstrate learning
Role of student	to acquire knowledge for production and application in examinations at some future time	to collect evidence to demonstrate performance as and when it occurs (self-pacing)
Mode of assessment	mainly timed, unseen terminal examinations (some coursework assignments)	mainly portfolios of evidence (some external tests)
Sample of domain	assessment items sample the subject content and elements within attainment targets as representative of the domain	total coverage required as evidence of mastery
Assessors	mainly externally set and marked	mainly internally assessed and verified
Quality assurance	external standardisation and moderation	external verification

It is a considerable challenge to ensure that there is a comprehensive structure of learning opportunities and that students progress through them appropriately.

This draws attention to the fact that when schools consider 14–19 progression they need to be mindful of two things: how to make the kind of provision that will enable students to follow pathways best suited to their needs, and how to support students in making these choices. In other words there are school-level issues and student-level issues to consider.

School-level issues and student-level issues

It is not my intention here to give detailed attention to the questions about how schools might plan their 14–19 provision. These are curriculum planning issues rather than assessment issues *per se* and much advice is available elsewhere[2]. In school-level planning it is important, however, to consider the implications of assessment issues. For example, the question of whether teaching staff have, or could acquire, the training and experience to provide and assess GNVQ units or courses is an important consideration to be set alongside a consideration of students' needs, and demands from local labour markets.

In contrast, questions about how students can best be supported to take advantage of the pathways that are provided engage more directly with aspects of assessment, recording and reporting policy in schools. In order to make appropriate choices, students need to have been given opportunities to learn and achieve those things that are necessary for progression to the next stage in their chosen route. Almost without exception this will mean learning not only in academic and vocational skills areas but also in the development of personal and social skills and qualities. They will need evidence of all these achievements and they will need to know how to use them and build on them as they move to the next stage of education, training or employment.

The National Record of Achievement, which became mandatory for all sixteen year olds in 1991, was an attempt to provide a record of qualifications, achievements, interests and experience for these purposes and to assist students in action planning. The relaunched NRA (PROFIL) is intended to go beyond this and more specifically to support the process of planning for lifelong education and from the important point of transition at age fourteen. What the new NRA might contain and how it could be used to support this purpose will be discussed further in Chapter 11.

Further reading

A recent book devoted entirely to the issues surrounding competence-based assessment was published by the Open University Press in 1995.

---

[2] See for example the 1995 SCAA booklet, *Managing the Curriculum at Key Stage 4*, also *Progression 14-19: serving all students well*, published in 1996.

The author is Alison Wolf, Professor of Education at the London Institute of Education, and the title is *Competence-based assessment*. Alison Wolf has been involved in evaluations of NVQs and GNVQs. This book is particularly valuable for its critique of criterion-referencing, which underpins the competence-based model, and I shall refer to it again in Chapter 5.

ACTIVITY

This chapter is mainly intended to map the territory and to raise issues for more detailed consideration in later chapters. It does not provide guidance or advice, as such, and practical activities do not arise as naturally as they might elsewhere. However, the following suggestion might be helpful to assessment co-ordinators or Key Stage 4 and Key Stage 5/Sixth Form co-ordinators.

Reviewing information for students and parents

If, as the Capey Report noted, one of the major problems for parents, students, and indeed teachers, is understanding the different language used and the different conceptions of teaching, learning and assessment underpinning the 14–19 pathways, it is important for managers and co-ordinators to review the accessibility of literature and oral presentations to parents and students.

Consider how information in this complex area might be made more user-friendly, perhaps by using cartoons or other illustrations based on the travel metaphor: maps, routes, pathways, mazes, junctions, destinations, signposts, languages, customs etc. Provide graphic ideas that might be used to help parents and students understand. You might also wish to adapt the kind of schematic representation I have used in Figure 4.2 on page 82.

5 Types of assessment 1: Assessments made in the course of teaching

Introduction

This chapter and Chapters 6 and 7 provide a review of the different types of assessment commonly used in secondary schools and they raise some of the important issues associated with each. My concern is that school assessment co-ordinators, heads of department and classroom teachers should be able to evaluate the relative strengths and weaknesses of various kinds of assessment before incorporating them into policy and practice, or before deciding to continue with existing assessment practices. The different forms of assessment that a school chooses to use should be based on a consideration of *fitness for purpose* rather than an uncritical acceptance of tradition or the blandishments of commercial companies with assessment 'products' to sell. Of course, as Chapters 3 and 4 described, there are some kinds of assessment which schools are required to carry out, but there is still much scope for school-based decision-making.

Taken-for-granted assumptions about the value of different kinds of assessment are widespread; some of these assumptions amount to myths that need to be challenged. Each type of assessment also raises a number of specific issues that need to be thought through. These are very large areas to deal with and my treatment of them will be necessarily brief but I will offer some practical suggestions about ways to deal with them.

Categories of assessment

Many writers on assessment classify the different types of assessment on a dimension of formality ranging from informal assessment to formal assessment. Almost invariably routine assessment in classrooms by teachers is described as informal assessment and standardised testing is at the opposite extreme. In my view this kind of classification has dangers because it often carries unjustified value judgements. For example, if we apply the Concise Oxford Dictionary definition of 'formal' as 'valid in virtue of its form, explicit and definite, not merely tacit', this would seem to imply that standardised tests are more valid than classroom assessments and that the latter are always tacit, never explicit. Because of the different nature of these two kinds of assessments, such a description could also imply that assessments that are expressed quantitatively are necessarily more valid than the kinds of qualitative assessments that teachers routinely make about their students' performance. In the discussion that follows I hope to show that these assumptions need to be questioned.

There is, of course, some justification for classifying types of assessments according to the degree of formalisation associated with their *procedures* (which is different from talking broadly of informal and formal assessment). My preference, however, is for broad categories that are drawn heuristically from the experience of teachers and students, rather than according to some logical scheme. In this respect it is interesting that teachers commonly use different terms for similar procedures used in different contexts, although the terms may be almost interchangeable according to dictionary definitions. 'Test' and 'examination' are obvious examples. In my view, *the contexts of use* are as important as the nature of the procedures and on this basis I propose to review five categories of assessment, each of which may itself incorporate a range of assessment procedures:

- assessment as part of classroom process;
- routine marking of classwork and homework;
- periodic tests and assessment tasks;
- standardised tests;
- examinations.

In this chapter I deal with the first two of these five categories, under the general heading of assessments made in the course of teaching.

Assessment as part of classroom process

It is stating the obvious to say that teachers make assessments all the time. From the moment new classes of students enter their classrooms at the beginning of a new school year, teachers observe their behaviour as groups and as individuals and, on the basis of these observations, they tailor their lesson plans and adapt their own teaching behaviour. In his 1991 book, *Classroom Assessment*, published by McGraw-Hill in New

York, the US writer Peter Airasian calls this 'sizing up'; others have called it 'spotting' and 'scanning'.

Observing the class

Typically such 'sizing up' will involve paying attention to a number of different aspects of what students do and what they say in various circumstances and drawing inferences from these observations. For example, teachers will take note of students who are noisy and those who are quiet; those who come prepared for the lesson and those who don't; those who ask or answer questions and those who never do; those who complete the work set and those who fail to finish in the time allotted; those who grasp certain ideas quickly and those who experience particular difficulties, and so on.

As teachers becomes familiar with their new classes, they will deliberately use techniques, such as asking questions, to elicit oral responses that will give them more information about a student's thought processes. Asking questions of students in the course of teaching is a vital tool in every teacher's kit of teaching methods. At the same time it is a form of ongoing assessment by which the teacher actively seeks information about students. In this sense, then, teaching, learning and assessment are intimately bound up together.

On the basis of *evidence* drawn from observations of behaviour and listening to oral contributions, teachers will draw *inferences* about a student's attitudes, personal qualities, abilities, motivation and commitment, learning speed and style, intelligence, attainments and progress. They may therefore describe students in general categories such as boisterous, reserved, disruptive, keen, disaffected, well-motivated, lazy, well-organised, chaotic, intelligent, bright, dull, slow, clever etc. Or they might refer to more specific skills and achievements: he speaks fluently; she has a good grasp of fair testing etc.

These inferences in turn will lead teachers to make certain *judgements* and *decisions* about the best ways to treat such pupils, e.g. controlling, challenging, encouraging, supporting, reinforcing, reprimanding. Often the sequence of *observing, inferring, judging* and *deciding* is almost instantaneous, especially for teachers who are able to draw on an accumulated store of experience of similar situations. Thus, a teacher might say that 'John is bright and I need to challenge him with more complex tasks if he is not to become bored and disruptive' without feeling any need to state the evidence on which she has made such an inference and judgement. This is part of the art or craft of teaching and it has been estimated that the average teacher makes hundreds of such decisions based on similar judgements every day. (Airasian's book begins with a list of 25 major decisions one teacher makes in one day.)

▇ Jumping to conclusions too readily

However, there are dangers in relying too heavily or exclusively on these kind of intuitions. Sometimes they can be wrong. Take for example a situation that I observed. A foreign languages teacher had given his class ten minutes to find the past tense of thirty irregular verbs in a wordsearch puzzle. At the end of that time, some of his students, mainly girls, had completed the task while some others, mainly boys, had hardly started, or had found very few correct words. On the basis of this evidence, the teacher inferred that the boys were less motivated, less able or slower than the girls.

However, observing at the back of the class, I thought there might be another explanation. At the end of the period of time allocated, the teacher read out the correct answers to the class so that they could check their own work. At this point the boys copied them down. Could it be that this lesson format was so familiar that the boys realised that they would be given the answers if they waited long enough? This would give them the revision material that they would need for the all-important end-of-term test without the hassle of having to do the work entailed in the task for this particular lesson. If this was their reasoning then it would be wrong to infer that they were less able, slower or even less motivated. They may have been sharp enough to know that it was the test results that really mattered; these went into the teacher's mark book, whereas the results of this class exercise were not recorded or used formatively.

What this example is intended to illustrate is that teachers' judgements can be wrong if they jump to conclusions too readily. And if they always respond to similar circumstances in identical ways they are in danger of developing stereotypes and biases. It would not be realistic, of course, to expect a teacher to ponder long and hard over every situation encountered. Given the number of situations requiring decisions every day, such a degree of reflection would inhibit action.

However, in recent years there has been considerable support for the idea that teachers should see themselves as 'reflective-practitioners'[1]. This concept emphasises the importance of teachers developing an attitude of mind and a new definition of their role which stimulates them

---

[1]This is a term coined by Donald Schön in his 1983 book *The Reflective Practitioner*, published by Basic Books in New York.

to 'think twice', by considering the evidence, before settling on a course of action. 'Reflection-in-action' does not mean that teachers have to become as systematic as scientists but it does argue that the practice of education is not only an art or craft but that it can, and should, have some of the characteristics of a science. For example, it would be reasonable to expect teaching decisions to be based on observations of students that are made with some degree of systematisation and objectivity and with due regard to the nature of evidence, inference and judgement.

Given the limitations of time and resources, what would it then be reasonable to expect teachers to do to strengthen and improve the quality of the assessments they make during the course of teaching? The following are some suggestions.

Improving the quality of assessments: sampling

First, it might be reasonable to expect teachers *occasionally* to select an *aspect* of students' responses to their classroom experience for closer scrutiny. This will involve *sampling* in at least three respects: lessons; students and events or behaviours. Even a very limited study, say, of one student's behaviour during the course of a single lesson, can provide valuable insights. Teachers should not feel obliged to study large 'representative' samples over long periods of time or only those behaviours that they feel are 'typical' and therefore 'generalisable' to all the students they teach. The biggest challenges to their professional skills are often from individual students who defy the norm and it is often worth making such students the focus of a more detailed study.

Non Worrall, the Curriculum Deputy at Queen Elizabeth's Girls' School, Barnet, with whom I have worked for some years, made such a study of one Year 7 girl in 1991. Eve, as I shall call her, arrived from her primary school with a record of poor behaviour and underachievement. She soon established her credentials as a disruptive influence. Something clearly had to be done so Non started by observing her behaviour more closely. She constructed an observation schedule with categories of different types of on-task and off-task behaviour and persuaded Eve's subject teachers to record her activities, along with those of the four other students in her friendship group, at five minute intervals during one lesson. Non also audio-recorded the group as they carried out a group activity in one of her English lessons. All groups were given a tape recorder so that Eve's group did not feel singled out. This audio-evidence revealed that Eve deliberately intervened in a way that annoyed others on eleven occasions during this one lesson. Her behaviour out of lessons was, however, very different. Non observed this too.

The whole class received a lot of attention as a result of this exercise and the climate in the classroom began to change as a result. But two explicit decisions were taken to improve the situation. First, Eve's friendship group was deliberately encouraged to become her support group. This improved the situation for Eve, for her group, and for the class as a whole. Secondly, Non decided to become her mentor, discussing progress and setting targets with her on a regular basis. The eventual outcome was an encouraging one. By Year 11 Eve had made such strides that she was awarded the school's prize for having made the most progress and she stayed on in the sixth form to take National Vocational Qualifications.

What I hope this illustrates is that studies of 'particular' cases are often just as important as studies of more 'general' situations and, indeed, solving a particular problem can lead to a more general benefit.

The value of collecting evidence systematically

A second thing that the above example illustrates is the value of collecting evidence in a somewhat more systematic way than is usual during the normal course of teaching. This might involve some kind of recording so that teachers can take the evidence away and think more deeply about what it might mean. I know that some teachers will claim not to have *any* additional time and space these days, but I also know many teachers, like the deputy headteacher mentioned above, who *find* the time because they believe that this kind of reflection is an important part of their professional role and has benefits that may eventually *save* them time in the longer term.

With respect to recording, teachers will have a number of decisions to make. Among the most important will be whether to record as much as they can in a fairly open-ended, unstructured way, perhaps by video-recording, audio-recording or keeping a diary or notes; or to record using a pre-structured observation schedule in the form of a checklist of behaviours in which they are particularly interested. Non Worrall recorded Eve's behaviour in both these ways.

The former has the advantage of allowing teachers to capture unexpected but nonetheless relevant data. (I recall that during my time as a school teacher I picked up a very interesting *sotto voce* commentary from one of my students when I tape-recorded a discussion-based lesson with a larger group!) The disadvantage is that a great deal of information is gathered in this way and the task of analysing it can be daunting.

Pre-structured observation schedules

The advantage of pre-structured schedules is that they are less demanding in terms of analysis because the categories have already been decided. The disadvantage is that teachers may be tempted to construct schedules according to their own preconceptions and the data may only serve to confirm these rather than to challenge them. This can sometimes be avoided by using schedules developed by other people for similar purposes. The possibility of biased interpretation can also be reduced by ensuring that the items in the schedule ask for *descriptions* of observable behaviour, e.g. 'Listens and responds to the ideas of other students when engaged in group tasks', rather than *evaluations*, e.g. 'Co-operates well with other pupils'. *Low-inference categories*, which do not require too much *interpretation* of what teachers see or hear at the point of recording, generally allow for a greater range of alternative interpretations than high-inference categories. They therefore are more helpful in the critique of taken-for-granted assumptions.

Figure 5.1 on page 92 and 5.2 on page 93 give parts of two observation schedules. (They are included here as examples, not as models.) The first has relatively low-inference descriptors and the second contains high-inference descriptors. You will notice that the schedule with high-inference descriptors is applicable to a wider range of behaviours. This is one of the arguments *for* more general categories although they require a greater degree of interpretation. They may only create real problems if a number of teachers choose to use the same schedule; in which case teachers will need to make sure that they are all interpreting the categories in the same way. (Chapter 8 deals with strategies for ensuring consistency in teachers' interpretations and judgements.)

Figures 5.1 and 5.2 also illustrate two different forms of recording: a rating scale and a check-list. I do not have space here to provide examples of all the different kinds of observation schedules that might be used but much advice about methods for collecting information about students' attitudes and achievements can be found in the many books on educational research methods that are currently available. Those addressed specifically to teachers are particularly useful and I give the full references to some of these at the end of this chapter on page 103.

▇ Interpreting the evidence

Once teachers have collected some information about their students, they will, of course, need to interpret it: to decide what it means. This will involve two things: *making inferences* about what the observed behaviours can tell them regarding a student's attitudes, abilities and

Figure 5.1 **Language inventory**

NAME:	WHEN OBSERVED
SPEAKING:	
1 Can deliver a message	
2 Can relate a story	
3 Can carry on a conversation	
4 Can develop a reasoned argument	
5 Can explain how something works	
6 Can give directions	
7 Can ask questions to find something out	
LISTENING:	
8 Listens to the teacher	
9 Answers questions	
10 Can recall what has been said	
11 Can respond correctly to instructions	
12 Responds to other students' requests for help	

achievements; and *making judgements* about the implications these inferences may have for planning learning and teaching.

In the United States, where English words sometimes carry different meanings, the term 'assessment' tends to be used for the collection of information about students' learning and the inferences that are drawn from it in terms of aptitudes, abilities and achievements. The term 'evaluation' is then used for the subsequent judgements and decisions that are made on the basis of these assessments. This is a helpful distinction which is somewhat blurred in the way we use the term 'assessment' in Britain, where it tends to be all embracing.

With respect to the inferences to be drawn from evidence of students' behaviour, the important point is that they should be fully *warranted*. For

Figure 5.2 **Qualities of 'good' students**

QUALITIES WE ARE LOOKING FOR IN STUDENTS Name:	Always	Usually	Sometimes	Seldom	Never
1 Shows interest in work					
2 Works consistently and is not distracted					
3 Is thorough					
4 Presents work tidily					
5 Meets the expected standard					
6 Makes progress					
7 Co-operates with the teacher					
8 Works well with other students					
9 Shows initiative					
10 Shows originality in creative work					
11 Takes care of school property					
12 Is punctual to lessons					

example, a familiar category in observation schedules relates to on-task and off-task behaviour. (Non Worrall used this category although she broke it down into specific behaviours.) If teachers use this as a single, generic description, they usually tick the 'off-task' box if they see students looking out of the window, walking around the room, or talking to other students when the teacher expects them to be reading or writing. However, they may be drawing mistaken inferences from what they assume to be 'off-task' behaviour. I remember feeling unjustly treated when a teacher once wrote in my report, 'She has a tendency to daydream'. I argued that I was actually thinking! It is therefore a good idea to break down high-inference categories, such as 'off-task', into more specific behaviours to avoid misinterpretation.

Checking inferences

It is difficult for teachers, of course, not to 'jump to conclusions' about the meaning of their observations. There are, however, a number of established ways for them to check their inferences. One is called *triangulation* and involves cross-checking with other sources of data. For example, a teacher who perceived a student to be 'off-task' because he was talking to other students might check her perception by asking the students what they were talking about. She might look at what the student had produced as a result of the task set before deciding whether her first impression was accurate.

Another strategy for enhancing confidence in the inferences made is to involve someone else in the process of interpreting the evidence. *Peer observation, peer audit, moderation and agreement trials* (see Chapter 8) require considerable commitment and organisation (and courage) but they can be invaluable in giving a critical edge to the way that teachers think about students' behaviour and learning outcomes. Anthropologists talk about the need to 'render the familiar strange' and a 'critical friend' or group can help teachers to do this with respect to their own classrooms and the students they think they know well.

The question of how judgements and decisions made on the basis of classroom assessments can enhance teaching and learning are dealt with more fully in Chapter 9 because this is a crucial issue that applies to other types of assessment as well. Indeed, many of the issues discussed above apply in some measure to other types of assessment, which I discuss below and in Chapters 6 and 7.

Routine marking of classwork and homework

In the section above I deliberately focused upon assessment based on students' behaviour in classrooms. (I use 'classroom' generically to mean all the places where teaching and learning takes place in the course of formal education, including gyms, workshops and on field trips.) Another important source of assessment evidence is, of course, what students *produce* in the course of their learning, i.e. their learning *outcomes*.

Built into every teacher's scheme of work will be opportunities for students to practice the skills that they have been taught, to demonstrate their knowledge, or to develop understanding by tackling tasks that require them to *apply* what they have learned. These opportunities take the form of tasks that teachers set for completion in class or at home. Often the product is written, although it could be some other kind of artefact.

How should work be marked?

The assessment of these student products is usually called 'marking' in Britain: a curiously vague word that implies little more than that teachers make some marks on students' work. This raises an important issue about the nature of marking: what kind of marks should they be? It would probably not be an exaggeration to say that, over the years, in most schools, there has been more discussion about this single matter than any other assessment issue. The questions seem to range from the seemingly trivial to the fundamental. For example:

- Should teachers actually put marks on students' work? Should they be recorded elsewhere, say, on an annotation sheet, or should they be given orally?
- Should teachers use red pen?
- Should teachers correct every mistake?
- Should teachers give narrative comments, or literal grades, or marks out of ten or twenty, or percentages, or some combination?
- Should they adopt National Curriculum levels for marking purposes?
- Should all teachers and departments adopt a common marking scheme?
- Who are marks for, and what purpose do they serve?

This final question is, of course, the most important and the answers to the others are contingent, to some extent, upon the answer to it.

Marking as feedback

Most teachers would say that they mark students' work to provide them with *feedback*. Why else would teachers go to the trouble? However, they are usually also mindful of pressure from parents and of a need to accumulate assessment results in mark books for other purposes, such as setting and reporting. In the marking of classwork and homework, as in other types of assessment, there is therefore still a tension between developmental and accountability purposes.

Even feedback to students can be seen to have two or more purposes. It can give them formative feedback on their successes and guidance on those areas where they need to improve. It can also provide a summative assessment of the standard achieved in a particular task. Many teachers attempt to meet both purposes by providing both a formative comment and a summative assessment in terms of a mark, grade or National Curriculum level. This approach seems commonsense and such practice is widespread. It should not, however, pass without careful scrutiny because research evidence is available to suggest *that the giving of grades can undermine the formative intention of narrative comments.* This evidence can be found in a very important review of research carried out in 1997 by Professor Paul Black and his colleague, Dylan Wiliam[2].

Black and Wiliam point out that the term 'feedback' has been borrowed by the behavioural sciences from the description of electrical circuitry in physics. In relation to education it has come to refer to *information about the gap between actual performance and desired performance (the 'standard') in a given domain which can be used to close the gap in some way.*

According to this definition the intention of *all* feedback must be primarily formative: to improve learning and performance. It is inappropriate therefore to regard any form of 'marking' during a student's course of study as devoid of formative intent. Even so-called 'summative' grades, levels and percentages can therefore be regarded as information about actual performance to compare with standards as an indication of the size of the gap that needs to be closed.

If this argument holds, then teachers might reasonably be less concerned about whether their assessments are summative or formative and more concerned to find out what *kind* of feedback will be most effective in helping students to close the gap between actual and desired performance.

On this issue Black and Wiliam's review is illuminating. They looked at recent research carried out in many different countries and discovered that findings were surprisingly consistent. First, in an important review of studies of the effectiveness of feedback, carried out by Kluger and DeNisi in 1996[3], there was evidence that feedback was almost as likely to have a negative impact on future performance as a positive impact. In order to explain why feedback should have negative effects it is necessary to look at the way that students respond to it. Kluger and DeNisi proposed four broad classes of action by students:

---

[2] The full review is entitled 'Assessment and Classroom Learning' and is published in the journal *Assessment in Education*, 5 (1), 1998.
[3] Kluger, A. N. and DeNisi, A. (1996) 'The effects of feedback intervention on performance', *Psychological Bulletin*, 119 (2), pp. 254–84.

- They attempt to reach the standard – this happens when the goal is clear, when the student's commitment is high and when the student believes that (s)he will eventually succeed.

- They abandon the standard completely – this happens when the student's belief in eventual success is low (which often leads to the development of an attitude of 'learned helplessness' described in the research of Carol Dweck[4]).

- They change the standard – students may lower the standard to make the goal more easily attainable, or they may actually raise the standard if feedback indicates that the gap is small or non-existent.

- They deny that an actual-standard gap exists.

Why students respond in these different ways requires a deeper level of explanation. Black and Wiliam, following Kluger and DeNisi, propose an important distinction between feedback that involves the student's self-concept and self-esteem and feedback that focuses strictly on the task.

Feedback involving the student's self-concept and self-esteem

Some forms of feedback draw attention to self in a way that affects the student's self-concept and self-esteem. Feedback in the form of rewards and punishments falls into this category. Most teachers try to avoid punishing students for failing to reach standards although sanctions exist in most schools for certain types of 'offences'. However, the giving of rewards in the form of merit marks, house points, or, most commonly, praise, is almost universal and is regarded as an essential part of good practice in most schools. Surprisingly – and this point is very important – Black and Wiliam's review reveals that praise, and other cues that draw attention to self-esteem and away from the task, generally have a *negative* effect. In fact the most effective teachers actually use praise *less* than the average.

This conclusion was supported in a number of experimental studies that compared different feedback 'treatments' with control groups. For example, a study by Ruth Butler in Israel[5] examined the effects of four types of feedback: comments, grades, praise, and no feedback. She found

---
[4] Dweck, C. S. (1986) 'Motivational processes affecting learning', *American Psychologist*, 41 (10), pp. 1040–48.
[5] Butler, R. (1987) 'Task-involving and ego-involving properties of evaluation: effects of different feedback conditions on motivational perceptions, interest and performance', *Journal of Educational Psychology*, 79 (4), pp. 474–82.

that students given comments scored one standard deviation[6] higher than the other groups on the post-test. There were no significant differences between the other three groups. Interestingly, those students given praise *thought* they were successful although they were *actually* significantly less successful than the 'comments' group.

This finding is consistent with other studies that suggest that while verbal praise and supportive feedback can increase students' interest and *attitudes* towards tasks, such feedback has no effect on *performance*. This finding will no doubt shock many teachers and they may wish to deny it because it undermines a basic tenet of much existing practice. However, the evidence is very strong and it must be taken seriously.

Feedback focusing strictly on the task

As indicated above, feedback that directs attention to the task is generally much more successful in helping students to reduce the gap between their actual performance and the standard desired. The key feature is that it must encourage 'mindfulness' in the student's response to the feedback. In other words, *feedback is most effective if it encourages students to think about the task rather than to think about themselves.*

This is especially important when tasks require 'higher-order' thinking. It may be less important when successful performance requires only the repetition of a particular behaviour, or the recall of information without the need to show deeper understanding, or the ability to apply knowledge in new situations. (There is an important link between different types of feedback and different theories of learning. This will be dealt with in more detail in Chapter 9.)

The *kind* of task-related feedback given is also important, and, according to Black and Wiliam, a number of points of practical advice can be extrapolated from the research evidence:

- Feedback is most effective when it stimulates *correction* of errors through a *thoughtful* approach.
- Feedback should concentrate on *specific* errors and poor strategy and make *suggestions* about how to improve.
- Suggestions for improvement should act as *'scaffolding'*, i.e. students should be given as much help as they need to use their knowledge but they should not be given a complete solution as

---

[6] Standard deviation is the term statisticians use to describe the distance of each mark from the mean (the average mark). In the curve of normal distribution most of the marks (68 per cent) fall within 1SD on either side of the mean.

soon as they get stuck or they will not think things through for themselves.

- Students should be helped to find *alternative solutions* if simply repeating an explanation continues to lead to failure.

- A focus on *process* goals is often more effective than a focus on product goals; and feedback on *progress* over a number of attempts is more effective than feedback on performance treated as isolated events.

- The quality of the *dialogue* in feedback is important and some research indicates that oral feedback is more effective than written feedback.

- Students need to have the skills to ask for help and to help others.

Implications for marking policy and practice

If the purpose of marking students' work is to improve their learning and raise their achievements – the ultimate goal of school improvement – then the research evidence on effective feedback deserves very serious consideration. The implications may not be comfortable, because they go against much common practice, but they can be set out in equally practical terms. For example, they offer some answers to all of the questions posed at the beginning of this section:

1 **Should teachers actually put marks on the students' work? Should they be recorded elsewhere, say, on an annotation sheet, or should they be given orally?**
Feedback given orally is probably best but this may not always be practicable. A dialogue can still be effective if carried out in writing but the important point is that it should indicate to students whether and, if so, *how* their performance has fallen short of the standard and what specific strategies they might use to improve it. They also need to be given opportunities to correct or improve their work. The question about making marks on the students' work often arises from a concern with the effect on self-esteem but, if the evidence is correct, this should not be a big issue if feedback is focused on the task rather than the person.

2 **Should teachers use red pen?**
The last sentence in question 1 above also applies here. Teachers are concerned with associations between the use of red pen and the kind of feedback that reduces self-esteem. It is not the red pen that needs

to be changed as much as the nature of comments. These should be task-focused and constructive. However, it may be useful to break the negative association by abandoning the red pen, bearing in mind, however, that any colour can acquire negative associations if used in a way that is destructive of a student's self-confidence.

3 **Should teachers correct every mistake?**
The evidence, suggesting that giving complete solutions discourages students from thinking for themselves, argues against this. A better approach would be to draw attention to more general categories of errors and to give suggestions for strategies for overcoming these.

4 **Should teachers give narrative comments, or literal grades, or marks out of ten or twenty, or percentages, or some combination?**
The overwhelming conclusion to be drawn from Black and Wiliam's review is that, in most circumstances, teachers should give narrative comments on classwork and homework but not grades or numerical marks. This is not to say that students should not know 'how they are doing' in relation to a standard (or even each other) but that information about standards can be given in other ways, for example in *descriptions* of standards which have *content* rather than just labels. (National Curriculum level descriptions are an attempt to provide this content and it is this – not the numbers – that teachers and students need to focus upon if they seek improvement.) The opportunity to study examples of work that demonstrate the standards is also helpful and the use of *exemplars* is discussed further in Chapters 9 and 11. Teachers' comments should therefore focus on the task, on pointing out gaps between the student's performance and the standard, on areas for improvement and on providing suggestions about the strategies that are likely to be effective in closing the gap. The use of grades, or equivalent, has not been found to be effective in raising students' achievements and, by being primarily 'ego-involving' rather than 'task-involving', they can actually have negative effects.

5 **Should teachers adopt National Curriculum levels for marking purposes?**
Following on from question 4 above, the answer to this must be 'No to the numbers' if we are concerned about the formative potential of routine feedback (but see also Chapter 6). If other forms of grading and numerical marking are inappropriate because they lack the capacity to contribute to improvement, so also may the giving of National Curriculum levels be undesirable *in this context*. Indeed, there is an added objection because the National Curriculum levels are so

broad and general that they are incapable of indicating much progress in specific areas. Even the average student is expected to progress by only one level every two years; a long string of, say, Level 5s is likely to engender very little enthusiasm in even the most diligent student. The potential to help students *know what to do* to achieve Level 6 is even less. However, this is not to say that marking should not be done with *reference* to the level descriptions; indeed this is important because they contain the criteria for assessment. At some point, preferably when it comes to summing up their performance (see Chapter 6), students will need to know how the narrative descriptions relate to the numerical levels, but for formative purposes it is narrative descriptions that matter because these communicate expected standards in direct, rather than symbolic, ways.

6 **Should all teachers and departments adopt a common marking scheme?**
This question usually arises because different practices are found in different departments in most secondary schools, and many teachers are reluctant to change time-honoured methods. Thus the English department may use narrative comments and literal grades whilst the maths department may give numerical marks and percentages. Would I be wrong to suggest that these practices owe more to the culture of subjects than anything else? If the argument propounded so far holds water, then schools would be well advised to adopt a classwork and homework marking policy based mainly, if not exclusively, on the use of formative comments. This would, however, allow them considerable scope to respond to the specific characteristics of subjects because comments will, by definition, be subject-specific.

I realise that what I am proposing is radical, and perhaps too radical for some schools to accept. The evidence, however, supports such a view and should be borne in mind before it is rejected. In this respect it is perhaps worth quoting directly from the conclusion to Black and Wiliam's review:

> ... *the case to be made here is firstly that significant learning gains lie within our grasp. The research reported here shows conclusively that formative assessment does improve learning. The gains in achievement appear to be quite considerable, and as noted earlier, among the largest ever reported for educational interventions. As an illustration of just how big these gains are, an effect size of 0.7, if it could be achieved on a nationwide scale, would be equivalent to raising the mathematics attainment score of an 'average' country like England, New Zealand or the United States into the 'top five' after the Pacific Rim countries of Singapore, Korea, Japan and Hong Kong.*

> *If this first point is accepted, then the second move is for teachers in schools to be provoked and supported in trying to establish new practices in formative assessment, there being extensive evidence to show that present levels of practice in this aspect of teaching are low, and that the level of resources devoted to its support, at least in the UK since 1988, has been almost negligible.*

What I am trying to do here therefore is to 'provoke and support' schools into establishing new practices with regard to marking, which is an aspect of formative assessment. (I shall deal with formative assessment again in Chapter 9.)

Of course, a comments-only approach to routine marking of classwork and homework has implications for recording and teachers may have to reconsider how they organise their mark books. Commercial publishers of mark books usually assume that marks will be given in the form of grades so they print pages for lists and grids of names, dates and grades with very little space for comments. If my recommendations are adopted then records are more likely to need space for names, dates, tasks, achievements, weaknesses, strategies and targets. Hard-pressed teachers will of course object that this kind of recording will take more time, which they do not have. My response would be to argue for quality rather than quantity and suggest that it is not necessary to record everything a student does but to sample or record only significant features of a student's progress in learning. (Issues in recording are dealt with specifically in Chapter 11.)

In 1996, the Association of Assessment Inspectors and Advisers published a broadsheet of principles and suggestions for *Teacher Assessment in Action*. The next page shows the section on 'Marking and providing feedback to pupils'. It is consistent with the arguments I have laid out above.

The penultimate point in this list is particularly important because parents are often mystified by the ways in which their children's work is marked. If schools genuinely wish to establish a partnership with parents in the support of learning then they should be explicit about their marking policy: about what its purposes are, and how marking should be interpreted and used by teachers, students and parents.

■ Further reading

1 There are very many books now available to help teachers collect and analyse data about students' behaviour in classrooms. Many of these include the terms 'reflective practitioner', 'teacher research' or 'action

> **In our classrooms marking and providing feedback to pupils will be effective when we:**
> - have practice which is consistent and in line with the overall policy on assessment, recording and reporting throughout the school;
> - provide feedback to pupils about their work promptly and regularly;
> - include both oral and written feedback where appropriate;
> - focus the response on the learning objectives and criteria for success;
> - provide pupils with opportunities to assess their own and each others' work and give feedback as appropriate;
> - ensure that pupils understand their achievements and know what they need to do next to make progress;
> - use the information gained together with other information to adjust future teaching plans;
> - share the policy with parents so that they can reinforce it;
> - regularly review our policy for marking, make sure it is understood by new members of staff and that our practice continues to reflect school policy.

From Association of Assessment Inspectors and Advisers (1996), *Teacher Assessment in Action*

research' in their titles. Two that teachers might find particularly helpful are *Teachers Investigate their Work: an introduction to the methods of action research*, by Herbert Altrichter, Peter Posch and Bridget Somekh, published by Routledge in 1993; and *Curriculum Action Research: a handbook of methods and resources for the reflective practitioner*, by James McKernan and first published by Kogan Page in 1991. These both provide an introduction to a wide range of techniques.

2 A shorter version of the review of research on assessment and classroom learning, carried out by Paul Black and Dylan Wiliam, has been written especially for practitioners and policy-makers. This specifically explores the implications for practice and will be of special interest to teachers and school managers. It is entitled *Inside the Black Box: Raising Standards through Classroom Assessment*. This was published in 1998 and can be obtained from Dylan Wiliam at the School of Education, King's College, Cornwall House, Waterloo Road, London SE1 8WA.

ACTIVITIES

1 Developing skills in classroom assessments

Improving the quality of assessments made during the course of teaching will depend on teachers being helped to refine the skills they already have and to develop new ones. They will need to be supported in this by opportunities for professional learning. This will be a role for the school assessment co-ordinator and the professional development programme. There are many activities that could be based on ideas in this chapter; the following is one. This could be the focus of a short in-service training session organised as a subject department or year group meeting.

(i) In preparation teachers should be asked to select one student each to focus upon. Ideally this should be a student whose progress is of some concern to them so that the outcome of the exercise might have really tangible results.

(ii) They should then collect some descriptive data about this student's behaviour in one lesson using two forms of recording: one structured such as in an observation schedule and one unstructured such as audio-recording/video-recording. Teachers should be encouraged to ask a colleague to do the recording for them if this would be more manageable.

(iii) They should bring the data to the in-service session and pair up with a colleague. They will each be expected to act as a 'critical friend' to the other.

(iv) Each pair should take one set of data at a time and discuss the inferences about the student's achievements and difficulties which might be drawn from the evidence. They should also discuss the usefulness of the different kinds of recording for this purpose.

(v) Next, they should discuss the kinds of interventions that the teacher might make to improve this student's experience and learning.

(vi) If there is time, the pairs of teachers might feedback their work to a larger group of staff; but if time is short the discussion could be limited to an oral evaluation of the methods used.

(vii) Teachers should be encouraged to try out the interventions that they propose. A brief follow-up session on another occasion might be used to evaluate the results.

2 Improving marking practice

This activity is also about developing new skills or refining existing ones. Once again it could be the focus of a short in-service session organised by the school assessment co-ordinator or working group.

(i) Each teacher should be asked to bring a piece of unmarked classwork or homework from one student. It need not be in written form; it could be an audio recording or photograph etc.

(ii) In groups of about four, teachers should discuss (1) the standard expected; (2) the standard actually achieved by the student; (3) what the student might do to improve, or, if the standard has been attained, what the next steps might be.

(iii) Individual teachers should then be given time to write comments for the student based on the discussion and to decide how best to make a record for themselves.

(iv) Teachers should then bring their comments and records back to the group for evaluation and discussion of the feasibility of using structured comments of this kind as a general marking policy.

(v) At this point, or alternatively at the beginning of the session, the group leader could provide a short input based on the findings of Paul Black and Dylan Wiliam's review.

6 Types of assessment 2: Periodic tests and assessment tasks

Introduction

In this chapter, I examine a range of activities designed by teachers specifically with assessment in mind. In this sense they may be somewhat different from the activities described in Chapter 5 although the distinction is, as I hope to show, somewhat tenuous.

A number of what might be termed 'periodic' assessments are considered here, ranging from the short test to the more extended assessment task. As in the previous chapter, I will concentrate on what I consider to be the most significant issues for schools. In this chapter, I give particular attention to two important ideas in the assessment field: the concept of *validity* and, again, *fitness for purpose*.

The use of tests is common practice in most secondary schools. These may take the form of short *ad hoc* tests with few items[1] incorporated into a lesson. Or they may take the form of end-of-unit or end-of-term tests. They may even involve a whole year-group of students taking a series of timed, unseen papers at the same time. National Curriculum tests at the end of Key Stage 3 have this character.

Ad hoc tests, at one end of this range, can be regarded as part of routine classwork and may be treated in much the same way as discussed in Chapter 5. The nature of the items may be such that students will be able to calculate how many responses they had correct, for example, in a ten-item vocabulary test. However, the emphasis, if the test is to contribute to teaching and learning, should be on task elements, especially any problems that students experienced with certain items, and how they might tackle these. Using the test as a competition, is, contrary to popular thinking, unlikely to lead to deep learning although it might encourage short-term memorisation (see Chapter 5 for the evidence). Large-scale tests, or combinations of tests, at the other end of the range, may be like

---

[1]'Item' is preferred to the term 'question' because test items are not necessarily put in question form.

examinations. Therefore I will deal with these in Chapter 7. My focus here is primarily on the middle range of activities in which end-of-unit tests and tasks feature strongly.

In the discussion about the marking of routine classwork and homework in Chapter 5, much of the evidence about the effectiveness of different forms of feedback was based on experimental studies. These involved pre- and post-testing in order to establish the relative effectiveness of different interventions. In much the same way, it would be reasonable for teachers to find out, at intervals, what progress students have made at critical points in their courses. It seems especially sensible to do some kind of 'dip-stick' testing when the end of a particular theme has been reached to provide a summative assessment and to consolidate learning before moving on to something new. Of course, modular examinations and those using other forms of continuous assessment also test attainment in this way. An issue worth considering, however, is whether end-of-unit testing is really necessary and desirable and, if it is, what form it should take.

The limitations of end-of-unit assessment

If the purpose of routine marking of classwork and homework should be primarily formative, as I argued in Chapter 5, then end-of-unit testing might be expected to fulfil a summative function. Some form of summative assessment is required of schools to fulfil public expectations and especially as a form of accountability to parents who have a right to know what progress their children are making.

There is a danger however that the end-of-unit or end-of-term test comes to assume such importance that it undermines the formative assessments that have been made on a regular basis throughout the period. Just as the giving of grades on ordinary classwork can affect self-esteem in such a way as to 'blind' students to the substantive advice given in comments, so also can the giving of grades and marks in end-of-unit tests have similar effects.

Reviewing existing evidence rather than testing

There is a way out of this dilemma. If routine marking involves commenting upon the standards expected in the execution of particular tasks *and* the students' actual performance in relation to learning objectives, there should be sufficient *evidence* available in classwork and homework for teachers to come to some overall judgement about students' achievements in relation to a particular unit of work. If these student outcomes are retained in work books, files or portfolios, then there should be no need to introduce a test to establish what students have achieved over a unit of work. What would be needed would be for teachers to *review* the existing evidence and come to a summative judgement (see also Chapter 11 on recording and reporting).

This, I firmly believe, is the intention behind the concept of teacher assessment in National Curriculum assessment. All the advice from the relevant government agencies suggests that the requirement for teachers to make a summative teacher assessment at the end of Key Stage 3 will be adequately fulfilled by teachers looking across the work produced by students over the key stage and using their professional judgement to decide which level description best fits each student's performance. This can be done without any additional tests. In the same way, end-of-unit summative assessments can be made without the introduction of special tests. Why then are so many teachers in so many secondary schools so committed to end-of-unit testing?

Why use end-of-unit tests?

There are several possible answers to this question. First, testing is part of the traditional culture of schools and it is difficult to change cultural traditions. Secondly, testing is a powerful mechanism of behavioural control; there are few things as effective as the administration of a test to ensure quiet classes and improve motivation (in the short term)! Thirdly, the end-of-unit test provides an opportunity for revision and the consolidation of learning. This is an important consideration. When I was a school student chemistry was a mystery to me until I settled down to sustained revision for 'O' level when it all began to 'come together'. Fourthly, tests can provide practice for examinations, including National Curriculum tests. This is especially important if students need experience of working in time-constrained conditions, without reference materials and on unseen papers.

The last two of these reasons are a legitimate justification for schools to use end-of-unit tests but teachers should be clear about their rationale and should not over-use them if they are to avoid the potential negative effects.

What form of test or task?

The term 'test' usually conjures an image of a list of questions requiring short answers to be completed by individual students working alone in a limited amount of time. The majority of questions require the recall of memorised information or the demonstration of skills that have been taught and practised. Students may be expected to write their own short answers to questions or to select an answer from a given range. This 'pencil and paper' mode of testing has its place and is widespread throughout the world. However, formal testing in Britain takes many forms, probably as a result of the influence of a relatively enlightened examinations system. Thus practical tests, oral and aural tests, and more extended essays, assignments and assessment tasks are usually considered as important modes of assessment for certain purposes. Once again the main criterion for choice must be 'fitness for purpose'.

In the sections that follow I examine some of the 'pros' and 'cons' of using different modes of assessment in the context of end-of-unit assessment.

Short answer pencil-and-paper tests

A number of different item formats are commonly used and a combination of item types often helps to maintain students' interest.

- **Multiple-choice items**   require students to make a selection from a number of possible answers, e.g. Who discovered the smallpox vaccine? (a) Louis Pasteur; (b) William Harvey; (c) Edward Jenner; (d) Joseph Lister?

- **Dichotomous items**   require them to make a choice of two opposites: True/False; Yes/No, e.g. The chemical symbol for gold is Ag. True/False.

- **Matching items**   require students to match two list of objects or characteristics in an appropriate way, e.g. Match places of worship to the religion. Places of worship: synagogue; mosque; church; temple. Religions: Hinduism; Judaism; Islam; Christianity.

- **Short answer or sentence completion items**   require students to supply a word, phrase or sentence in response to a question, e.g. What is the name of the current Leader of the Opposition?

Pencil-and-paper tests of this kind are useful for assessing students' acquisition of factual knowledge. Although their construction takes time and extreme care, they can usually be administered, completed and scored relatively quickly. Answers are usually either correct or incorrect so they enable fairly objective and reliable comparisons to be made between the performance of students. Correct answers simply need to be counted; scores can then be compared.

These features make pencil-and-paper tests attractive to teachers although the same features are also a potential source of problems. For example, such tests tend to overemphasise the recall of factual information and therefore rarely sample the content of a subject in a representative way, or assess higher-order concepts or skills. This can be a source of *content invalidity* if the test fails to sample appropriately all the different types of learning outcomes that teachers aim to develop in their students during a course of study, including knowledge, skills, understanding, application and personal qualities. If students perceive that they are only assessed on their knowledge of factual content then they are, understandably, tempted to limit what they learn accordingly – they rapidly become 'test-wise'. (The concept of validity is crucially important and I deal with it in more detail in Chapter 8.)

A good short answer test is therefore more difficult to construct than most teachers imagine. For example, questions need to be clear and unambiguous and framed in language of an appropriate level. Students also need to be clear about what they have to do. They need good instructions. It is not always easy for teachers to anticipate the problems of misunderstanding that can arise, which is why it can be important for someone else to scrutinise the questions with a 'fresh pair of eyes'. It is also a reason why the 'piloting' of test items is standard practice by the test development agencies that construct these kinds of tests for other purposes.

In Peter Airasian's book on *Classroom Assessment* (full reference on pages 86–7), which deals with these technical matters in detail, there are interesting examples of the way in which poorly written test items can 'cue' students to give correct answers when they actually know little or nothing about the subject matter! Such cues may be grammatical, such as using the indefinite article 'a' or 'an' before a word to be added. The inclusion of implausible options in a multiple-choice item may encourage students to dismiss them and opt for the most plausible response. Similarly, students may realise that the option with the most detail is often the correct one because test designers tend to pay less attention to the wording of the incorrect options. In true-false questions, words such as 'always', 'never' tend to appear in statements that are false. On the other hand, 'sometimes', 'often' and 'may' appear in statements that are true because most things in our world happen sometimes, but not always.

Students can rapidly become 'test-wise' to such cues – and can even be taught how to 'read' such cues by teachers who wish their students to do well in external 'high stakes' tests and examinations of this kind. The effect is to improve artificially the performance of students who become test-wise and artificially depress the relative performance of those who don't. Research evidence indicates that boys generally perform better on multiple-choice tests than girls (see Chapter 10), suggesting that boys may be better at raising their performance by reading these cues.

Essay tests

Another form of pencil-and-paper test, and one that is more familiar in Britain than in many other countries, is the test with a limited number of questions requiring essay-type answers. Often students are permitted a choice of questions to answer and questions are framed in an open-ended way giving considerable scope for interpretation. Examples of such questions might include: 'How far has your study of the past helped your understanding of the present?' 'What are the recurrent themes in the novels of Thomas Hardy?' 'To what extent does organic farming represent a move towards an environmentally-sustainable form of agriculture?' Sometimes such questions are followed by sub-questions or headings which guide students towards themes that they should consider in their answer.

The strength of essay questions is that student are often encouraged to demonstrate higher-order thinking skills such as comprehension, application, analysis, synthesis and evaluation[2]. It is rarely sufficient simply to reproduce factual content knowledge. Usually, there is a requirement to apply knowledge to a particular problem or issue and to organise knowledge in some way according to the student's construction of salient features or dimensions.

Furthermore, students are often encouraged to come to some view of their own about the particular theme based on their evaluation of the evidence. This enables them to show individuality, creativity and originality in their thinking. These are sophisticated skills and the open-ended form of question is therefore usually more appropriate to older and more advanced students. However, its value as a means of measuring complex cognitive outcomes is considerable and probably accounts for its popularity at A–level and in British university education.

Drawbacks of the essay test

The essay has drawbacks of course. First, performance is dependent on writing skills. Students with limited writing skills, such as those with

---

[2] This list is derived from Benjamin Bloom et al. (1956), *Taxonomy of educational objectives 1: cognitive domain*, New York: David McKay. He regarded this as a hierarchy of six levels with memorisation of knowledge at the lowest level and evaluation at the highest level.

specific learning difficulties, e.g. dyslexia, may have difficulty in demonstrating the extent of their knowledge and understanding if the essay form is the only mode of response available to them.

Secondly, the essay is a very specific genre governed by certain rules of structure, composition and style. If students are to perform well in this mode they need to understand these rules as much as they need to understand the substantive content of the subject with which they are dealing. In other words, in order to write a good essay in response to the question about sustainable agriculture (above), they need to understand what would constitute a good essay on this theme as well as knowing the geographical ideas they need to draw upon. It is rarely adequate to expect students simply to transfer the essay-writing skills they have learned in English lessons to another subject area without additional support for this within the specialist discipline.

The requirements for good essays in different subject fields are varied and students need to understand this. For this reason, the skills of learning how to learn and how to demonstrate one's learning, what educationalists often call 'meta-cognitive skills', need to be taught by *all* teachers, irrespective of their subject specialism. This can present an additional challenge because teachers will need to incorporate meta-cognitive learning objectives into their lesson plans.

Most teachers do this already even if they have not referred to it in this way. For example, at some point they usually take students through exemplars or model answers or show them how to structure essays in preparatory exercises. Undoubtedly, this kind of activity can be as important for student success as 'getting through the syllabus' and more conscious attention may need to be given to this aspect of teachers' work with students. (This theme is elaborated upon in Chapter 9.)

A third drawback of the essay test is the difficulty associated with marking. All students' essays will be different in some way and when teachers come to assess them they will not be counting correct answers but making more qualitative judgements of a student's understanding. This requires teacher-assessors to have some clear criteria and standards by which the piece of work can be judged. Usually this requires an explicit 'marking scheme' although 'impression marking' is still fairly prevalent in many schools. I can think of very little justification for the latter practice because it hides teachers' judgements from scrutiny by their colleagues and, perhaps more importantly, students simply have to accept the authority of the teacher's judgement without learning anything from it – they can rarely find out why a teacher made an impression-based judgement or what they need to do to get a different one.

Often multiple criteria need to be considered in marking essay questions and teacher-assessors may have to make judgements about the relative weighting of criteria and whether strength in one area should be allowed to compensate for weakness in another. For example, should a strong and convincing argument compensate for the fact that a student has got some of his facts wrong? This is not a problem if, as discussed in Chapter 5, the assessment is made in the form of detailed comments. Relative strengths and weaknesses can then be discussed with advice about where improvements can be made. It does matter, however, if the assessment has to be reduced to a single level, as in National Curriculum assessment, or a single summative grade, as in GCSE.

Practical, oral and aural tests

In many areas of the school curriculum, some learning objectives are expressed in terms that cannot easily or validly be demonstrated in written outcomes. Perhaps the most obvious example is National Curriculum Attainment Target 1 in English: speaking and listening. It is hard to imagine how this could possibly be assessed using paper-and-pencil tests although, conceivably, listening might be assessed by a test paper that asked questions about students' knowledge and understanding of something that they had heard.

In Japan, where all learning up to first degree level appears to be assessed using short answer or multiple-choice tests, even language pronunciation is assessed in this way. For example, a question in an English language paper might ask: 'What is the correct pronunciation of the word 'cough': (1) cow; (2) coh; (3) coff; (4) cuff?' This example may seem ludicrous to those of us who are familiar with alternative forms of language assessment but it highlights the need for us to question whether the forms of assessment used are suited to particular learning objectives. If they are not, they can distort learning and become a source of invalidity.

In Britain we have long been accustomed to preparing students for the oral component in foreign languages examinations at 16+ and an aural component in music examinations. The introduction of AT1 in the English subject order has also encouraged more extensive use of oral and aural assessments. In the assessment of physical education the necessity of a practical component is more or less taken for granted. In science and technology the National Curriculum subject orders and 16+ examinations have also contributed to wider use of practical tasks as a basis for the assessment of practical skills such as the manipulation of equipment and tools.

Teachers are generally well aware of the need to match the assessment to learning in this respect and will usually endeavour to assess oral skills by means of an oral assessment, and practical skills by means of a practical assessment etc. This undoubtedly strengthens the validity of assessment results.

Problem areas such as the assessment of IT competence

However, there remain some 'grey' areas where an appropriate choice of assessment mode is not so obvious and further consideration needs to be given to the importance of matching the form of assessment to learning objectives. I have in mind, particularly, the assessment of skills in information technology.

Information technology is now a subject of the National Curriculum and a 'key skill' in all post–16 courses. It is expected to be taught 'across the curriculum' and therefore integrated into work in other subject areas. If it is taught in this way, it is logical that it should be assessed in this way also. This means that *all* teachers are expected to assess the IT skills that students demonstrate in the context of the courses they teach, although the IT co-ordinator in the school might be expected to provide guidance, support and co-ordination.

Different subject areas are likely to encourage the development and use of particular IT skills. For example, the use of word processors might feature strongly in English, spreadsheets in mathematics and science, databases in business administration, graphics packages in art and design, and multimedia CD ROM packages in the humanities. It is just conceivable that a special end-of-term or end-of-year test might be constructed to assess competence in most of these areas but this would probably separate the assessment from the context of use, require an inordinate amount of time to cover all relevant skills, or be so cursory and reductionist that the validity and reliability of the test would be doubtful. The only valid way of assessing students' IT competence is therefore to make some assessment *in situ* – in the context of practice.

This can pose considerable difficulties for both IT co-ordinators and subject teachers. The ideal situation might be for co-ordinators to work alongside subject teachers at the point in the course of study when a summative assessment is sought. This would enable them to construct a practical test, observe the processes students use in tackling it and discuss both the subject-specific and IT-specific criteria they bring to bear when judging the process and the products.

This process of discussion can be very important because subject teachers, working alone and perhaps lacking some IT skills themselves, might be tempted to evaluate the *products* made by students rather than the *process skills* that they use. For example, an English teacher might set up a 'practical' test asking students to word process a letter to the editor of a newspaper arguing for a new arts and community centre in their small town. In marking this test, the English teacher would probably look at the finished product and assess it in relation to subject criteria to do with conventions of letter-writing, the structure of reasoned argument, style, expression, spelling, punctuation and grammar. He might also look at layout to determine the extent to which the student has used the word processor effectively.

The trouble is that the product alone is incapable of revealing how effectively the student has used the technology. The appearance of the final product is not a good indicator. For instance, an acceptable layout can be produced by using only the 'Tab' and 'Return' keys or it can be produced by using Rulers, Toolbars, Menus and Shortcut keys.

The former amounts to using the word processor as little more than a typewriter and is inefficient and slow; the latter shows more familiarity with the technology and evidence of IT skills. However, the difference can only be assessed if students are *observed in the process* of using it. Like all practical tests, including oral and aural tests, this requires teachers to pay great attention to what students actually *do*. This is time consuming and labour intensive and requires great organisation. However, it is really the only valid way of collecting the evidence to make judgements about practical skills and processes.

The question for teachers therefore is how to build such assessment opportunities into their teaching programmes without squeezing the latter or trivialising the former. This is not an easy question to resolve but my advice again would be to go for quality not quantity. A limited number of high quality assessment activities carried out in a thorough way are likely to be of more value than frequent tests that do not actually assess what they are supposed to do. This applies not only to the assessment of IT skills but also to most other areas of the curriculum.

■ Authentic assessment tasks: an important alternative

For some years now many schools and teachers have been moving away from an exclusive focus on short tests as the dominant form of periodic assessment towards including more extended assessment tasks in their repertoire. Undoubtedly they have been influenced in this by the introduction of coursework assignments in 16+ and 18+ examinations and by the need to assess the 'process' attainment targets (AT1s) in National Curriculum English, mathematics and science. Indeed in the original formulation of the National Curriculum, 'standard assessment tasks' (SATs) were proposed which were conceived by TGAT as extended tasks of a similar nature to the kind of activities that might be a regular part of teaching and learning.

However, under pressure from traditionalists in government (but admittedly also in some teachers' unions and some schools), the concept of the SAT was soon discarded and replaced by national tests which reverted to the more familiar short, written, timed, unseen format. It is interesting therefore that extended tasks have re-emerged from SCAA in the form of *Optional Tests and Tasks* to support teacher assessment (TA) in the non-core subjects at Key Stage 3. In 1996, sets of these were sent to all schools.

Under these influences, the concept of the assessment task is therefore alive and well in many schools and represents an important alternative to other types of assessment. It has particular strengths which lie in its claims to validity. Unlike other forms of testing, which often reduce the complexity of what it means to show competence or understanding in a particular area, the assessment task preserves that complexity and invites the student to approach the task as a problem to be solved having many dimensions. Similarly, the assessor is also required to recognise this complexity and to tease out the various aspects and layers of performance that a student demonstrates in executing such a task.

Tasks that have relevance to the 'real world'

In the sense that tasks which are valued in the adult world have this multi-dimensional quality, they can be described as 'authentic'. This contrasts with most other forms of testing which have few correlates in the real world. What adult, for example, performs work that depends upon sitting alone at a desk, producing written material in a very short space of time, but having no access to other people or reference material? Civil servants and lawyers, for whom the traditional examination system was first devised, may come close but even they are not so constrained in their daily work.

In the United States, where for many years the dominant mode of assessment has been the standardised test which gives scores that are an exceedingly narrow indicator of what a student might actually be able to do, there is now considerable interest in what is called 'performance assessment' or 'authentic assessment'. The examples of 'authentic assessments' that are given in American books and journals[3] bear a strong resemblance

---

[3] The December 1996 and January 1997 edition of *Educational Leadership*, 54 (4), the Journal of the American Association for Supervision and Curriculum Development, was devoted to the theme of 'Teaching for Authentic Student Performance'.

to what in Britain we would simply call 'assessment tasks'. However, the North American addition of the adjective 'authentic' is a useful reminder that the tasks that have most value in both learning and assessment are likely to be those that approximate to 'real world' tasks.

There are occasions when it is possible to set students real problems to solve with real outcomes. For example, when my son was in year 7 at comprehensive school, the science department made an arrangement with a local builder's merchant to provide a new design for their site. The object was to redesign the existing site in a more environmentally-friendly way, taking account of budget constraints and the existing and immovable position of the roads, the buildings and the neighbouring housing estate. Groups of students worked together on their plans, paying particular attention to the need to encourage wildlife and minimise pollution. The process of planning was assessed by their teachers and their products were evaluated by the building company which chose one of the designs to use.

This project was enormously motivating for the students because it was real; students who had just left primary school saw that their ideas were valued, which made them feel grown up. Of course, it is not always possible to create such realistic tasks so simulated activities often serve as substitutes. This is not a problem if students are able to accept that there is a close association between the simulated task and the kind of activity that might require similar application of their knowledge, skills and understanding in the real, adult world.

An example of an authentic assessment task

In the early 1990s I did some work with education advisers in the London Borough of Enfield. During an in-service day for teachers on assessment, the mathematics adviser introduced an assessment task that might be used as a basis for assessing a number of aspects of learning in mathematics. The task was along the following lines.

Tea Time

A tea firm wants to make presentation boxes of 200g of tea.
The card used to make the boxes costs 20p per square metre.

Make three different boxes they could use.

Write a report for the managing director to explain your conclusions.

Although simply written, tasks such as this can have a number of advantages over more traditional forms of testing:

1. **Authentic tasks require students to perform a series of operations which can provide evidence in relation to a number of different learning objectives.**

    In this example, students need to be able to calculate the volume of 200g of tea, probably based on measurements of a standard packet. Then they need to create two-dimensional 'nets' for three boxes of different shapes that would each provide the same volume capacity. They need to work out how these could be cut from the card most economically and then calculate the cost of each design. They are also expected to explain these operations and evaluate the products in a written report.

2. **Authentic tasks permit students to work more at their own pace and demonstrate achievement at their own level. In this sense differentiation is achieved by outcome rather than by task.**

    In this example, it is possible for students to create the nets for the new boxes in different ways according to their level of mathematical sophistication. They could either calculate the shapes entirely by measurement and calculation or they could dismantle a standard tea packet and use the net of this to cut and paste shapes until they produced something satisfactory. They could therefore respond to the demands of the task at their own level and perhaps demonstrate a deeper level of understanding than teachers might expect of them. This contrasts with many other forms of assessment in mathematics, such as in National Curriculum tests or GCSE, which require teachers to estimate a student's level of performance before it is tested in order select a tier of papers. In these circumstances, differentiation is by task which can handicap certain individuals. For, instance there is some evidence that teachers are disinclined to enter girls for higher tier papers for fear that the possibility of failure will be too stressful for them. (See Chapter 10 for more detail on this issue.)

3. **Authentic tasks enable important aspects of achievement to be demonstrated and assessed other than those strictly associated with only one subject domain.**

    Although the tea firm task and the builder's merchant task, described above, were developed by mathematics teachers and science teachers respectively, they both incorporated elements of design and technology, English and, possibly, art and personal and social education. Achievements in these other domains also deserve to be acknowledged.

Opportunities for cross-curricular assessment

Many truly authentic tasks would be carried out by teams of workers. Simulating this team situation would provide opportunities for students to demonstrate skills of communication, co-operation and leadership. Most schools claim to promote the social and personal education of students and authentic activities of this kind provide legitimate contexts in which the outcomes of social and personal learning might also be assessed (see also Chapter 10). It would not be unreasonable, therefore, to expect teachers to focus upon four different aspects of achievement in the assessment of authentic tasks:

- evidence of the acquisition of knowledge of facts and the understanding of concepts (propositional knowledge);
- evidence of understanding and skills in implementing processes (knowledge of application);
- evidence of personal and social skills and qualities;
- evidence of motivation and commitment (including effort)[4].

In real life, human activity is rarely confined to a single subject domain; likewise authentic tasks are almost inevitably 'cross-curricular'. There are strong arguments therefore for exploiting this characteristic and using such tasks as a focus for cross-curricular assessment. (An annotation sheet, which might be used to record evidence and judgements in relation to these aspects of achievement, is given on page 216.)

This poses organisation problems, however, because it implies that more than one assessor should be involved. Other assessors might be needed to assess those achievements which would be beyond the expertise of some specialist teachers. If such assessments are thought to be important enough this problem is not insurmountable. As in the example of the assessment of information technology, described in the section on practical tests on pages 113–15, it might be possible on a limited number of special occasions to arrange team-assessment as one might arrange team-teaching – but this does have implications for the organisation of schools.

---

[4] These four aspects of achievement derive from the influential Hargreaves Report on *Improving the Secondary School*, which was published by the Inner London Education Authority in 1977. These categories are used again in Chapter 11.

The concept of an Exhibition

Examples of team assessment of integrated, cross-curricular tasks can be found in the work of Ted Sizer, who founded the Coalition of Essential Schools to improve the quality of student learning in American schools. In *Horace's School: Redesigning the American High School*, published in 1992 by Houghton Mifflin in New York, Sizer presents a model of assessment in which a number of learning outcomes are combined in one assessment task called an Exhibition. This word describes its purpose which is to enable the student to exhibit the outcomes of his or her learning. The Exhibition brings together a number of important dimensions of learning and meaningful assessment:

- It asks students to work across traditional scholarly disciplines in a respectful way by creating 'real' learning activities. Tasks are not necessarily devised by teachers; students can devise them for themselves, providing they understand the principles that underlie their construction. Helping students to acquire this meta-level understanding is also a valued teaching and learning objective.

- It asks students to practise using accumulated knowledge and to apply it to new situations.

- It insists on effective communication in a number of forms of expression, e.g. oral, written and graphic.

- It requires that students be reflective, persistent and well organised.

- It creates a focus for their learning by describing the destination for their journey, although this is not to say that precise learning outcomes are tightly pre-specified. The concept of an Exhibition has little to do with the behavioural objectives model of curriculum planning, which has been heavily criticised for its limited view of worthwhile learning outcomes.[5] The best teachers usually want to see their students achieving more and going beyond what they might have pre-specified. In other words, they want to be delighted and perhaps surprised by the learning that their students can demonstrate.

---

[5] See Stenhouse, L. (1975) *An Introduction to Curriculum Research and Development,* London: Heinemann, for perhaps the best known criticism of the objectives approach.

Assessment of the Exhibition by a panel of assessors

Given the multi-disciplinary nature of the Exhibition, a panel of assessors is considered to be most appropriate. This panel might be made up of the teacher who acted as the main tutor or supervisor for the work, another adult but not necessarily a teacher (a business representative would be appropriate for tasks such as the science- and maths-based tasks discussed above), and a peer of the student's own choice.

The student will be aware of the broad criteria by which the Exhibition will be assessed because these are presented or negotiated at the beginning of preparation for the task and Exhibition. They became *planning guidelines*. About 50 minutes is allocated to each Exhibition, half of which is devoted to the student's presentations and the other half to discussion with the panel. The panel would be expected to ask penetrating questions about what had been learned, the completed research, reflections on the work covered and its relationship to the broader field, tentative hypotheses and ideas about further work, and reflections on the learning process itself (meta-cognition). In some ways the process might be compared to the *viva voce* for the award of PhD degrees!

One observer of this process, Gerard Calnin, a teacher-fellow visiting my institute from Australia in 1995 and making a trip to the USA during this time, said that the process was impressive. High school students had learned their material in such depth that they were able to respond to some difficult questions which might have challenged an undergraduate. Moreover, they were able to talk knowledgeably about the different perspectives offered by the different disciplines on particular themes, such as immigration and settlement in nineteenth century America.

On his return to Australia he introduced some of Sizer's ideas about learning and assessment to his colleagues in the Peninsula School in Melbourne. In 1996 a group of staff began trailing an integrated programme for Year 9 focusing on the theme of twentieth century Australian immigration and using alternative assessment strategies including the Exhibition.

Teachers in England might protest that given the constraints of the National Curriculum, such developments would not be possible in British schools. I am not convinced by this argument. There are clear points of overlap in the programmes of study for the different subjects which would permit some integrated approaches to both teaching and assessment if teachers felt there was value in developing them. The argument for authenticity would provide a good reason for taking this line.

Implications for the organisation of schools

There is no doubt, however, that such approaches are likely to have repercussions for the school as a whole and may even point to the need for some 'restructuring', as the title of Sizer's book suggests. The integration of both learning and assessment across subject domains may require change in the structure of the curriculum, of departments, classes, the timetable and of the use of space. Subjects taught to classes of 30 students by subject specialists in 40- or 50-minute periods may need to be replaced by integrated, resource-based learning, supported by teams of teachers working with large groups, small groups or individuals as the need arises and using longer blocks of time to work on extended projects. These are big issues and are really beyond the scope of this book. However, a cursory exploration here serves to emphasise the extent to which assessment, rather than being an 'add on' to curriculum, teaching and learning, is in fact inextricably linked to the primary educational processes and has wider implications for the organisation and management of schools.

Are special assessments for summative purposes really necessary?

This discussion also brings us back to some important questions that we should ask in relation to the title of this chapter. If the most valid kind of assessment that we can make is based on authentic assessment tasks; and if authentic assessment tasks integrate learning and assessment rather than simply provide opportunities to display the knowledge and skills that students have learned earlier (the Blue Peter model!), is it appropriate to use them only as end-of-unit, summative assessments? Should they not be used formatively and at any appropriate point in a course of study? Indeed, should they not become the backbone of the course of study itself? If this is the case, should we dispense with the idea that it is necessary to devise some special assessment activity to provide a summative assessment at the end of a unit of work?

My view on this issue is the same as that expressed earlier in this chapter. If students have produced evidence of their learning in tasks that they accomplish during their course of study, and if these outcomes have been assessed formatively with due regard to criteria and standards, then teachers and students should be able to *review* this evidence periodically to come to a summative judgement for reporting purposes. There should be no real need for anything additional, such as a specially devised end-of-unit test, to furnish a summative judgement.

ACTIVITY

1. Creating a bank of assessment tasks

Whether teachers wish to develop end-of-unit assessments, or whether they wish to integrate assessment fully into teaching and learning, they will find it useful to develop a resource bank of assessment tasks. The optional tests and tasks supplied by SCAA might form part of this. These can be used in several ways: as normal classroom tasks to be assessed formatively as described in Chapter 5; as sources of evidence on which to base periodic summative assessments; as standard tasks that can be used by a number of different teachers to check the consistency of their judgements (see Chapter 8).

Individual teachers can create their own personal resource bank but this activity is likely to be more productive if teachers pool their ideas. Ideally, then, this activity should be the focus of a series of departmental or faculty meetings. However, if schools wish to be more ambitious, it could be done in cross-curriculum working groups. The sequence of the activity might look something like this:

(i) Look at the programmes of study and attainment targets for the curriculum area and identify a number of what might be termed 'key learning objectives'. If departments intend to work together they might look for areas of close association or overlap, e.g. the use of co-ordinates in mathematics, geography and science, or the study of life in pre-twentieth century British society in English literature and history.

(ii) In relation to each learning objective, think about *how* students will be expected to demonstrate the intended knowledge, understanding or proficiency. Use these ideas to establish clear *performance targets*.

(iii) Design tasks which call on students to *apply* their knowledge and skill. Typically the result will be a tangible *product* or a *performance*. These products and performances should have an explicit *purpose* and be directed towards an identified *audience*. In the real world, problems are rarely limited to a single content domain so authentic tasks usually provide opportunities to make connections across subjects.

(iv) Next devise an assessment scheme, or rubric, setting out the *criteria* by which performance will be judged. This will spell out the qualities that will be considered most significant or important in students' work. It may be presented in the form of a list of questions, e.g. Are assertions supported by evidence? Is the structure likely to withstand normal wear and tear?

(v) Criteria alone, because they are generalised, are not usually sufficient to give students (or teachers for that matter!) a clear enough idea of what standards are sought. This can be done better by providing *exemplars* derived from products and performances produced by others. These do not always have to be 'models of excellence' although it is useful to have some. Students can also learn from exemplars that demonstrate weaknesses.

(vi) In order to create a bank of exemplars, to put alongside the bank of tasks, it will be necessary to try out the tasks – to *pilot* them. This is an important activity in its own right because most tasks will need some adjustment when the pitfalls of implementing them have been discovered. I would expect both the bank of tasks and the bank of exemplars to change frequently as teachers become familiar with them and add new ones, discard those that are not well designed, and refine those that are 'tried and tested'.

(vii) Once the tasks have been created, check again that they fulfil the learning objectives of the curriculum, then work out the *implications for teaching* the knowledge and skills that students will require in order to perform the tasks. This is a kind of 'backwards design' which starts from the question: 'What do we want students to be able to know, understand and do?' Only then does it ask: 'What does this mean for our teaching?' It is in some ways a very different way of looking at learning from that embedded in the National Curriculum programmes of study which give priority to what teachers should teach and deal with attainment targets in very generalised ways.

This looks a great deal of work. It is! But there should be no expectation that a bank of such tasks is created overnight. It can be built up gradually over many years and become a store of tried-and-tested activities that will eventually make teachers' work easier but more effective.

The notion of exemplars has only been introduced here in a cursory way. It is dealt with more fully in Chapters 8, 9 and 10.

7 Types of assessment 3: Standardised tests and examinations

Introduction

In this chapter I deal with types of assessment that are commonly used in schools but which teachers have a limited role in constructing, if they have any at all. Unlike classroom assessments and internal tests and assessment tasks, which teachers construct, administer, mark and interpret, standardised tests and public examinations (in which category I include National Curriculum tests) often require teachers only to make a choice of test instrument or examination syllabus, administer the test or examination papers, and interpret results. The construction of the test itself and the marking are usually carried out externally by a test development agency or examination board. This has advantages and disadvantages.

The processes of test construction and marking are often difficult and time-consuming and it is helpful to have some 'off the shelf' assessments to use. On the other hand, because they are developed for use by large numbers of teachers in large numbers of very different schools, they cannot give teachers detailed information on the specific achievements of their students in relation to particular aspects of the 'curriculum as taught'. The American writer Peter Airasian, in his book *Classroom Assessment* (see pages 86–7 for full reference), includes a strong 'health warning' that is worth repetition. He refers both to standardised tests and state-mandated tests which in the British context can be compared to National Curriculum tests.

> Because standardised norm-referenced tests and state-mandated tests are constructed by agencies outside the classroom, there is a tendency to view them as more important and more sophisticated than teachers' own assessments. Because the tests are constructed by professional test constructors, people often overestimate their precision. Regardless of the assessment device, score differences of a few points or percentile ranks usually

> do not indicate real differences in the achievement of pupils and should not be interpreted as if they do.
>
> Norm-referenced and state-mandated achievement tests are infrequent visitors to the classroom, appearing once or so a year to take a quick reading of pupil achievement on a small subset of the objectives pupils have been taught. The information they provide should not be ignored, but in many cases it will add little to what the classroom teacher already knows about pupils.

As in Chapters 5 and 6 my discussion of these types of assessment will focus upon the issues that teachers need to understand. As in all types of assessment the concept of *validity* is central. Similarly important is an understanding of the basis on which assessment judgements are made. Teacher assessments are usually criterion-referenced and student-referenced (ipsative), by which I mean that teachers compare a student's performance with his or her own previous performance. Standardised tests, however, are invariably norm-referenced. Examinations usually combine criterion-referencing with norm-referencing in some way. The description of the tests and examinations given in this chapter will therefore be used to explain and explore some of the issues associated with what is often called the *'basis of comparison'*.

Standardised tests

Standardised tests are of many kinds and are designed to measure many different qualities. Three broad categories can be distinguished:

Achievement tests

Achievement or attainment tests[1] seek to determine what students have actually learned in relation to either a specified or an assumed curriculum. In this sense they are curriculum-related. National Curriculum tests might be described as achievement tests but they are not 'standardised' in the strict sense of the word because, as I explain below, they have not been subjected to a rigorous process of 'norming' which is a defining characteristic of standardised tests. It is significant therefore that they are called 'standard' tests and not 'standardised' tests.

---

[1] 'Achievement' and 'attainment' are often used interchangeably although some prefer to use 'achievement' when reference is being made to the progress that is made from one occasion to another. 'Attainment' has a more static connotation and is useful when reference is to performance on a single occasion without attention being paid to prior levels of performance.

In 1997 there were pilots of mental arithmetic tests and tests of grammar, punctuation and spelling for eleven and fourteen year olds that are supposed to render more finely discriminated, age-related scores. This would provide standardised tests as a component within the national testing scheme. However, difficulties have been encountered with the grammar test and its nationwide introduction has been deferred until 1999.

Other standardised achievement tests with which teachers will be familiar might include test batteries, such as the *Richmond Tests of Basic Skills*, and tests of attainment in particular areas, such as reading. Some tests, such as the so-called diagnostic tests used by educational psychologists, are designed for use by professionals who are specially trained, but many are supplied with detailed guidance on procedures so that teachers can administer them to their own students.

Schools in Suffolk, for example, administer the local education authority's Suffolk Reading Scale to all students. In so far as this involves only sentence completion, by selecting the correct response from a list of five words, there are serious worries about whether this is a valid test of 'reading' as such (whether it possesses 'construct validity'). However, the test is valued because it seems to have predictive validity: it is a fairly accurate predictor of students' future performance. In this sense it acts very much like a test of cognitive ability (see page 129) and is used extensively within the county for value-added and monitoring purposes (see Chapter 12).

Diagnostic tests to help identify problems

When a student has been identified by teachers as having special educational needs, an educational psychologist may be called in (at Stage 3 in the Code of Practice) to administer some diagnostic tests to help identify the nature of the problem. Usually a battery of tests will be administered which provide a *profile* of achievements and weaknesses. Two approaches to measurement are most common. One focuses on failure to master one or more end-of-instruction objectives (deficit measurement); the other focuses on error analysis. This latter requires a trained observer, usually the educational psychologist, to examine the pattern of errors a student makes and infer the nature of the student's difficulties based on an understanding of how learning typically develops. On this basis, suggestions about a programme of future instruction can be made to the teacher and used as a basis for an Individual Education Plan (IEP). (An example of a psychologist's report is given on pages 139–41.)

There are a number of problems with the concept of diagnostic testing that should perhaps be noted at this point. First, the term 'diagnostic' has been borrowed from the powerful medical model to legitimise educational usage in a way that is often unsustainable. Far less confidence can be placed in these tests and the interpretation of results than can be claimed for X-rays or blood tests in medicine.

Secondly, the link between diagnosis and action is often very fragile. Suggestions about what teachers should actually do about problems that have been identified often pay insufficient attention to the realities of schools and the need for teachers to have time, material resources and additional skills.

Thirdly, the association between diagnostic testing and particular forms of standardised test seems to deny a diagnostic element in routine assessments carried out by teachers. Surely, if teachers are to engage in formative assessment, as described in Chapters 5 and 9, then diagnosis of weaknesses will be an important element of this. It is curious that TGAT described four purposes of assessment and distinguished formative assessment from diagnostic assessment. I suspect that this was a legacy of the association of diagnostic assessment with certain forms of psychological testing.

Aptitude tests

Aptitude tests differ from achievement tests in that the items in the test are not derived from the knowledge and skills that are assumed to be explicitly taught in schools. In this sense they are not curriculum-related. Instead they are based on the characteristics of the outcome that is to be predicted.

In the USA, for instance, the Scholastic Aptitude Test (S.A.T.), devised by the prestigious Educational Testing Service (ETS), is widely used to select applicants for college admission. S.A.T. items include questions that require students to demonstrate their knowledge and skills but these are not chosen to reflect *current* learning but to represent the kind of skills that will underlie effective performance *in the future*, i.e. in further and higher education. In this sense the content of the test is expected to have criterion-related validity but its chief value derives from its predictive validity – its capacity to predict future performance.

Aptitude tests are little used by teachers in British schools although the careers service may use them with some students for particular purposes. However, they are increasingly used by employers who wish to assess whether potential employees are likely to be able to develop the specific skills required in a particular job. These may be skills that are not explicitly taught in schools. Insurance companies, the civil service and the armed forces, for example, often give aptitude tests to applicants to see whether they possess the kind of qualities that will favour the development of particular characteristics, e.g. adaptability, information-handling, communication skills, leadership, goal-oriented motivation, initiative, interpersonal skills, teamwork.

Aptitude tests are also useful for identifying potential that may remain undisclosed in achievement tests, the results of which may be heavily influenced by a student's particular experience in a particular school. History abounds with stories of high achievers in adult life whose school achievements were mediocre or poor: Winston Churchill and Richard Branson spring immediately to mind. Aptitude tests are therefore used to guide recruitment because they claim to be able to discover potential that is sometimes hidden or not explicitly assessed in achievement tests.

Tests of cognitive ability

Tests of cognitive ability are among the most common forms of standardised testing to be found in British secondary schools. Although there is little in the dictionary definitions of the words to distinguish between achievement, aptitude and ability, in educational circles the term 'ability' has come to be associated with possession of certain enduring mental faculties. Moreover, although the relative contribution of genetics and environment has always been a source of much controversy, the assumption in the western world has usually been that, after due account is taken of the influences of different 'nurturing' practices, differences in ability are the result of different 'natural' endowment.

I emphasise that this is a western conception because eastern cultures under the influence of Confucianism make no such assumptions. In Pacific Rim countries, for example, the homogeneity of students' mental endowment is emphasised and it is thought that differences in attainment (except for those who are obviously 'handicapped', which is seen as a medical condition) is attributable not to natural differences in their ability but to the degree of *effort* that they are prepared to put into their studies. Hence the seemingly excessive hard work and long hours that the Japanese, Koreans and Taiwanese devote to scholastic work. It is significant also that achievement testing is ubiquitous in these countries but tests of presumed mental ability are used rarely, if at all.

Measuring mental qualities in the past

The idea that differences in attainment are related to differences in innate ability has been powerful in the West for almost a century. This is undoubtedly due to the influence of psychometricians who, as their name implies, developed a science to measure mental qualities, and in particular the general cognitive ability known as intelligence, sometimes referred to as *g*.

They were encouraged in their task by the need to devise a system for the allocation of scarce public resources. Both Alfred Binet, who developed the first intelligence test in France in 1905, and Cyril Burt, who used a modification of this test in London around the time of the First World War, were asked to identify those children who needed special provision. Tests were therefore used to identify children who were 'educationally sub-normal', 'mentally defective' or 'feeble-minded'. None of these descriptions is acceptable today but psychometric tests are still used to measure mental abilities and place individuals in rank order by means of a score.

Current definitions

For the most part, the idea of mental faculties has now been defined more precisely as *cognitive abilities,* to emphasise those abilities associated with the kind of *thinking skills* required in academic study and in recognition of the existence of other aspects of mental life, such as the affective or emotional domain, which are not explicitly measured by most tests of mental ability.

Similarly, although intelligence tests still exist, and the general public can buy books to test their own IQ (Intelligence Quotient), most psychometricians acknowledge that 'intelligence' is a slippery concept which is still ill-defined and difficult to measure. The saying, 'Intelligence tests measure what intelligence tests measure', implies that it is impossible to be confident that questions such as those which ask students to match 'knife' to 'sheath', not 'fork', as 'sword' is to 'scabbard', are really tests of an underlying ability called intelligence. 'Intelligence' is a human construct and its existence is as much a matter of belief as of science.

Moreover, many psychologists now believe that intelligence is not a unitary quality but that there are several distinct intelligences. The work of Howard Gardner[2], at Harvard University, on multiple intelligences is particularly influential at the present time. Drawing on research involving people who for various reasons have limited mental ability in some areas but have other kinds of ability in abundance, such as autistic children who draw brilliantly, he has proposed that there are at least seven distinct kinds of information processing: language; logic and mathematics; spatial

---

[2] Two of his most important books are *Frames of Mind* (1983) and *The Unschooled Mind* (1991).

thinking; musical intelligence; bodily-kinesthetic problem-solving; interpersonal intelligence; and intrapersonal intelligence.

In recognition that cognitive ability is multiple rather than singular, cognitive abilities tests are often made up of a number of separately administered and separately scored test batteries. For example, the *Cognitive Abilities Test* (CAT), published by NFER/Nelson, which is used in many secondary schools for monitoring purposes (see Chapter 12), consists of three test batteries: verbal, quantitative and non-verbal. Others such as *The British Ability Scales*, used frequently by educational psychologists, have even more.

Although it is possible to compute a single score by aggregating scores across these batteries and finding the mean, there are objections to doing so because this irons out the peaks and troughs in a profile, and these are often the most useful for diagnostic purposes. The 1973 *Teachers' Book* accompanying the first edition of the CAT stated quite explicitly that: '... the averaging of scores on the three batteries of the *Cognitive Abilities Test* is *not* recommended.' However, in the second edition (after restandardisation in 1984), this sentence had been deleted although a caution remained:

> ... *the averaging of scores on the three batteries of the* Cognitive Abilities Test *is likely to obscure an individual's differences in cognitive abilities in the three areas tested. For instructional and guidance purposes, the information provided by the separate scores is generally more useful than that provided by an average, although this may serve a useful purpose in predicting future achievement in some subjects.*

The final clause in this statement was a significant addition to this version of the handbook and was the result of a follow-up project carried out in 1978 which correlated CAT scores with subsequent performance in GCE/CSE. The study found that some of the highest correlations were with the mean CAT Standard Age Scores of all three batteries. Thus, for the purposes of GCSE prediction, the CAT now supplies mean scores as well as scores for the separate batteries.

The 'predictive validity' of cognitive ability tests

The validity claimed for tests of cognitive ability tests rests almost entirely on their ability to predict future scholastic achievement. Face validity is important because a test should at least look as if it tests what it claims to test. Construct validity is also important because if a test claims to tap a particular ability, such as the ability to think quantitatively, it should test this and not something else such as the ability to read verbal instructions.

But people value tests of cognitive ability most for their capacity to predict future performance. This 'predictive validity' is the source of the test's usefulness to schools because it can alert teachers to students who are probably underachieving in some area and would benefit from additional support. (The concept of validity is taken up again in Chapter 8 and the use of such tests for monitoring purposes is considered in more detail in Chapter 12.)

Test construction

Norm-referencing

Whether the standardised test is a test of achievement, aptitude or a cognitive ability, the process of test construction is more or less the same. All are norm-referenced so, underpinning the whole process, is another crucial *assumption*: that attainments and mental characteristics are distributed across a population in much the same way as physical characteristics such as height. It is possible to measure a person's height in a relatively objective and reliable way, by using a tape measure with fine divisions and getting someone else to check the measurements. If the results for a large sample of the target population are then displayed in rank order, a pattern emerges which usually approximates to the 'bell curve' of 'normal distribution' (see Figure 7.1 on page 137).

Psychometric tests attempt to mimic this measurement process which is why standardised tests are sometimes called 'objective tests'. In fact there is very little that is objective about psychometric tests except the scoring process which can be accomplished by machine. All other stages in the process are vulnerable to the influence of human subjectivity: the definition of the domain to be tested, the choice of items, the interpretation of scores[3].

For example, even if there is such a thing as general cognitive ability or intelligence, it cannot be directly observed in the way that physical characteristics can, so there is no certainty that mental characteristics are 'normally distributed'. Test developers have to assume that they are, simply because of the analogy with the physical world. On this basis they then define the domain to be tested and develop test items that will render results which conform to the bell curve. In other words, *in the process of construction, the test is manipulated until it produces the desired pattern of results*. This procedure is acceptable if, when the test is used, it fulfils the purposes for which it is designed, for example, if it predicts

---

[3] The objectivity of the scientific method in the natural sciences has also been questioned in recent years.

future performance accurately, or enables comparisons to be made between students. In this sense the ends justify the means.

Test development agencies and their procedures

The prime objective of norm-referenced, standardised testing is therefore to *compare* a student's performance with a much larger group of students, usually a national sample of students of the same age. For this reason, teachers are not in a position to construct standardised tests for themselves and they have to rely on the efforts of test development agencies. These agencies will go through the following procedures in sequence when they produce such a test:

1 Define the domain and identify the content or objectives to be tested.

2 Write and try out (pilot) test items; usually three times the number will be written than will be eventually needed.

3 Try out the items on a national representative sample and monitor the spread of scores along the possible range.

4 Make a selection of items for the final version of the test based on their content appropriateness and their capacity to *discriminate* between students. Items are usually chosen which approximately 50 per cent of candidates will answer correctly and 50 per cent will get wrong. The idea is to produce a test which will *spread* scores as finely as possible (like the fine gradations on a tape-measure), therefore items will be discarded which validly test domain content but which most students will get right.

5 Administer the final version of the test to a large national sample of students. The sample will be designed to represent different categories of students (according to age, gender, ethnic group, socio-economic status, geographical location, type of school etc.) in the same proportions as they are found in the total population. The test will also be administered in the way that is proposed when it is marketed, i.e. using the same directions, booklets and answer sheets.

6 Develop test 'norms' on the basis of the results of this national trial. This is a crucial element of the test development procedure because the spread of scores produced by this national representative sample supply the 'norms' against which future individual scores will be compared. It is vital therefore that the 'norming sample' is adequate. Four criteria are used to judge adequacy: the size of the sample (it should be large); representativeness; clarity in the description of

procedures (they should be unambiguous); and recentness. This last criterion is especially important but is the most often neglected. In the same way that a generation of children may be substantially taller, on average, than the previous generation, it is reasonable to assume that norms in attainment, aptitude or ability will change over time. Therefore, standardised tests should be 'renormed' every eight years, or so, to keep up with such changes. This means that *schools should check when tests were last renormed before using them and treat with caution scores based on norms over eight years old.*

7   When norms have been established, the test development agencies will market the tests for use in schools.

Test administration

Ensuring reliability of results

Another characteristic of all standardised tests is that the way they should be administered to individuals or groups of students is specified in great detail. This is intended to enhance the reliability of the results. If teachers administer the tests in different ways, this would influence scores in such a way that they could not reliably be compared with the norms or with the results in other schools. It is usual, therefore, for the test developers to supply booklets which spell out the following:

- how to prepare for the test;
- how to arrange the room;
- how to distribute the tests and answer sheets;
- how to time the tests;
- what to say when administering the test;
- what to do whilst students are taking the test;
- how to collect the test booklets and answers sheets;
- how to score the answers, or send them off for external scoring.

Do standardised tests produce valid results?

The fact that so much of the administration is pre-specified in such a detailed way makes the procedure very artificial and quite unlike anything that the student will encounter in the normal course of teaching and learning. The validity of such tests has therefore been questioned because the unusual pressures created by the artificial situation can distort student performance.

For example, some students may become so anxious about the need to work in isolation and silence and under time constraints that they 'go to pieces'. If this happens the test may not measure what it is supposed to measure but rather a student's ability to keep a cool head under pressure! Moreover, performance in the 'real world' rarely has the same character as tests; this is another reason why tests may be considerably less valid than the authentic assessments described in Chapter 6. The danger with many forms of standardised tests is that validity is often sacrificed on the altar of reliability (an issue I return to in Chapter 8).

Interpretation of test results

The whole point of standardised tests is to enable teachers to *compare* the results of their student(s) with the results of students in a much wider sample – usually a national one. This is intended to give them some measure of how well their students are doing in relation to others elsewhere, or an indication of what their relative strengths and weaknesses may be. This can be very important because working for long periods of time with a particular group of students in a particular school can make it difficult for teachers to acquire a wider picture of the range of attainment or ability across the population as a whole. They may therefore have little sense of whether their students should be considered as underachieving or not. In order for comparisons to be made between the score of an individual student and the distribution of scores across the norming sample, a number of operations have to be performed.

Types of standardised scores

First, a *raw score* has to be obtained. This is simply the total number of correct answers given by the student. These scores are then converted by means of tables into various kinds of normalised scores. This is done by reading off scores which relate raw scores to the students' ages in years and months. The resulting standardised scores can be expressed in a number of different ways. The following are the most common:

1 **Standard age scores** These enable comparison between an individual's performance and others in the same chronological age group by representing scores on a scale where the average (the mean)

is given a value of 100. Thus a student with a score of 112 would be above average, a student with a score of 130 would be well above average, and a student with a score of 80 would be below average. This kind of scoring will be familiar to most people because it is the way that IQ scores are usually represented.

2 **Percentile ranks** The standard age score can be further interpreted by being converted, again, into a percentile rank which describes the percentage of students who attained a lower score than the student whose attainment, aptitude or ability is being scored. For example, if a student is given a 75th percentile rank then she scored higher than 75 per cent of the students in the norm group.

3 **Stanines** Stanine scores indicate the group in which any given percentile rank falls. These are scores on a nine-point scale ranging from 1 to 9. Scores of 1 to 3 are considered below average; 4 to 6 are considered average; and scores of 7 to 9 are considered above average. Stanine scores are now quite commonly used to report pupil performance, probably because they place scores in broader bands. This recognises that raw scores are unlikely to be 'error-free' because they record only how a student performs on a single occasion; it is unlikely that scores would be identical if the test were to be taken at other times. Stanine scores are therefore deliberately less finely differentiated than standard age scores and percentile ranks, whose seeming precision can be quite spurious. Schools also find stanines useful because they are a convenient way of grouping pupils for various purposes. However, the cut-off points can seem fairly arbitrary and care needs to be taken about assigning students on the boundaries to one group or another if this is going to have profound consequences for them, e.g. in assigning them to teaching sets or entering them for tiered papers in examinations.

4 **Age equivalents** Another way of comparing the scores of an individual with the scores of the norming group is to represent the student's score in terms of the approximate age at which the average student attains the same level. Scores on reading tests are often represented in this way and students are assigned 'reading ages' to compare with their chronological ages. Thus a student with a chronological age of eight years four months may be described as having a 'reading age' of eleven years six months because he has performed in the test at the level expected of the average eleven and a half year old. This so-called 'developmental' scoring is popular with teachers and parents but it is open to misinterpretation, especially if the score indicates that the student is performing at a higher level than

the test was actually designed to assess. This will be the case if the test does not assess performance in relation to the curriculum and learning experience of eleven year olds. Although they are not strictly standardised tests, as such, this has been a major problem with National Curriculum tests, which by allowing the allocation of a Level 4 at age seven implies that Level 4 students aged seven are working at the same level as the average eleven year old. This is misleading because the curricula on which seven and eleven year olds are assessed are very different.

As can be seen, there are numerous ways in which standardised test scores can be interpreted statistically. Indeed, a single set of raw scores can be subjected to various treatments. For example, the *Cognitive Abilities Test* enables four different scores to be recorded for each test battery: the raw score; standard age score; percentile rank; stanine. Figure 7.1 shows the relationship of standard age scores, percentile ranks and stanines to each other and to the normal curve of distribution.

The various ways in which the scores can be handled provide some very satisfying tables and graphs to the mathematically inclined and deeply impress those who are not. However, it should be remembered that this elaborate edifice of statistical manipulation may simply serve to hide some fairly shaky foundations. After all, the scores that are derived are only as good as the assumptions on which they are based. If the

Figure 7.1 **Normal curve of distribution**

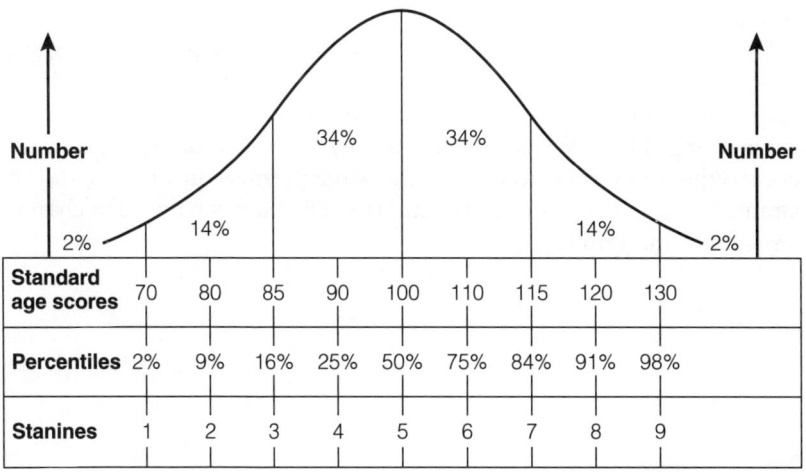

questions that students are expected to answer lack validity, or if the assumption of a bell-curve of normal distribution cannot be sustained, then the scores must be questioned.

I do not intend to demolish the claims made for standardised tests. They have undoubted value in any portfolio of assessment techniques available to schools. In particular they can help schools and teachers challenge their own assumptions about how well their students are doing. However, they should always be used in conjunction with what teachers know about students from their own classroom assessments. *No single type of assessment is so valid and reliable that it dispenses with the need for any other.*

■ Explaining and drawing implications from test results

There is a further issue about the interpretation of standardised tests which I should deal with at this point. The interpretation of raw scores in terms of some form of 'normalised score' is only one stage of interpretation. Teachers still need to know what these *mean* for the student and for subsequent teaching and learning. In other words they need some *explanation* for the scores that a student achieves and some way of working out the *implications* for future teaching.

Standardised tests that are administered by teachers to classes or large groups are usually accompanied by teachers' handbooks that provide some guidance, but this can only be given in the most general terms: about differentiated teaching, learning support for special needs, or student guidance etc.

The results of tests administered to individuals by professionals, such as educational psychologists, are usually reported in more detail and reports go some way towards working out the implications for teaching and learning. Take, for example, the following educational psychologist's report which is reproduced with the kind permission of the child, his parents and the local education authority. The names have been changed to preserve anonymity.

As part of my assessment I used British Ability Scales (BAS) subtests in order to look at the balance of his skills and abilities.

SUMMARY OF TEST INFORMATION

BRITISH ABILITY SCALES   On: 13-06-94

	Centile	Approximate Age Equivalent at 9 years 11 months
Reasoning		
*Matrices	91	14y 0m – 14y 5m
+Similarities	97	16y 11m – 17y 0m
Spatial Imagery		
*Block Design (Level)	95	13y 6m – 13y 11m
*Block Design (Power/speed)	73	11y 5m – 11y 6m
Short Term Memory		
*Recall of Designs (visual)	88	12y 0m – 12y 5m
+Recall of Digits (auditory)	40	8y 5m - 8y 6m
Retrieval and Application of Knowledge		
Basic Number Skills	15	8y 0m – 8y 5m
+Word Definition	99	16y 0m – 16y 5m
Word reading ('sight' words)	17	7y 11m – 8y 0m
Spelling	16	7y 8m – 7y 9m

NEALE ANALYSIS OF READING ABILITY
    Accuracy: 9y 2m
    Comprehension: 10y 11m

* Tests used to calculate visual ability
\+ Tests used to calculate verbal ability

Overall Adam's measured verbal skills were good and placed him at centile 97 in the well above average band of ability. His auditory short term memory span (Recall of Digits) was weak in comparison with his other scores and characterised by auditory sequencing difficulties. It lay, however, within the average band and because of his good language skills should present no difficulties to Adam in acquiring spoken information.

Adam is right-handed and right-eyed. On the Word Reading Test, Adam's score was weak. His errors were characterised by letter sequencing difficulties, omission and addition of syllables to multi-syllabled words and misreading of words of similar shape e.g. 'leather' for lethal, 'curtain' for criterion. Adam attempted every word in the test and used 'word building' skills.

On the Neale Analysis of Reading Ability Adam used his knowledge of syntax and semantics to aid his reading and achieved an accuracy score when reading the stories of 9y 2m level and a comprehension score of 10y 11m level. Many of his errors consisted of a wrong final syllable e.g. verb endings.

Interestingly, in general conversation with me earlier Adam had said,

'I think I'm up to my age in reading now.'

Adam's measured spelling skill lay at 7y 8m – 7y 9m level. He has been working on a spelling programme, 'Alpha to Omega', with Mrs Smith (LEA support teacher) and can manage a number of digraph combinations when learned, but Mrs Smith informed me that Adam has difficulty in generalising these digraphs; they tend to be specific to the words he has learned.

Adam has a neat cursive handwriting style with well formed letters. His written work is not always legible because of his weak spelling skills.

On the Basic Number Skills test Adam understood simple addition, subtraction, multiplication and division. He was able to carry forward groups of tens and hundreds but had difficulty with some simple subtraction and stated that he couldn't do more complex subtraction which required him to 'decompose' groups of tens. In multiplying a two-digit figure by a single digit, Adam appeared to use both multiplication and (erroneously) addition in the same sum.

Adam has specific reading and spelling difficulties with associated difficulties in mathematics.

Recommendations

1. Adam needs access to the National Curriculum.

2. Adam needs a continuing individual programme of reading skills designed to use his strengths and build up his weak skills. This will need to:

   a) develop further his knowledge of consonant and vowel digraphs. (This can be approached through families of words, e.g. each, peach, teach. 'Alpha and Omega' materials by B. Hornsby and F. Shear, 'Attack' materials, or any programme which steadily builds through levels of difficulty can be used.) 'Look, cover, write, check' techniques should be used, based in a programme of cursive handwriting skills. If a computer spelling programme is used it will still be necessary to develop the learning of spelling within a cursive handwriting programme;

   b) develop his word analysis skills so that he can recognise syllables/morphemes in words and deal with these as meaningful units – e.g. locate, location. Particular attention should be placed on final syllables;

   c) continue to use 'top-down' reading skills for 'informed guessing' (being able to use knowledge of the meaning of words (semantics) and form of words (syntax) with emphasis on the informed aspect);

   d) continue to develop the above areas in parallel with a programme of reading for pleasure and meaning.

3. The reading skills programme should be developed in the context of a meaningful relationship between primary communication skills (listening and talking) and secondary communication skills (reading and writing). Planning skills for written work need support and development.

4. Adam needs an individual programme of maths skills, where emphasis should be put on the sequence of stages needed to carry out the basic processes.

5. Adam needs an individual programme based on the above points. This will involve some daily individual or small-group work within the timetable. The details of the programme and the day-to-day, week-to-week adjustment would best be planned/carried out by the Learning Support Centre (LEA) staff, school's special needs teacher and class teacher working closely together, and liaising with his parents. Support and development of Adam's confidence is an important part of this programme.

In this example the educational psychologist used a range of standardised tests to describe the strengths and weaknesses of a primary school student who had been identified by his teachers as having some learning difficulties. Scores are reported in two forms: percentile ranks and age equivalent scores. The psychologist also aggregated the scores on some subtests to produce scores for more general verbal and visual ability. The resulting profile conveys a picture of classic dyslexia although some people prefer not to use this term because it tends to 'medicalise' an educational problem; it is significant that the report speaks only of 'specific' learning difficulties.

Looking beyond the scores

Information about those areas where Adam is significantly above or below the norm for his age is helpful in identifying where he has specific problems, but the report does not leave it at that. The educational psychologist goes on to say something more about the nature of Adam's problems, drawing on other kinds of evidence such as accounts given by the support teacher and the student himself. She also gives some reasons why Adam may be experiencing difficulty. Here she is using a form of criterion-referencing because judgements of Adam's performance are made in relation to criteria, for example a checklist of skills, rather than simply the comparative performance of other students.

In reality, most types of assessment combine elements of both criterion- and norm-referencing, although one or the other tends to predominate. In the educational psychologist's report on Adam, where norm-referencing predominates, there are still a number of criterion-referenced diagnostic comments, concerning, for instance, what is required for fluent and accurate reading. It is also this understanding of what characterises the effective development of reading, writing and computation that enables her to make recommendations for a future individual educational plan for Adam.

What this illustrates, then, is the *need for interpretation to go well beyond the scores in order for educational value to be derived from standardised testing procedures.*

Examinations

Strictly speaking, examinations are not a separate type of assessment because they usually combine a number of the different types of assessment already described. For example, they may combine coursework assessment based on assignments (assessment tasks) with end-of-course or end-of-module test papers (as in GCSE and A–level), or assignments, portfolios and end-of-unit tests (as in GNVQ). For this reason, the issues raised and the advice given in Chapters 5, 6, and the first part of this chapter, broadly apply to examinations also.

What distinguishes examinations, therefore, is the larger scale of the exercise, the formal context in which they are conducted, and their purpose, which is primarily summative. Moreover, examinations often have a more obvious role to play in certification and selection. This is certainly true for external examinations which lead to qualifications. Internal examinations, conducted within the school, can have similar importance if they are used to inform decisions about the courses that students will subsequently follow.

In this sense, most examinations have 'high stakes' associated with them and it is most important to consider the *consequences* for the student. An American researcher, Samuel Messick, has argued that 'consequential validity' is as important a consideration as other more technical definitions of validity because much of the value claimed for assessment practices will be undermined if their impact is destructive for the student. ('Consequential validity' is dealt with in more detail in Chapter 8.)

As I mentioned in the Introduction to this chapter on page 126, most examinations combine criterion-referencing with norm-referencing in some way. Since issues associated with this feature of examinations underlie the disputes about 'grade inflation' or falling standards that habitually accompany the annual publication of examination results, I focus on these in the final sections of this chapter.

Norm-referencing and traditional examinations

In England and Wales the traditional route to qualifications through GCSE and A–level has been based on predominantly norm-referenced examination systems. Thus both examinations are designed to rank the performance of individual candidates and award a spread of grades. The grading system is based on assumptions about the spread of achievement conforming to the bell-curve of normal distribution in much the same way as scoring of standardised tests (see Fig 7.1 on page 137).

A comparison between the spread of GCSE results and mean CAT scores is given in Figure 7.2. The GCSE curve is skewed slightly to the upper end of the range because approximately ten per cent of the total cohort is not entered for GCSE.

Figure 7.2 **Distribution of GCSE results compared to distribution of CAT scores: 1996**

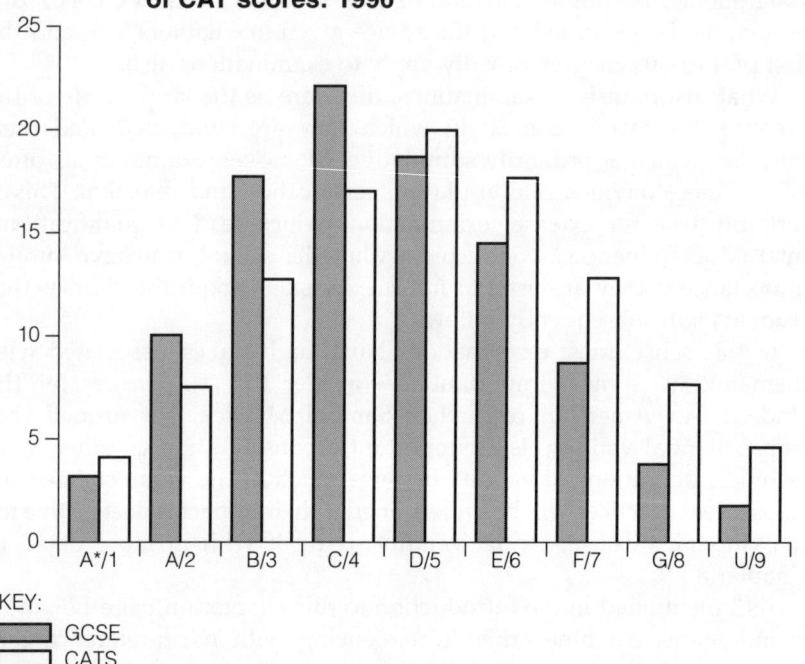

KEY:
- GCSE
- CATS

Times Educational Supplement, 23 August 1996

Figure 7.3, below, averages the results of a number of GCSE subjects, but the pattern sometimes varies considerably across subjects.

The unusual pattern of results in physics and Latin is easily explained: much smaller and highly selective groups are entered for these subjects. For example, in 1997 only 11,673 candidates took Latin GCSE in contrast

Figure 7.3 **GCSE results in some subjects in 1997**

Subject	Percentage of candidates obtaining grade						
	A*	A	B	C	D	E	F	G
English	2.0	8.7	18.8	26.5	22.1	12.4	6.8	2.3
Mathematics	2.1	7.5	14.6	23.1	16.5	15.6	12.2	6.3
Combined science	3.5	7.0	17.6	20.4	21.8	16.2	9.1	2.8
Technology	1.8	7.6	17.0	20.5	20.5	16.3	10.2	4.6
Geography	3.9	12.4	18.5	20.2	16.8	13.2	9.0	4.3
French	4.1	15.1	14.9	17.2	18.5	13.4	10.8	5.2
Physics	13.6	22.7	29.4	20.6	7.5	3.8	1.5	0.1
Latin	26.8	32.5	20.5	11.7	5.1	0.9	0.4	0.3

to the 649,559 students who took English; and only 44,892 took physics in contrast to the 1,007,640 who took combined science.

Consistency of standards: are the examinations getting easier?

The fact that the patterns differ across subjects and from year to year does, however, indicate that other factors operate on the basically norm-referenced examinations systems. For example, the steady improvement in the proportion of candidates achieving the higher A*–C grades since the introduction of the GCSE would probably not occur if grades were purely norm-referenced year on year. The truth is that although early attempts to develop grade criteria for GCSE were aborted, the GCSE possesses general criteria and the National Curriculum provides attainment criteria in NC subjects. Marking schemes for examiners also include detailed criteria by which candidates' responses to particular examination papers or elements should be judged.

Thus both the GCSE and A–level embody criteria in their grading schemes and this combination of criterion-referencing and norm-referencing provides the grounds for examination boards to claim that standards are consistent over time, even when there is a general improvement in results. The 'bell-curve' is, however, so entrenched in the national psyche that the public – and the media in particular – find this difficult to believe; if a higher proportion of candidates are achieving higher grades then the examination, in their view, must be getting easier.

In order to lay this ghost, SCAA and OFSTED commissioned a report on *Standards in Public Examinations 1975–1995*. This was published by SCAA in 1996 and looked at both 16+ and 18+ examinations and focused on three subjects: English, mathematics and chemistry. The study, involving 50 independent specialists, did two things: it analysed the demands of syllabuses and examinations over time, and it analysed direct evidence (e.g. exam scripts) of candidates' work associated with particular grades.

The conclusions reached by the six panels of experts were broadly similar. Although the *nature of the demand* made by the examinations had changed over time with different emphasis given to different content and skills, the *level of demand* was broadly comparable with some losses compensated by other gains. Thus in all subjects at both levels the standard of the examinations in 1995 were comparable to standards in 1975. When the improved GCSE and A–level results were reported in the summer of 1997, it was noticeable that accusations of 'grade inflation' were more muted, perhaps because this report had gone some way to allay the usual fears.

There were some, however, who remained unconvinced. The Institute of Directors, for example, issued a press release on 14 August 1997 cautioning against treating the one per cent rise in the A–level pass rate as an indicator of rising standards:

> *The IoD said that rising pass rates are frequently assumed to indicate improved educational achievements, but all too often they are associated with easier marking and lowering academic standards – in other words 'grade inflation'. . . 'A' level pass rates have risen significantly in recent years and yet our surveys suggest businessmen (sic) believe standards have been falling. . . The 'A' level should be the gold standard but there are increasing suspicions that standards are being watered down. And this is in spite of public assurances to the contrary.*

It seems that anecdote will always outweigh evidence in some quarters!

Ranking giving rise to elitism

One of the most serious concerns associated with these traditional examinations, in which the *ranking* of candidates is a basic principle, is their inherent *elitism*. This is especially so with A-level (the 'gold standard') but is also evident in GCSE where the pressures for school improvement have focused on the proportion of students achieving A*–C grades. This effectively disenfranchises those students whose efforts to achieve even a G grade should be encouraged and celebrated. This issue will be looked at again in subsequent chapters, but it is worth pointing out here that the concept of winners and losers is built into norm-referenced assessment systems, with unavoidable consequences for all concerned.

Criterion-referencing and vocational qualifications

This concept of winners and losers is not necessarily in evidence with criterion-referenced systems, where the assumption is that anyone who fulfils the requirements specified in criteria, and meets the standards, will have their achievement recognised. The need to compare performances and discriminate between candidates has not the same value as in norm-referenced assessment and the basis of comparison is a candidate's performance against the criterion.

In essence, therefore, criterion-referencing is more *egalitarian* because everyone is regarded as having the potential to succeed. In practice, however, criterion-referenced systems of assessment have their own difficulties. This has been particularly evident in attempts to introduce criterion-referenced vocational qualifications, such as GNVQ and NVQ.

The architects of the NVQ system of competence-based assessment, for example, built their model quite explicitly on criterion-referencing[4] on the grounds that it could provide information about a candidate's competence that is substantive, specific and highly reliable. A key characteristic of NVQs is that they are part of a decentralised assessment system: the criteria and standards for competence are determined by 'lead bodies' for each industry and the assessment of candidates is made by work-based assessors. The quality of these assessments is checked by 'external verifiers' from the awarding bodies.

This looks fairly straightforward but Alison Wolf, in her book *Competence-based Assessment*, published by the Open University Press in 1995, has described the system as fraught with difficulty. Some of the problems are very similar to those encountered in the attempt to implement criterion-referencing in the National Curriculum.

Problems associated with criterion-referencing and NVQs

The first problem has been the perceived need to develop unambiguous performance criteria. This has required the 'domain' of behaviour to be so carefully and clearly specified that anyone involved in assessment, as either assessor or assessed, will understand what performance is expected in order to fulfil the criterion. The assumption is that, provided assessments conform to the requirements in the elements of competence and in their performance criteria, they will automatically be valid, and being valid they will necessarily be comparable and reliable. Wolf argues that this goal has proved elusive:

> . . . *English competence-based awards have become ever more complex in structure, and ever more weighted down with detail. This is not because of some problem specific to competence-based assessment or NVQs in particular. On the contrary. Once we see them as examples of a 'criterion-referenced' approach, we can also see that this ever-receding goal of total clarity derives not from bad luck or incompetence, but is actually inherent in*

---

[4]See Jessup, G. (1991) *Outcomes: NVQs and the Emerging Model of Education and Training*. London: Falmer Press.

the methodology adopted. The more serious and rigorous the attempts to specify the domain being assessed, the narrower and narrower the domain itself becomes, without, in fact, becoming fully transparent. The attempt to map out free-standing content and standards leads, again and again, to a never-ending spiral of specification.

Secondly, even when the domain and performance criteria appear clearly specified, the tasks generated to test performance will inevitably differ somewhat, from place to place and occasion to occasion, in terms of format, context and problem content. Therefore, assessment tasks that authors believe will make the same demands in terms of the skills and competences required may prove to have different levels of difficulty when tackled by candidates. (For example, 11×11=? is easier than 99×99=? although the procedures required are the same.) In other words, there is no justification for assuming a one-to-one correspondence between assessment and objective.

Thirdly, the whole edifice of competence-based assessment underpinning NVQs (and GNVQs similarly) rests on an assumption that a consensus exists about 'standards of competence' in an industry. According to Alison Wolf this, too, is questionable. She makes another telling point:

. . . one of the motives behind the introduction of a competence-based system, and the establishment of lead bodies, was to improve the quality of training and to spread best practice throughout the industry. But if lead body definitions have, as one of their objectives, the encouragement of change in people's conceptions, it is obviously unwise to predicate our assessment system on the assumption that conceptions are stable and uniform.

Finally, despite the rhetoric about the robustness of criterion-referenced systems, they are operated by human beings who tend to 'interpret', using their own internalised, holistic conceptions about what constitutes competence when faced with the job of ticking off performance criteria.

Wolf presents evidence that assessors do not simply 'match' candidates' behaviour to assessment instructions in a mechanistic fashion, but 'make allowances' or 'compensate' for performances in certain contexts to bring assessments in line with their perception of what the candidate is really capable of.

In other words, even in a competence-based system, assessors make complex, non-mechanistic judgements in much the way that they might in more conventional academic assessment systems, such as in GCSE and A–level. The evident tension between the need to identify separate elements of competence and the need to come to an overall judgement is another example of the dilemma facing teachers engaged in National Curriculum assessment.

Inevitably assessors draw on their knowledge of the performance of other candidates in making assessments so they rarely, if ever, make purely criterion-related judgements. Thus the point made by an American writer, Angoff, over twenty years ago still rings true in these newer circumstances: a norm-referenced interpretation can nearly always be placed upon a criterion-referenced assessment, simply by making comparisons.

In conclusion, then, it should be acknowledged that in the same way that traditional examinations are not purely norm-referenced, neither can vocational qualifications and National Curriculum assessments be described as purely criterion-referenced. Most types of assessment contain elements of both in different proportions. Consequently it is important to be aware of the issues associated with both sources of judgement in relation to all types of assessment.

Further reading

1. Throughout Chapters 5, 6 and 7, I have made frequent reference to Peter Airasian's book entitled *Classroom Assessment*, first published in 1991 in New York by McGraw-Hill Inc. Although this is written for teachers in America, and relates to a context which is somewhat different from Britain, it is both practical and accessible and gives more detail on types of assessment than I have space for here. American books are sometimes difficult to get hold of and expensive so this might be one to obtain through inter-library loan.

2. Another book to obtain through inter-library loan, because it is out-of-print, is an important review of standardised tests by Philip Levy and Harvey Goldstein. This was published in 1984 by the Academic Press and is entitled *Tests in Education: a book of critical reviews*. Unfortunately this has not been updated but, since many of the tests have not been updated either, it is still a useful reference.

3. An authoritative analysis of the technical issues in assessment and testing, which is based on an extensive review of research, is *Assessment and Testing*, by Robert Wood. This was published by Cambridge University Press in 1991.

4. There are also a number of more general guides to the issues surrounding assessment and testing that have been published recently. The following draw on experience both in the UK and internationally, or across phases:

Black, P. (1998) *Testing: Friend or Foe? Theory and Practice of Assessment and Testing.* London, The Falmer Press.
Broadfoot, P. (1996) *Education, Assessment and Society.* Buckingham, The Open University Press.
Stobart, G. and Gipps, C. (1997) *Assessment: a teacher's guide to the issues.* 3rd edition, London, Hodder and Stoughton.

ACTIVITY

Reviewing the use of standardised tests

Schools may find it useful and important to review their use of standardised tests in the light of the discussion in this chapter. This could be a task for the assessment co-ordinator or assessment working group. An audit can be carried out by collecting information about all the standardised tests known to be used in the school, including those used by educational psychologists and the careers service. The following questions can be asked about each:

(i) What is this a test of: attainment, aptitude or ability?

(ii) Do the items in the test have face validity: do they appear to test what they purport to test?

(iii) When was the test constructed and last 'normed'? If this was longer than eight years ago is there a reason for this, and what are the implications for continued use?

(iv) Are there cautions in the handbook for administering the test and does the way it is used in the school take account of these cautions?

(v) How are the scores interpreted in the school: what efforts are made to explain the scores and work out the implications for future practice?

(vi) What attempts are made to relate the results of such tests to teachers' own assessments of students' performance?

(vii) Does the way the school uses the tests fit with the purposes for which they were designed? If not, is the way they are used really legitimate?

(viii) What are the consequences of using these tests: for students, for parents, for teachers and for the school as a whole?

Such questions should simulate discussion about the relative benefits of using such tests and consideration of the ways they can best be integrated with other forms of assessment into a coherent school policy.

8 Creating confidence in assessments

What makes a 'good' assessment?

In Chapters 5, 6 and 7 a number of criteria for judging the quality and usefulness of assessment systems have been mentioned: *fitness for purpose, validity* and *reliability*. Another criterion that schools consider to be crucially important is *manageability*. In this chapter I draw together some of the references I have already made to validity and reliability and examine them in a little more detail. The discussion is sometimes difficult and quite technical but I would encourage teachers and managers to grapple with it because these are the criteria on which the value of any assessment procedure ultimately depends. If assessments do not possess these qualities in good measure they are not worth doing.

I have used the terms validity and reliability in the previous chapters but some writers now prefer to use the terms *trustworthiness* or *dependability* to refer to the extent to which assessment procedures are sound and the information they generate can be relied upon with confidence. Dependability in the assessment context refers to an acceptable blend of the two other properties already mentioned: validity and reliability. Ideally, all assessments would possess maximum reliability and maximum validity but this is rarely possible; in the real world of assessment practice, some compromises have to be made. Before I discuss the relationship between these two it might be helpful if I deal with them separately. I take validity first because issues surrounding this concept have featured prominently in Chapters 5, 6 and 7.

Validity

The term validity is broadly taken to mean *the extent to which what is assessed is what the assessor set out to assess.* Several types of validity are often distinguished in classical test theory: face validity, predictive validity, concurrent validity, criterion-related validity, content validity, construct validity, internal validity, external validity, ecological validity etc. etc. For the purpose of giving practical guidance to teachers, it is not necessary to describe all of these but I will mention those that I consider to be the most important in the school context.

Face validity

At the most simple and basic level is *face validity*. This requires that the assessment *looks* as if it assesses what it claims to assess. One might think that this requirement is obvious and easily fulfilled but examples tell a different story. Take, for instance, reading tests that require children to complete sentences by selecting from a choice of five or so words in a list. This bears very little relation to the way that children learn to read, i.e. by reading stories in books. For them the face validity of such a test may be negligible because it has very little to do with what they know reading to be. Hence their responses to the test may reveal their confusion. Face validity is therefore important because it is desirable for students to understand the purpose of assessment in an effort to secure their co-operation.

Predictive validity

As mentioned in Chapter 7, standardised tests are usually developed by test development agencies that have little knowledge of the particular curriculum and learning experiences of individual students or classes. Indeed, this has little interest for them because the main objective of the test is not to assess how much an individual has learned of what she has been taught but to compare her attainments or skills with those of other students. Thus items in a test are chosen because of their capacity to *discriminate* finely between the performance of different pupils. This is described as an item's *facility*. Items that most children would get right would be discarded because they would not possess the facility to discriminate in the way desired.

Ultimately, the validity of such a test rests on its power to predict future attainment, in other words, to *generalise* from the interpretation of the test result to other outcome criteria. This is called *predictive validity* or *criterion-related validity* (the latter has a slightly wider scope of reference than the former) and is a chief kind of validity claimed for many standardised tests of basic skills, abilities and aptitudes.

As explained in Chapter 7, during the process of test development the test would be adjusted until the rank ordering of a representative sample of students is highly correlated with their future attainment. New generations of students can then be given the 'validated' test as a means of predicting how they, too, will perform in similar circumstances.

Whatever the problems associated with them, IQ tests continue to have their advocates because of this capacity to predict future performance. To the end of his life in 1997, Hans Eysenck, their foremost proponent, consistently claimed that:

> *IQ testing has been extremely successful on the practical level - predicting academic success from early childhood to university degree, selecting officers in the armed forces, correlating effectively with almost any activity using cognitions of one kind or another*[1].

The mention of *selection* is significant. One could argue that the fact that IQ was widely used as a means of selection for certain kinds of education and training makes it hardly surprising that IQ and eventual achievement are highly correlated. Those selected for grammar school or the armed forces etc. on the basis of high IQ scores were given the *opportunity* to achieve whilst others were not! These sort of cautions should be taken into account when using similar tests of ability for such common practices as setting and streaming in schools.

Predictive validity is also the reason why some approaches to the value-added analysis of school effectiveness have used tests of cognitive abilities as base-line measures for the analysis of examination results at sixteen. The argument is that such tests are still the best predictors we possess of examination success at the end of compulsory schooling and are therefore the most useful measure of whether a school has helped students to fulfil their potential. The strength of this claim is examined further in Chapter 12.

Content validity

Examinations, as we know them at school level, are not supposed to be tests of underlying abilities or aptitudes but measures of *attainment:* the extent to which candidates can demonstrate their acquisition of knowledge, skills and understandings in relation to a curriculum that they have been taught. To be a valid assessment, therefore, it is important that the examination is inclusive of all the relevant subject matter and not just a few selected aspects of it. This is called *content validity* and is perhaps the most important kind of validity for teachers to consider in developing classroom assessments and internal end-of-unit tests and

---

[1]*Times Higher Educational Supplement*, 25 January 1995, pp. 15–6.

examinations. In particular they need to consider all those skills, qualities and understandings they try to develop in their students during a course and how they might assess them.

The easiest option is often to assess content knowledge, i.e. knowledge of facts. But if knowledge of processes (e.g. of investigation, of putting knowledge into practice) and requisite social and personal attitudes are neglected then the content validity of an assessment can be seriously threatened. This has been a major concern with National Curriculum assessment as the government has moved progressively towards pencil-and-paper tests of subject knowledge and away from the more broadly based and practical 'standard assessment tasks' as TGAT originally conceived them.

Ensuring content validity is, however, about more than simply checking that all the relevant content is sampled in test questions. If content validity could be established simply by looking at the questions asked, it would differ little from face validity. But content validity is also concerned with the answers elicited and their relationship to the questions. For this reason, validation has to take place in the setting in which the assessment is carried out so that comparisons can be made between what was being sought and the behaviours that were actually elicited.

Content validity, therefore, is not only concerned with whether the test *appears* to assess what it purports to assess, but also the extent to which it *actually* does so. In this respect, teachers who design their own assessments have some advantage over test development agencies because they are 'on site' when the tests are used and can often monitor the responses elicited more easily.

Construct validity

Closely related to content validity is *construct validity*. Indeed many writers regard construct validity as the unifying concept. Construct validity requires a clear and accurate definition of the domain being assessed so that the assessments test the construct and not something else.

For example, the assessment of the construct called 'reading' requires an agreed definition of what constitutes reading. Older standardised reading tests (such as the Schonell Graded Word Reading Test) often test word recognition but neither comprehension nor fluency and expression. Similarly, in mathematics, assessments should have the power to assess mathematical competences and not something else, such as the ability to comprehend complex written instructions. In science, the construct can be defined by considering the range of contents covered (which might include knowledge of facts, knowledge of processes, skills and scientific attitudes). For this reason assessments that reflect the construct 'science' would also reflect the content of science. Therefore, construct validity incorporates content validity.

Consequential validity

The above descriptions imply that the responsibility for ensuring the validity of assessments is placed upon the developers of the tests, examinations or assessment tasks. However, recent debate has gone beyond test development to take on board issues of values and ethics. This represents something of a paradigm shift from an exclusive concentration on the scientific and technical issues associated with psychometric assessment, firmly grounded in a positivistic, 'natural science' approach, to a consideration of issues of interpretation and meaning more commonly associated with humanistic or hermeneutic approaches in social research. What is perhaps most interesting is that this transformation has come from within the ranks of the measurement experts who are generally steeped in the science of psychometrics.

A 1975 paper by the American researcher, Lee Cronbach, called 'Beyond the Two Disciplines of Scientific Psychology', is often quoted as having started the ball rolling but it is another American, Samuel Messick, who in 1989[2] formulated a new concept of validity which is now regarded as being as important as content and construct validity for assessment design and use. This is known as *consequential validity* and refers to the worth of assessments in terms of their *social, personal and educational consequences*. The following is a relevant, if difficult, passage from Messick's seminal paper.

> *Hence, what is to be validated is not the test or observation device as such but the inferences derived from test scores or other indicators – inferences about score meaning or interpretation and about the implications for action that the interpretation entails.*
>
> *(. . .) To validate an action inference requires validation not only of score meaning but also of value implications and action outcomes, especially of the relevance and utility of the test scores for particular action purposes, and of the social consequences of using the scores for applied decision making. Thus <u>the key issues of test validity are the meaning, relevance, and utility of scores</u>*

---

[2]Messick, S. (1989) 'Meaning and values in test validation: the science and ethics of assessment', *Educational Researcher*, 18 (2), pp. 5–11.

as a basis for action, and the functional worth of scores in terms of the social consequences of their use (my emphasis).

This kind of definition stresses the importance of assessment *utility*. In other words, whether an assessment or test is of any use – and whether these uses are worthwhile – must be a prime consideration. Teachers will no doubt be pleased to hear this because they will view assessment as a waste of time if the information it provides is irrelevant and does not afford a basis for meaningful educational action, i.e. for teaching and learning and school improvement.

The concept of consequential validity also gives recognition to the political dimension of assessment and acknowledges the role of 'stakeholders' in deciding whether or not the use of a particular form of assessment is of genuine value or whether the negative effects outweigh the potential good. For many years concerns have been expressed about the potentially destructive influence of the 'backwash' effect of certain forms of assessment on children's lives. As a child who failed the 11+ examination in the 1950s, and who had to resist the labels associated with secondary modern schooling in order to improve her 'life chances', I feel strongly about this issue! The social consequences of assessment are therefore a vitally important consideration – perhaps the most important – and should be taken seriously before any decision is made on adoption of a particular assessment regime.

When an assessment system, such as National Curriculum assessment, is imposed on schools by government, teachers may feel powerless to do much about it. There is evidence, however, that when they voice their concerns they are listened to by even the most autocratic administrations, if for no better reason than that, without their co-operation, the system cannot be made to work.

In the early days of the National Curriculum in England, for instance, teachers questioned the fairness of the requirement that every school should publish its NC test results in cases where the numbers of children involved were so small that individual children could be identified. They feared that the consequences of exposure could be harmful. An agreement was later secured from government that comparative data would not be expected in these circumstances, thus alleviating one of the problems of the 'backwash' effect.

This kind of consideration takes the issue of validation out of the controlling influence of test developers and acknowledges a much greater role for teachers, students, parents and the public in deciding whether an assessment procedure should be used. Technical 'soundness' continues to be important but added to this are questions about whether assessments are fair and worthwhile in an ethical, social and educational sense.

Reliability

The term *reliability* has a technical meaning, referring to the quality of the assessment procedure itself. A reliable assessment is one which gives *consistent* results by eliminating errors arising from different sources. For example, inconsistencies might arise from differences in how the same assessment task is *presented* to different students. This could significantly affect the way that students respond and is the major reason why the administration of standardised tests is specified to the extent of telling teachers what words to say to students who are taking the tests.

Inconsistencies in the *interpretations of assessment criteria and standards* are another source of error. In the early days of National Curriculum teacher assessment (TA), reports soon emerged that the evidence required to fulfil what were then called 'statements of attainment' had been interpreted in different ways by different teachers.

Ideally, it should be possible for another assessor, or the same assessor on other occasions, to repeat the assessment and get the same results. Two main types of reliability are therefore distinguished: *inter-judge reliability*, which refers to the degree of agreement between two assessors; and *intra-judge reliability*, which refers to the consistency of an assessor's judgements on different occasions. This is how reliability is traditionally defined, although other specific types of reliability are also distinguished:

- **Test-retest reliability** If the same student is assessed twice on the same test, the marks should be the same.
- **Mark-remark reliability** If the student is assessed by two different teachers, their marks should agree.
- **Parallel forms reliability** If a different but similar test is used, the student should get the same marks.

Each of these types of reliability creates its own set of problems when carried out as a procedure. For example, if an assessment is used frequently, students may memorise questions from one occasion to the next; if more markers are required, the costs of assessment will rise; and if tests are carried out in parallel forms, the time taken for assessment is lengthened which may limit time for teaching and reduce the motivation of the student.

All of these procedures for estimating reliability can be misleading for another reason. They give the impression that it is possible to guarantee the reliability of results for an *individual*. In practice, traditional procedures for estimating the reliability of an assessment involve statistical techniques which define reliability in terms of the spread of marks of *all* students who take the test. Dylan Wiliam, in an accessible article called 'Some technical issues in assessment: a user's guide', published in the *British Journal of Curriculum and Assessment* in 1992 (volume 2, number 3, pp. 11–20), explains how meaningless this may be at the level of the individual:

> *A teacher administers a test to a class and, using one of the standard methods (. . .), finds that the reliability of the test, for the class, is 0.95. Because of the high reliability (reliability is measured on a scale from 0 to 1), we would assume that we could depend on these marks to mean something.*
>
> *Instead of handing the test papers back to the students in the class, however, the teacher writes down each test mark on a different piece of paper and hands these pieces of paper out to the students randomly as they arrive for the lesson. Each student has got a mark on the test that is achieved by somebody in the class, although it is unlikely to be theirs. Nobody who knew what had happened would place much faith in the marks that the students were given, and yet the reliability of the test would still be 0.95! This is because the reliability is a measure of how much the spread of marks in the class is due to genuine differences in the ability being measured, and how much is due to other factors. Because the spread of marks has not changed, and because the spread of ability in the class had not changed, the reliability of the test will not change even though the marks that students get are almost completely meaningless.*

Wiliam concludes that traditional techniques for estimating reliability have little relevance to the typical use made of tests and assessments in schools. In his view reliability is only a small part of the dependability of an assessment, which also requires a measure of validity.

■ The relationship between reliability and validity

In the previous sections, I have tried to describe and explain some of the facets of two difficult but important concepts that determine whether an assessment is considered a 'good' assessment, and whether we can have confidence in what it tells us about students. Broadly speaking, *reliability is a property of the assessment procedures themselves, whereas validity is a property of the information they produce*. I have treated these two properties separately but I have also mentioned that they are linked and need to be examined in relationship to each other. The blend of reliability and validity is what is referred to as the *dependability* of an assessment. This idea can be expressed as:

$$\text{reliability} + \text{validity} = \text{dependability}$$

However, there remains a question about the *relative importance* or *weighting* that should be attached to the two elements.

Most people would argue that validity is the first consideration: an assessment which is not valid is useless whether or not it is reliable. On the other hand, an assessment that is not reliable cannot, by definition, be valid. This relationship between reliability and validity, and the dangers of satisfying one condition but ignoring the other, can be illustrated by an analogy with archery.

An archer may be very reliable in his aim in that all his arrows hit the target in close proximity to one another. However, his aim may fall short in terms of validity because the arrows fall nowhere near the bullseye (which is equivalent to the domain to be assessed). Another archer may succeed in hitting the bull with an arrow or two but at other times the arrows are scattered all over the target, sometimes missing it completely. Since this archer's aim is unreliable, nothing much can be claimed for its validity. High validity and high reliability would only be achieved if *all* the arrows hit the bullseye.

The trouble with this illustration is that it gives the impression that high validity and high reliability can be achieved simultaneously. Theoretically there seems no reason why this should not be so, but in practice this ideal has often proved elusive. As I pointed out earlier, the technical procedures for estimating reliability do not provide information on the dependability of individual results. They also tend to impose limitations on the definition of the domain to be assessed and the ways in which assessment can be carried out, thus threatening validity.

On the other hand, assessments that are fully capable of sampling a complex domain of learning, in settings which do not introduce artificial conditions and therefore additional threats to validity, are unlikely to be replicable. In such situations validity may be high but reliability will be weak. In any assessment, therefore, there is likely to be some trade-off between validity and reliability. The best one can strive for is the highest degree of each property which is attainable in a given context and with respect to a particular purpose. In an important book in this field (reference given on page 167), Wynne Harlen has concluded that the best one should expect is that *an assessment should possess both high validity and optimum reliability.*

Implications for schools

The implication of this discussion of the relationship between validity and reliability is that schools need to consider *both* properties when evaluating the quality of their assessments. They therefore need to examine their assessments *from a number of different angles* in order to judge their overall quality. The various interpretations of the concept of validity point to two different implications for schools, depending on whether assessments are developed internally, within the school, or whether they are adopted or imposed from outside.

Establishing the validity of internally designed assessments

When schools develop their own assessment systems, they must assume responsibility for validation in much the same way as professional test development agencies. This means that they should make efforts to ensure that their assessments have at least face validity and content validity and that they are satisfied with the consequences that flow from assessment practice.

With regard to consequential validity, perhaps the most important thing for teachers to consider is how they *actually* use assessments for the planning of teaching and learning and for school improvement generally. With this concrete evidence they are then in a position to make judgements about their utility and their ethical consequences.

Teachers should also make sure that assessment tasks are designed to sample all the relevant content of the curriculum. However, bearing in mind the second aspect of content validity mentioned on page 154, they should also observe students' *actual* responses to these tasks to make sure that the tasks are capable of eliciting the kind of responses expected. There is much evidence that people who design assessment tasks often have mistaken ideas about how students will tackle them.

An interesting example of this is given in an article by Patricia Murphy[3], drawing on evidence from the now defunct Assessment of Performance Unit. Students were asked to test the insulating properties of a selection of fabrics to decide which would make the best jacket for mountaineering. The people who designed the task expected the students to heat water to boiling point in beakers, wrap the fabrics around the beakers and measure the rate of cooling. Some students

---

[3] Murphy, P. (1996) 'Integrating learning and assessment – the role of learning theories?' In P. Woods (ed), *Contemporary Issues in Teaching and Learning*. London: Routledge/Open University.

perceived that this was what the assessors really wanted them to do, but others (notably girls) took all aspects of the given context into account and were observed blowing air from hairdryers through the fabric, soaking the fabrics in water and trying to construct little jackets.

In other words, this latter group had interpreted the content of the task to be much broader than the assessors had intended. Either the assessors needed to recognise this and assess this wider spectrum of knowledge, skills and understanding, or they needed to rewrite the task to a narrower specification.

Monitoring the validity of externally designed assessments

When teachers adopt assessment systems that are offered or imposed by external agencies, their role in validation is somewhat different. They are not in a position to build validation into the design process but they can have a powerful voice in commenting on assessment design in the light of their experience of implementation.

This critical function is important and most external assessment developers will welcome feedback – and some explicitly invite it – because they usually have limited resources for piloting. However, teachers are sometimes reluctant to provide such feedback for a number of reasons: they may regard test development agencies as 'the experts' whose 'science' is almost beyond comprehension; or they may feel that there is no point in challenging something with the weight of government legislation behind it. However, they should be encouraged to offer critique if critique is warranted. In the long term it is students who will benefit.

An example of such critique was offered by teachers of English in 1997 who were vociferous in their criticisms of the Shakespeare paper (Paper 2) in the national tests at Key Stage 3. In essence their argument was about its content and consequential validity.

In the study of English at Key Stage 3, students are expected to read a wide variety of plays, fiction and poetry by writers living before and after the year 1900. However, of the two test papers set for fourteen year olds in 1997, one was entirely devoted to the assessment of students' understanding of Shakespeare. The Subject Order states:

> Students should be encouraged to appreciate the distinctive qualities of these works through activities that emphasise the interest and pleasure of reading them, rather than necessitating a detailed line-by-line study.

In recent years many teachers have achieved some considerable success in this, partly through the influence of Rex Gibson and his teacher associates who, in conjunction with the Cambridge University Press, have produced school editions of Shakespeare's texts with class activities to emphasise that Shakespeare wrote his plays to be acted, watched and enjoyed.

Unfortunately, the national tests have not fully reflected this new approach and although there is usually a question about how a director might direct a scene, most of the questions have asked students to analyse the meaning of a pre-set passage. Inevitably then, some teachers feel constrained to spend more time on Shakespeare than on other writers and to abandon their dramaturgical approach in favour of close analysis of set text, at least as the time for the tests comes near.

The protests from teachers of English focus on two linked concerns: the fact that the test does not reflect the content of the curriculum but samples it in an unrepresentative way; and the evidence that this is already having a 'backwash' effect on teaching and learning. At the time of writing the outcome of this protest has yet to be determined, but these teachers are making an important contribution to the debate about what should count as evidence of learning and achievement in their subject. In a democratic society, they have every right to do so.

Establishing consistency in assessments through moderation

As the quotation from Dylan Wiliam's article on page 158 makes clear, reliability has a particular connotation in classical test theory and the statistical procedures for establishing it are beyond the resources of most schools. Moreover, it has only limited relevance to teachers who are more interested in the value of assessments for individual students.

It is interesting therefore that recent government documentation relating to National Curriculum assessment rarely mentions 'reliability' but rather the need for 'consistency' in the assessments carried out by teachers in schools. This may be a deliberate way of saying that statistical precision is not what is being looked for but an attempt by teachers and schools to ensure that the assessment judgements they make, with respect to individual students, as well as groups, can inspire confidence because attempts have been made to eradicate obvious sources of bias.

Procedures for promoting consistency are often referred to under the general heading of *moderation*. In 1994, Wynne Harlen and colleagues produced a book reviewing moderation procedures in various assessment systems in the UK and across the world (reference on page 167). In her introductory chapter, Harlen drew a helpful distinction between those procedures concerned primarily with the *quality control of assessment results* and those procedures whose main concern is the *quality assurance of assessment processes*. The latter assume that sound results will follow from sound procedures.

Drawing on Harlen's book, the following is a summary of those procedures that are used, or might be used, by schools. In some cases the choice of procedure lies outside their control, as in the moderation of examination scripts or coursework samples, where the procedure is mandatory.

Summary of moderation procedures for use in schools

1 Approaches to quality control in assessment

These typically take place after the assessment event.

(i) **Use of reference or scaling tests for statistical moderation** This is a device used in the development of many standardised tests and by examinations boards. Students' marks are adjusted using the results of another externally marked test of known reliability. Sometimes it is used to compensate for systematic variations in teachers' judgements when they are being used as internal markers. The marks of a teacher who is known to be 'lenient' will be moved down and the marks of a 'harsh' marker will be moved up although the rank order will remain the same.

There is some indication that teachers are implicitly invited to use National Curriculum tests as reference tests in a similar way because they do not have to submit their teacher assessment (TA) results until test results are known. They can therefore adjust them accordingly. The evidence of the 'leveller perspective' given in the 1996 national evaluation conducted by Exeter University (see Chapter 3) suggests that this is a use made of tests in some schools.

(ii) **Inspection of samples by post** In this procedure, work assessed internally by teachers is sampled by an examination board or assessment agency to check that the tasks have been set and marked according to instructions. This is the principal method used by examination boards for the moderation of coursework in GCSE.

(iii) **Inspection of samples by visiting moderators** This is similar to the above procedure but it enables a wider range of products to be inspected, including artefacts, tapes and

▶

photographs of ephemeral evidence and students' portfolios of work. It also facilitates more professional discussion between moderator and teacher. It is the normal procedure used in the award of vocational qualifications (see the reference to 'external verifiers' in the section on the NVQ, in Chapter 7 page 147). This is a procedure that could be more widely used in secondary schools if they were willing to involve LEA advisers/inspectors or colleagues in other schools. This may seem unrealistic in times when resources are stretched and schools are engaged in competition with each other, but the professional and educational benefits of such collaboration could be considerable.

(iv) **Teacher-requested moderation (appeals)** In most certification procedures, some provision is made for appeals if the assessment result is not what was expected. Usually an appeal can only be made on the grounds that the examination procedures have not been carried out correctly. However, until 1993, it was possible to invoke moderation procedures in National Curriculum assessment when test results did not correspond with teacher assessment results and when teachers felt that the latter should have had priority over the former, rather than vice versa. A moderator was then brought in to 'reconcile' the results and to decide, on the basis of evidence presented, whether the teacher's judgement should be upheld. Now that both teacher assessment and test results are reported separately, this procedure has been discontinued although teachers still can, and do, challenge some national test results, notably in English.

(v) **Group/consensus moderation of internal assessment results** This involves a review of work that has been internally assessed. The intention here is for a group to ensure, *post hoc*, that assessment judgements have been assigned as previously agreed.

2 **Approaches to quality assurance in assessment**

These usually take place before or during assessment to ensure the quality of the *process*. The focus tends to be on the opportunities for learning and assessment and on increasing shared understandings of criteria and procedures.

(i) **Defining criteria for assessment** The attempt to specify key learning objectives and performance criteria by which the

▶

attainment of objectives can be judged, is intended to provide a basis for consistency in assessments. This is then a kind of 'intrinsic moderation'. However, the account of NVQs given in Chapter 7 makes the point that the clear and unambiguous specification of learning outcomes can be problematic (see pages 147–9. If this specification is done by external agencies such as industry lead bodies or assessment agencies, it is often remote from the influence of teachers. This often dilutes the impact of such statements on their assessment practice. If, however, teachers are involved in the *collaborative* development of specifications of performance criteria in relation to their internal assessments, this can be an effective way of enhancing consistency in their assessments, across time and across classrooms.

(ii) **Exemplification**   The provision of examples of students' work which has been assessed, preferably with commentary on the features used in making the judgement, can be helpful in indicating the kind of tasks that provide opportunities for students to demonstrate their achievements. They also help to make abstract criteria concrete and therefore strengthen consistency in interpretation. The *Exemplification of Standards Materials:* Key Stage 3, published by SCAA in 1995 and 1996, were of this nature and generally highly valued by teachers. However, examples produced centrally cannot reflect all the variable contexts in which teachers work and many schools like to produce their own portfolios of exemplar material to reflect their own particular contexts and schemes of work.

(iii) **Approval of institutions/centres**   This procedure, often called accreditation, is a process whereby a body responsible for an award approves an institution or centre to carry out assessment for these awards. Usually centres are accredited after a visit from the accrediting body for the purpose of inspecting documents and facilities relating to curricula, staffing, resources and assessment arrangements. Some LEAs have offered schools accreditation of their assessment procedures in relation to their National Curriculum teacher assessment arrangements or in relation to their provision of records of achievement.

(iv) **Visits by verifiers or moderators**   This is distinguished from the inspection of samples by visiting moderators – see 1 (iii) above – by the fact that visits are made to observe the

▶

> way in which assessments are *carried out,* in order to influence the process and to inform the interpretation of assessment criteria and standards. However, the two procedures can be combined.
>
> (v) **Group moderation** These are meetings of teachers, from one school or clusters of schools, at which samples of work are discussed in order to arrive at shared understandings of what performance on criteria looks like in practice. These are sometimes known as 'agreement trials' or 'agreement panels'. They have become an important part of National Curriculum assessment training in many schools and sometimes result in the production of highly valued school, cluster or regional portfolios of exemplar material to illustrate agreed evidence of performance at the different levels.

In concluding her commentary on moderation processes, Wynne Harlen points out that all forms of moderation have costs and benefits and that a choice of an appropriate procedure for a given assessment system should be based on weighing up these advantages and disadvantages. Harlen identifies the following aspects as particularly important in this respect:

- the extent to which moderation procedures are bureaucratically controlled;
- their contribution to the professional development of teachers;
- the demands they make in terms of time;
- their financial cost;
- their impact on the assessment process;
- their impact on the product of assessment, i.e. results.

She also provides an analysis of the costs and benefits of each of the moderation procedures mentioned above in relation to these six aspects. The resulting profile (Figure 8.1, opposite) can be used as a rough guide to choice of moderation procedures.

What emerges from this analysis is not totally unexpected. Those procedures that have the greatest impact on results but are also cheap, have no impact on professional development or the quality of assessment processes because they are purely bureaucratic. Those procedures that have the greatest impact on the professional development of teachers and

Figure 8.1 **Profiles of moderation procedures**

Procedure	ASPECTS OF MODERATION PROCEDURES					
	Bureaucratic	Contribution to professional development	Time	Cost	Impact on process	Impact on product
Reference tests	***	–	*	*	–	***
Inspection of samples	*	*	*	*	–	**
Group moderation of results	*	**	**	***	**	**
Defining criteria	–	**	**	*	*	**
Exemplification	–	**	*	*	**	**
Centre approval	–	**	*	*	**	**
Moderator visits	–	**	***	***	***	*
Group moderation	–	***	***	***	***	**

After Harlen, 1994, p.143

the assessment process also tend to be the most costly in terms of time and money. This is because they are people-intensive.

In the context of National Curriculum assessment, TGAT argued for a model of moderation involving group moderation (agreement trials), moderator visits and exemplification. However, the government abandoned this in favour of a system of external checks (based mainly on externally set and marked papers) that are less costly, more bureaucratic but likely to have a focused impact on assessment products (results).

Many secondary teachers welcomed this change in policy because they thought that it would be less time consuming. They were right, of course, but Harlen's analysis indicates that while this change serves the accountability (and political) purposes of assessment well, it is less able to promote the educational goals of assessment – improvement in teaching and learning – that are of equal or greater importance.

Further reading

Wynne Harlen's edited collection of articles on the issue of quality in assessment is an up-to-date account of approaches to moderation across a number of systems, in Britain and elsewhere. Most of the contributors were members of the Assessment Policy Task Group of the British Educational Research Association. The full reference is: Harlen, W. (ed.) (1994) *Enhancing Quality in Assessment*, Paul Chapman Publishing Ltd.

ACTIVITY

Developing quality assurance procedures for internal assessments

Since moderation procedures for examinations are externally determined, schools will find it most useful to work on developing their internal mechanisms. This can be done *at departmental level* but using a common framework, which I outline below. Schools would be well advised to start in a modest way with something containable and concrete. They can expand the scope of their procedures, gradually, having evaluated the results of their first efforts. I suggest that departments begin to establish procedures on the basis of an initial trial with *a single assessment activity*. This could be a common assessment task or end-of-unit test to be used by all teachers of a particular year group. (Some schools may, of course, have some procedures already in place, in which case what I am suggesting may simply be an extension of these.)

The framework has three stages:

Stage 1: Before assessment
(ideally involving all teachers in the department or a smaller working group)

(i) *Design the assessment*

- Clarify the domain to be assessed – what constructs and content are to be covered? What are the key learning objectives of the curriculum?
- Define performance criteria and the standards expected on the criteria but avoid over-specification – what dimensions of achievement (knowledge, skills, understanding) will be assessed and what standards are expected in relation to each? What provision should be made for students who meet criteria other than those specified?
- Design a marking scheme incorporating these criteria;
- Check that the assessment *looks* as if it has face validity and content validity.

(ii) *Plan how the task will be presented to students*

- Decide how, where, when, and by whom the assessment will be administered;
- Decide what degree of standardisation of procedures will be necessary, bearing in mind the problem of creating inauthentic conditions which could invalidate results.

Stage 2: During assessment
(ideally involving individual teachers and a 'critical friend', or appointed 'moderator' from within the department)

(iii) *Monitor the administration of the assessment*

- Observe the presentation of the assessment to students – does the teacher deviate from the agreed procedure? If so, why?
- Observe what students actually *do* – do they behave as expected?
- Observe what impact the assessment has on students – do any get anxious? Do they enjoy the task?

Stage 3: After assessment
(ideally involving all departmental colleagues)

(iv) *Group moderation (agreement trial)*

- Study a *selected range* of student 'products' and try to apply the performance criteria and standards;
- Attempt to come to a consensus judgement based on the evidence of student outcomes but take into consideration the observations made during the administration of the assessment;
- Annotate the student's work (perhaps on an attached annotation sheet) with judgements of the standard achieved, referenced to the evidence, together with comments about the context in which the work was produced.

(v) *Create a portfolio of exemplars*

- Begin to make a collection of exemplars which illustrate a range of assessments in relation to key learning objectives and a range of responses from students, with consensus judgements about the achievements demonstrated;
- Use these as illustrations of agreed standards in future group moderations.

(vi) *Evaluate the assessment process*

- Discuss the extent to which the assessments were able to assess what they were supposed to assess;
- Discuss the extent to which teachers' assessments were consistent in terms of (a) the way the assessments were presented and (b) the way standards were interpreted;

- Decide any changes needed to assessment tasks and procedures if this particular assessment activity is to be repeated.

If teachers find this framework helpful they could be encouraged to use it when an occasion arises – perhaps once or twice a year. Gradually they would build up a bank of 'agreement trialed' assessments and a departmental portfolio of exemplar material. 'Going through the process', even in relation to one specific assessment activity, is also likely to give them some awareness of quality assurance issues that will, hopefully, transfer to their everyday assessments in classrooms.

If schools develop an enthusiasm for this approach they could profitably involve colleagues from other schools in agreement trials and moderation.

9 Assessment, learning and the involvement of students

Assessment *of* learning or assessment *for* learning?

Any assessment is only as good as the action that arises from it. This is what is meant by 'consequential validity'. In other words, measurement for its own sake has no value; it is the inferences that are drawn from it and the actions that are taken on the basis of these inferences that determine the value of assessments. Since the purpose of schools is the education of children, assessments have little value unless they contribute to that purpose. They should help students to learn better and, in so doing, raise their achievements and contribute to school improvement. Assessment results alone cannot do this because, as the saying goes, you cannot fatten the pig simply by weighing it. Something has to be *done* with assessment data. Assessment *of* learning is therefore insufficient for educational purposes; assessment *for* learning is necessary.

This idea – that assessments can be built into teaching to enhance learning – is at the heart of the concept of formative assessment which was introduced in Chapters 2 and 5. Some people prefer to call this simply 'educational assessment'. In this chapter I unpack this idea further and look in more detail at the implications for teachers' practice.

Formative assessment

As discussed earlier, formative assessment is usually taken to refer to the process of identifying what students have, or have not, achieved in order to plan the next steps in teaching. It will usually involve the diagnosis of learning difficulties, although this is not synonymous with the kind of standardised, psychometric, diagnostic assessments described in Chapter 7. Within formative assessment, the term 'diagnosis' usually possesses a more colloquial and less technical meaning.

Formative assessment is also distinguished from other forms of assessment in that it is, by definition, carried out by teachers. This is important if it is to inform the decisions teachers make in the classroom. The aspiration is that assessment should become fully integrated with teaching and learning and therefore part of the educational process rather than a 'bolt-on' activity.

In an important article published in 1989, Royce Sadler, an Australian writer, outlines a theory of formative assessment[1]. In this he explains the nature of the relationship between formative assessment and teaching. He considers that *feedback* (see also Chapter 5 pages 95–9) is the key element in formative assessment and he sees two audiences for this: the teacher and the student. Feedback to the student, mediated by the teacher, is particularly important because no learning can take place without the active involvement of the student. According to Sadler:

> *The indispensable conditions for improvement are that the* student *comes to hold a concept of quality roughly similar to that held by the teacher, is able to monitor continuously the quality of what is being produced* during the act of production itself, *and has a repertoire of alternative moves or strategies from which to draw at any given point. In other words, students have to be able to judge the quality of what they are producing and be able to regulate what they are doing during the doing of it. (. . .)*
>
> *Stated explicitly, therefore, the learner has to (a) possess a concept of the* standard *(or goal, or reference level) being aimed for, (b) compare the* actual *(or current) level of performance with the standard, and (c) engage in appropriate action which leads to some closure of the gap.*

Sadler writes about 'standards' rather than 'criteria' in order to distance himself from the sophisticated technical approaches that have grown up around criterion-referenced assessment (see Chapter 7 pages 146–9). His interest is in the kind of qualitative judgements that competent teachers make using multiple criteria to appraise the work of students over a series of assessment tasks. For him, it is the configuration or pattern of performance that takes precedence. This is particularly relevant to the British context because it is the kind of judgement that teachers are expected to make in teacher assessment using 'level descriptions'.

Students monitoring themselves

Sadler says that such qualitative judgements can be made dependable by the development of natural-language descriptions and by exemplar

---

[1] Sadler, D. Royce (1989) 'Formative assessment and the design of instructional systems', *Instructional Science*, 18, pp. 119–44. This is not an easy article but it has been very influential and is often referred to.

material to which both teachers and students should have access. He wants the goal of formative assessment to move eventually from a system of teachers giving students feedback to one in which students monitor themselves. This requires the development of an evaluative language, shared by teachers and students, based on the development of *meta-cognitive skills*, i.e. the skills that enable the kind of reflection on performance that Sadler mentions in the quotation above.

Sadler argues that such skills can be developed by providing 'direct authentic evaluative experience' for students. He suggests that the provision of examples of students' work which have been assessed, preferably with commentary on the features used in making the judgement, has an important role to play in this. In other words, not only can exemplar material help teachers to gain an understanding of standards in a given area (see Chapter 8 page 165), but it can fulfil the same role for students. Conversely, he is sceptical of the usefulness of grades or scores for communicating anything of formative value (see also Chapter 5 pages 96–103).

> *In any area of the curriculum where a grade or score assigned by a teacher constitutes a one-way cipher for students, attention is diverted away from fundamental judgements and the criteria for making them. A grade therefore may actually be counterproductive for formative purposes.*

■ The involvement of students in assessment

The description of formative assessment given above indicates that student self-assessment and peer-assessment should not be regarded as an optional extra but should be an essential part of any assessment that aspires to have a positive impact on learning. However, the kind of self-assessment implied is far removed from the practice of simply allowing students to 'mark' their own work using the teacher's grading scheme. When students do the latter they often simply mimic what they have seen teachers do without any real understanding.

In order to make self-assessment effective, students have to be 'let into the secrets' of teachers' professional practice so that they acquire some of their skills and understandings. This is a major task because students can be a very conservative influence and may be resistant to taking over any part of what they see as 'the teacher's job'. Moreover, it assumes that teachers have a firm grasp of the principles of formative assessment, which is not always the case.

When I recall my own experience as a school teacher, I am embarrassed when I think of the times that I introduced a lesson with such words as, 'Today we are going to look at a poem by Ted Hughes'. I would set some homework based on questions about the poem, and I would mark the work produced. I might have said something about the quality of students' work when I handed it back and I might have indicated what I was looking for, but it did not always occur to me to build this kind of discussion deliberately into the lesson *before* I set the task. I was teaching Ted Hughes rather than teaching students how to learn. Many things have changed since I was a schoolteacher, but I still hear teachers worrying about 'getting through the syllabus' when they should perhaps be more focused on what students actually learn.

In what ways should students take part?

So what involvement should students have in the assessment process if it is to be formative for learning? The following are indicated by research (see the review by Black and Wiliam, referenced in Chapter 5, footnote to page 96).

1 **Access to criteria.** Students should have an understanding of what would be regarded as mastery or desired performance in an area of learning. This means that teachers need to discuss the criteria and standards for assessment with them. If existing 'official' criteria are couched in teacher language then it is worth spending some time translating these, with students, into a form that they can more easily comprehend. This is possible, even with students with learning difficulties. While I was involved with the national evaluation of records of achievement pilot schemes in the 1980s, I observed a teacher in a special school work with his class to produce a set of criteria for science, based on published criteria for teachers. These were made into a poster and pinned to the classroom wall. When students thought they had achieved one of the criteria they asked their teacher to come and discuss the evidence with them prior to recording the achievement. A similar set of criteria are given on the next page in Figure 9.1. These are from the science department of a Cambridgeshire Village College and relate to Science Attainment Target 1.

2 **Access to assessed examples** Criteria and standards are often phrased in generalised ways, so it is also important that students have access to examples of assessed work so that they can see what the standards look like in practice. This argues for the use of exemplification material with students, for learning purposes, as well

Figure 9.1 **Student-friendly science criteria**

INVESTIGATION PLANNING AND ASSESSMENT SHEET		
Investigation _____ Name _____ Form _____ Date _____	Your Assessment	Teacher Assessment
1 Planning Have you described the main things (*variables*) that could affect the experiment? Have you picked one or two variables to test, and said which they are? Have you made any predictions about what will happen? Have you tried to explain your predictions scientifically? Did you need to carry out any trial runs to help sort out your method? Have you said how many different values of your variables you will test? (Try to use at least 5!) Have you written a detailed method? Have you made this a fair test? Has your plan dealt with any possible safety problems?		
2 Carrying out Are your measurements as accurate as possible? Are there enough measurements? Did you repeat any measurements and have you said why? Have you written the results down as you go along?		
3 Analysing and making conclusions Are your results clearly presented (tables, charts etc.)? Could you draw a graph or chart of your results? Did the graph need a line of best fit? Have you written a conclusion? (What have you found out?) Have you described any pattern shown in your results? (Something like. . .the bigger the voltage the brighter the light. . .) Have you explained your conclusions as scientifically as possible? If you made a prediction do your results match what you predicted would happen? (Say why and why not.)		
4 How good is your evidence? Do you think you have a big enough range of results to support your conclusion? Explain what you mean! Have you got any odd results? Have you tried to explain these odd results? Can you suggest any improvements to your method?		
SWAVESEY VILLAGE COLLEGE		

as with other teachers for establishing consistency in marking. This should not impose an additional burden on teachers if they have already created a portfolio of exemplars as suggested in Chapter 8 (see page 165). This, and any exemplification material from SCAA/QCA, could be used for this purpose with students. Exemplars do not always have to provide 'model answers'; a great deal can be learned from evidence of shortcomings and mistakes. Indeed, some of the Key Stage 3 national tests in mathematics have attempted to be formative by asking students to analyse mistakes in the computations of others, rather than simply asking students to do computations themselves.

3 **Opportunities to set their own tasks** It is usually assumed that assessment tasks will be designed and set by the teacher (see Chapter 6). However, if students understand the criteria for assessment in a particular area, they are likely to benefit from the opportunity to design their own tasks. Their motivation will be increased and thinking through what kind of activity would meet the criteria and standards will, itself, contribute to learning. Within GCSE coursework and GNVQ there is some opportunity for students to choose their own projects. The important thing to consider, however, is not only the choice of theme but also what will meet the assessment criteria.

4 **Self-assessment and peer assessment** If students are to learn from their own performance in order to improve, they need to be able to assess and evaluate their *actual* performance against standards. They need to identify any gaps between actual and desired levels and they need to be able to work out why these gaps have occurred. Then, they need to identify the strategies that they might use to close the gap and meet the standard on another occasion. This is a complex activity but it has to be done *by* the students because it is they who are the learners and they need to internalise the process. Learning cannot be done *for* them by the teachers.

Teachers have an important role, however, in teaching students the meta-cognitive skills to carry out this process. They can do this by working through examples with individuals or groups and making clear to them the thinking processes that they go through, and which they want students to acquire. Students can then be given examples to work on themselves (their own or those from other people) in much the same way that they might be given tasks in the subject field. Teachers might protest that this addition to their professional role takes time from teaching their subject, and they have little enough time as it is. My response would be that spending some time on developing students' meta-cognitive skills is likely to have very positive outcomes in terms of raising students' achievements.

Perhaps the most crucial aspect of training students in self-assessment and peer assessment is enhancing the *quality of the discourse*. Most students are imbued with a culture that values the ability to give 'correct' answers quickly through rapid recall of stored information. What is needed for self-assessment is quite different. Students need to be trained to ask thoughtful questions of their own work and that of their peers; they need to be helped to admit problems without risking the loss of self-esteem; they need to take time to puzzle over the reasons why problems have arisen; and they need know that it is acceptable to look at a number of possible solutions before opting for a particular course of action.

Dialogue with someone else can be very valuable to raise awareness of hidden possibilities or challenge taken-for-granted assumptions. The teacher can be one partner in this, and should be on some occasions, but given the numbers in the average class this is not always practicable. Peers can often take this role and, by acting as a critical friend to a fellow student, they will almost inevitably enhance their own understandings as well.

5 **Opportunities to implement strategies for improvement** If students have identified areas for improvement and decided strategies for achieving better outcomes, they need opportunities for putting strategies into practice. This argues for self-assessment to be integrated into an interim stage in the completion of assessment tasks (perhaps at final draft stage and earlier). Otherwise it may be some time before students have opportunities to improve their performance on a particular set of criteria in a particular area of the curriculum.

The process of formative assessment involving students in the way described here may require learning to be slowed down so that it can be deeper, more thoughtful, and more secure. Time will also be needed to induct students into the processes and understandings associated with good assessment practice. So be it. In my view, there is little to be gained by racing through the syllabus and achieving only partial, superficial or surface learning. Such an approach, however, may require teachers to strip away some of the detail in their schemes of work in order to concentrate only on *key* learning objectives and *essential* knowledge and understandings.

The arguments for student self-assessment

All these suggestions may constitute a fairly radical departure from existing practice for many teachers and change will need to be supported by senior managers and an appropriate staff development programme. Teachers will also need to be convinced that it is likely to be worth taking the risks associated with innovation. Some very compelling evidence that such an approach will actually work, and have substantial benefits, can be found in the review of research carried out by Paul Black and Dylan Wiliam (see page 96).

A study in Portugal, reported by Fontana and Fernandes in 1994[2], involved 25 mathematics teachers taking an INSET course to study methods for teaching their pupils to assess themselves. During the 20 week part-time course, the teachers put the ideas into practice with a total of 354 students aged 8–14. These students were given a mathematics tests at the beginning and end of the course so that their gains could be measured. The same tests were taken by a control group of students whose mathematics teachers were also taking a 20 week part-time INSET course but this course was not focused on self-assessment methods. Both groups spent the same time in class on mathematics and covered similar topics. Both groups showed significant gains over the period but the self-assessment group's average gain was about *twice* that of the control group. In the self-assessment group, the focus was on regular self-assessment, often on a daily basis. This involved teaching students to understand both the learning objectives and the assessment criteria, giving them an opportunity to choose learning tasks, and using tasks that gave scope for students to assess their own learning outcomes.

Other studies in Black and Wiliam's review report similar achievement gains for students who have an understanding of, and involvement in, the assessment process. Moreover, there is strong evidence that the gains for customarily 'low attainers' are higher than for 'high attainers', although these latter also make gains. In other words, the long tail of underachievement (an especially worrying feature of British education for many years) is reduced in these studies. If implemented nationwide, strategies to promote formative assessment, incorporating student self-assessment have the potential to raise standards generally and the achievements of 'low attainers' in particular.

Those schools and teachers who were involved in the records of achievements movement in the 1980s will probably say that this is what

---

[2] Fontana, D. and Fernandes, M. (1994) 'Improvements in mathematics performance as a consequence of self-assessment in Portuguese primary school children', *British Journal of Educational Psychology*, 64, pp. 407–417.

they were arguing for all along, believing that the *process* was central for motivation and improved learning. The artefact called a 'Record of Achievement' was in some senses always of secondary importance.

This argument was never really understood by government, however, and the National Record of Achievement fell short of its promise. The relaunch of the NRA as a 'formative' document will need to take on these ideas about processes if it is not to go the same way. However, in contrast to the record of achievement pilot schemes in the 1980s, we now have, in Black and Wiliam's review, a strong empirical base for arguing for the efficacy of formative self-assessment for improving students' learning. *Carpe diem*: we should seize the day.

Formative assessment and theories of learning

In arguing that processes of formative assessment contribute to improved student learning, I have largely drawn on theoretical accounts, such as Royce Sadler's (see pages 172–3), and empirical evidence, such as that collected by Black and Wiliam. In order to convince teachers and help them in their practice, it may also be important to explain how assessment interacts with learning and why it is so important. Any formulation of formative assessment really needs to be grounded in both empirical evidence and learning theory. I realise that theory became unfashionable, even despised in certain quarters, during the 1990s, but we all have at least informal theories about how the world works. If we did not, we could not act, except instinctively. According to Kurt Lewin, 'There is nothing so practical as a good theory'; there are a number of good, if competing theories, about how learning takes place and the role of assessment in this process.

Two different theoretical perspectives appear to underlie most approaches to formative assessment although they often involve superficially similar practices and procedures, such as the specification of criteria for achievement within a domain. These two main perspectives are derived from *behaviourist* theoretical positions or *constructivist* theoretical positions.

Formative assessment from a behaviourist perspective

Formative assessment within a behaviourist tradition emphasises the clear specification of performance criteria and the kind of evidence needed to demonstrate performance. Assessment is therefore integrated with teaching and learning in that:

- specific, achievable, and often short-term goals are set;
- appropriate curricular experiences are provided;
- tasks or tests are constructed in which performance can be assessed;
- assessments are made against performance objectives;
- feedback is provided to students on whether they have achieved the targets, which gives them information about what is expected next time.

This kind of approach has underpinned much work in the graded assessment field and is the acknowledged foundation in vocational assessment, especially National Vocational Qualifications. A case can also be made for saying that this was the basis of SEAC and SCAA's interpretation of the formative role of teacher assessment in National Curriculum assessment during the period when assessment was focused on statements of attainment (1990–95).

In memorising facts and learning skills it is indeed useful to find out what facts or skills have been acquired. The feedback it provides to help further learning is in terms of what has not been learned and what should be tried next time. The action to be taken usually involves further practice and reward or praise when the goal has been achieved. In this context a behaviourist approach may be quite acceptable with its notions of stimulus, response and reinforcement.

Learning and assessment of ball-control skills in PE provides an example. Whilst it may be helpful to understand something of the physics of motion, a student's ability to control the speed and direction of a ball will largely depend on practising certain techniques. When the ball fails to reach its target, the student may be able to say what went wrong but, if not, an observer can provide feedback and suggest what to do next time. If the next shot reaches its goal, this will be reward in itself, but if the goal is not so obvious a word of praise will indicate to the learner that the movement was correct and should be repeated on another occasion. In this context, praise rarely gets in the way of learning because it will reinforce a correct sequence of movements. However, when understanding or deep learning is involved, praise may be counter-productive (see Chapter 5 page 98).

Formative assessment from a constructivist perspective

From a constructivist perspective, formative assessment is viewed rather differently. It focuses not so much on behaviour as on cognition (thought), generated in a social context[3]. In particular it is interested in promoting *learning with understanding*, which is actively understood and internalised by the learner.

Contemporary cognitive psychology supports the notion that understanding involves creating links in the mind and that *making sense* of something depends on these links. Isolated pieces of information do not have links to existing mental frameworks and so are not easily retained. The identification and creation of links to existing frameworks depends on the active participation of the learner and on the familiarity of the context of the material to be learned.

Understanding, in this view, is the process of construction and reconstruction of knowledge by the learner. What is known and understood will, of course, change with new experience and as new ideas and skills are presented to help make sense of it. Thus the characteristics of this learning are that it:

- is progressively developed in terms of big ideas, skills for living and learning, attitudes and values;
- is constructed on the basis of previous ideas and skills;
- can be applied in contexts other than those in which it was learned;
- is owned by the learner in the sense that it becomes a fundamental part of the way he or she understands the world; it is not simply ephemeral knowledge that may be memorised for recall in examinations but subsequently forgotten.

Relating new knowledge to existing understandings

Constructivists therefore argue that an assessment system intended to improve the quality of learning should not treat students as imperfect learners, but as people who are actively trying to make sense of what they are taught. For this reason, it is important that teachers should try to discover how students have related new knowledge to their existing understandings, and, more importantly for self-assessment, students

[3]Constructivism has several variants. The most recent emphasise that the structures of thinking are generated in interactive processes between people in specific contexts of action. These versions are called social constructivism, situated cognition or socio-cultural approaches.

should learn to do this for themselves.

Many teachers will be familiar with the practice of 'concept-mapping' and this is similar to what I have in mind. Teachers and peers can only do this by observing student learning and asking students to 'think aloud' about what they have learned and understood. The information gained allows teachers and students, in dialogue, to analyse misunderstandings or the extent to which previous experiences, attitudes and values, or expectations, have influenced learning. On this basis, appropriate next steps in both teaching and learning can be planned.

Drawing on a similar analogy to that of archery, which I used in Chapter 8, Mary Simpson, a constructivist researcher from Scotland, argues[4]:

> *Assessment must therefore extend beyond the simple determination of the extent to which [students] have learned as intended to the discovery of what they have actually learned, right or wrong. Teachers, like marksmen, may have clear objectives, but if they are to improve the quality of their performance then – like marksmen – they will want to know where all their shots went, and not merely how many find their target. Indeed, the patterns of 'wrong' learning, like the distribution of off-target shots, will provide the clearest cues to improvement.*

Later in the same article she makes another important point:

> *But pupils do not learn only what they have been taught, only within school, or only from their teachers. Any system of assessment which is to make a positive contribution to pupil learning must be one which allows pupils' actual knowledge structures within specific topic domains to be adequately mapped. Since this involves pupils in volunteering information about their uncertainties, it can only be carried out in a setting which allows that information to be confidential between pupils and teacher and in which the latter is not a judge or even an accessory to the judging process, but a participant in an informal contract with pupils to share the responsibility for learning.*

Since students often bring different experiences, attitudes and structures of knowledge to any task, particular attention needs to be paid to the construction of the assessment tasks themselves. There is little justification for assuming that the task will be interpreted precisely as the task-setter intended because there will be no one-to-one correspondence between the contents of any two peoples' minds. Given this, teachers are probably in a better position than many external test developers to construct appropriate assessment tasks for their students and to interpret the results. They are in a good position to question and find out how

---

[4]Simpson, M. (1990) 'Why criterion-referenced assessment is unlikely to improve learning', *The Curriculum Journal*, 1(2), pp. 171–83.

students' previous experiences frame their thinking and therefore what will stimulate students to reveal their knowledge and understandings. This also supports the idea that students themselves should have a role in task design and choice.

Of course, a great deal of time is required for this kind of effort. The pressures imposed by the National Curriculum, even in its reduced post-Dearing form, allow little space or resources for truly reflective practice or the professional development needed to support reflective teaching. Hopefully, as things settle down and provided that no major new 'reform' is introduced, teachers may be able to develop their practice incrementally along these lines.

Assessment for learning in the twenty-first century

Teaching pupils to become good learners will be a key role for teachers as the information revolution and the restructuring of employment continues to have an impact on people's lives and on the relevance of traditional knowledge and skills. In this context, it is unlikely that simply learning quantities of information or acquiring practical skills will be adequate to deal with rapid change.

Whilst numeracy, literacy and IT skills (the so-called 'key-skills') will continue to be a foundation, learning beyond the basics will require a considerable measure of conceptual understanding, and intrapersonal and inter-personal skills and understandings of a similarly high order. Without this 'learning with understanding', young people are unlikely to possess the strategic vision, self-motivation, problem-solving capacity, flexibility and adaptability that will be required for 'lifelong learning' in the 'learning society' of the twenty-first century. Therefore, the second kind of formative assessment described here, grounded in a constructivist theory of learning, will need to become part of the professional practice of most teachers.

Distinguishing formative from summative assessment[5]

As I mentioned in Chapter 2, summative assessment has a quite different purpose, which is to describe learning achieved at a certain time for the purposes of reporting to parents, other teachers, the students themselves and, in summary form, to other interested parties such as school

---

[5] The remaining sections of this chapter are an edited version of an article by Wynne Harlen and myself entitled 'Assessment and Learning: differences and relationships between formative and summative assessment', published in *Assessment in Education*, 4 (3), 1997, pp. 365–79. I am very grateful to Wynne Harlen for allowing me to reproduce some of her words in this text.

governors. It has an important role in monitoring the overall educational progress of students but not in day-to-day teaching, as does formative assessment.

Unlike summative assessments, which may be either criterion-referenced or norm-referenced, formative assessments are always made in relation to where students are in their learning in terms of specific content or skills. To this extent, formative assessment is, by definition, criterion-referenced. At the same time, it must also be *student-referenced* or *ipsative*. This means that a judgement of a student's work or *progress* takes into account such things as the effort put in, the particular context of the student's work and the progress that the student has made over time. In consequence the judgement of a piece of work, and what is fed back to the student, will depend on the student and not just on the relevant criteria.

The justification for this is that the individual circumstances must be taken into account if the assessment is to help learning and to encourage the learner. If formative assessment were purely criterion-referenced it would be profoundly discouraging for many students who are constantly being faced with failure. This hybrid of criterion-referenced and student-referenced assessment is acceptable as long as this information is used *diagnostically* in relation to each student, which is consistent with the notion that formative assessment is essentially part of teaching.

The claim that criterion-referenced systems often only thinly disguise norm-referenced systems would lead to the contentious notion that there is some degree of norm-referencing in formative assessment. It is true that any attempt to articulate a trajectory of development of knowledge, skill and understanding in any subject domain often implies assumptions about 'normal' stages of development and progression. Also, judgements about an individual's progress in relationship to others is sometimes helpful in identifying whether there is an obvious problem that needs to be tackled urgently. This is probably a main reason why parents continue to be so concerned about where their child is in relation to the attainments of others of the same age.

The point to be made here in the context of formative assessment, however, is that whilst norm-referenced assessment might help teachers recognise the existence of a problem, it can offer them no help in knowing what to do about it and may simply have a deleterious effect by labelling students. In order to contribute to learning through teaching, assessments need to reveal the specific nature of any problems; this can only be achieved by a combination of criterion- and student-referenced assessments.

Using evidence appropriately to improve performance

It is important to recognise that the reality of formative assessment is that it is bound to be incomplete, since even the best plans for observing activities or setting certain tasks can be torpedoed by unanticipated events. Moreover, the information will often seem contradictory. Students are always changing and may appear to be able to do something in one situation but not in another. Such evidence is a problem where the purpose is to make a judgement about whether a student fits one category, criterion, or one level or another. However, where the purpose is to inform teaching and help learning, the fact that a pupil can do something in one context but apparently not in another is a positive advantage, since it gives clues to the conditions which seem to favour better performance and thus can be a basis for taking action.

In this way the *validity* and usefulness of formative assessment is demonstrated and enhanced. Validity is vitally important to formative assessment because it cannot claim to be formative unless it demonstrably leads to action for improved learning – the point that I made at the beginning of this chapter.

However, it is not necessary to be over-concerned with *reliability* in formative assessment since the information is used to inform teaching in the situations in which it is gathered. Thus there is always quick feedback for the teacher who usually has opportunities to use observations of the response to one intervention as information in making the next one. Through this rapid loop of feedback and adjustment between teacher and learner, the information inevitably acquires greater reliability. This is not to say that teachers do not need any help with this important part of their work, but the help required is to be found in how to identify significant aspects of students' work and to recognise what they mean for promoting progress.

In summary, formative assessment can be distinguished from summative assessment because:

- it is essentially positive in intent, in that it is directed towards promoting learning; it is therefore part of teaching;
- it takes into account the progress of each individual, the effort put in and other aspects of learning which may be unspecified in the curriculum; in other words, it is not purely criterion-referenced;
- it has to take into account several instances in which certain skills and ideas are used and there will be inconsistencies as well as

patterns in behaviour; such inconsistencies would be 'error' in summative evaluation, but in formative evaluation they provide diagnostic information;

- validity and usefulness are paramount in formative assessment and should take precedent over concerns for reliability;
- even more than assessment for other purposes, formative assessment requires that pupils have a central part in it; pupils have to be active in their own learning (teachers cannot learn for them) and unless they come to understand their strengths and weaknesses, and how they might deal with them, they will not make progress.

In contrast, the characteristics of summative assessment are that:

- it takes place at certain intervals when achievement has to be reported;
- it relates to progression in learning against public criteria;
- the results for different pupils may be combined for various purposes because they are based on the same criteria;
- it requires methods which are as reliable as possible without endangering validity;
- it involves some quality assurance procedures;
- it should be based on evidence from the full range of performance relevant to the criteria being used.

■ Linking formative and summative assessment

It would be wrong to suggest that information gathered by teachers for formative purposes should not be used when they come to make summative assessments. This would be wasteful and, in any case, impossible in practice, because teachers cannot ignore knowledge that they have of students. Instead it is essential to distinguish different ways of *arriving at an assessment judgement* for different purposes.

At this point it is useful to keep in mind that the kind of information that is gathered by teachers in the course of teaching is not tidy, complete and self-consistent, but fragmentary and often contradictory. The unevenness, as mentioned above, is not a problem but an advantage for formative purposes, helping to indicate what supports or hinders achievement for a particular pupil. However, these uneven peaks and troughs have to be smoothed out in reporting performance for summative purposes. Thus although some of the same evidence can be used for formative and summative purposes, for the latter it has to be reviewed and aligned with criteria applied uniformly across all pupils. This means looking across the range of work of a pupil and judging the extent to which the profile as a whole matches the criteria in an holistic way.

The alternative to using the same *results* of assessment for both purposes is, therefore, to use relevant *evidence* gathered as part of teaching for formative purposes but to review it, for summative purposes, in relation to the criteria which will be used for all pupils. This means that formative assessment can remain a mixture of criterion-referenced and student-referenced assessment, as is required for providing a positive response to students and encouraging their learning. At the same time the use of information gathered as part of teaching, appropriate for formative assessment but which could be misleading or even confusing if used directly for summative assessment, is filtered out in the process of reviewing information relevant to the criteria being applied, in the National Curriculum level descriptions, for example. In other words, summative assessment should mean summing up the evidence, not summing and averaging across a series of assessment judgements that have already been reduced to letter or numerical grades. Similarly, formative assessments should not be recorded in the form of mini-summative judgements; rather there should be records of work completed with observations and notes of how these have been used to help progress.

Using evidence to maximise value: an illustration

If opportunities to distinguish between the formative and summative use of the evidence are missed, the formative value of information about students' learning can be neglected. For example, one element of the 'Exemplification of Standards' material, distributed to all schools in England and Wales in 1995 by the Schools Curriculum and Assessment Authority (SCAA) and the Advisory Council on Assessment and the Curriculum for Wales (ACAC), was a video and booklet containing evidence of pupils engaged in speaking and listening (English Attainment Target 1) and judged to be at various levels from 1 to 8. The Key Stage 3 material includes footage of a girl named Nicole, for whom English is 'an additional language', who is seen contributing to four different activities.

A teacher viewing this video might notice that Nicole watches the faces of peers very closely, although sometimes obliquely, and sometimes angles herself so that she can read the text from which they are reading. She is often to the side of group interaction and has difficulty breaking into a fast verbal exchange. Occasionally her contributions are 'talked over' by others who are more forceful. However, when the activity gives her an opportunity to 'have the floor', she speaks quietly and slowly but more confidently and her contributions are structured and comprehensible.

This kind of evidence might be used formatively by the teacher to indicate how Nicole's learning in this area might be extended by building on her listening skills; by acknowledging the tremendous progress she has made in competent use of her second language; by helping her with sentence constructions that she finds especially difficult; by providing her with more opportunities to speak in formal presentations where she cannot be interrupted by more confident peers; and by working with the whole group on their understanding of the nature and dynamics of group discussion to allow better pacing; turn taking, listening, inclusion etc.

None of this is mentioned in the material accompanying the video because it is 'designed to help teachers make consistent judgements about which level best describes a pupil's performance'. Thus the commentaries on Nicole's contributions relate strictly to the general criteria embedded in the level descriptions. The peaks and troughs and idiosyncrasies of her performance are ironed out for the purpose of coming to the following summary and overall judgement:

> *Although she perhaps lacks confidence, Nicole contributes clearly and positively in discussions. She makes substantive points, gives reasons and is able to argue for her views when challenged. She is beginning to ask questions of others and take account of their views. She adjusts her speaking to more formal situations although she is not fully confident in standard English. Overall, Nicole's performance is best described by Level 5.*

Many other examples similar to this last one indicate that the fundamental distinction between formative and summative assessment has not been fully articulated. Formative and summative assessment may relate to each other in that they share a set of common criteria which are agreed expectations in terms of desired outcomes, but beyond this they are essentially different phenomena with different purposes, different assumptions and different methods. Some of the same evidence may be used for the different purposes but it will be used in different ways.

Developing this new approach

It is essential to provide help for teachers with both formative and summative assessment and in a way which disentangles the two and enables teachers to use assessment in a genuinely formative way to help students' learning. This would include guidance on types of feedback from teachers necessary to maintain pupil motivation as well as on identifying specific aspects of attainment or good performance and what to do to help further improvement. For formative assessment, teachers may need assistance in identifying 'next steps' in learning, perhaps more in relation to some subjects, such as science, than in others.

The further development of exemplar materials may be important here, but only if the materials are directed towards the need to make 'next steps' decisions, as well as the need to make overall summative judgements. Teachers may also value examples of techniques for gaining access to students' ideas and for involving the latter in self-assessment and in deciding their 'next steps'. As we have seen, there is now considerable evidence that such collaboration between teacher and students facilitates learning in a very direct and positive way (see page 178).

Further reading

Teachers who are interested in finding out more about current thinking on how children learn, might like to read the following texts. The first is *How Children Think and Learn*, by David Wood and published in 1988 by Basil Blackwell, in Oxford. The second is *Experiential Learning: experience as the source of learning and development*, by David Kolb, published in 1984 by Prentice Hall, in Englewood Cliffs, USA. The latter is a popular reference for those working in post-compulsory education.

ACTIVITIES

Activities to promote formative assessment will usually focus on the work of the individual teacher in his or her classroom. However, it will be important to provide support and training for these activities within the department and the school development programme. This chapter has indicated a number of areas for the development of teachers' practice, especially with respect to the involvement of students. The best strategy would probably be to develop the steps outlined in the section on student involvement (pages 174–7), one at a time, before a teacher attempts to put them all together.

1 **Generating assessment criteria in student-speak**

   Individual teachers or groups of teachers could be asked to identify a small unit within their scheme of work (perhaps a single lesson) that has clear learning objectives. These learning objectives should be discussed with the class or student group before the unit is taught. Teachers should make clear what it is that they expect students to learn and then discuss with them what criteria would be appropriate to judge achievement. If there are published criteria, such as National Curriculum level descriptions or GNVQ criteria, these can be incorporated and 'translated' into natural language descriptions if needed. The resulting criteria can be presented as a poster or assessment sheet (see page 175) and used by students to plan their work and to assess it. The use of such criteria should be evaluated and changes made as necessary.

2 **Using examples of assessed work with students**

   If departments have begun to build a portfolio of exemplar material for the purposes of developing consistency in judgements across teachers (see Chapter 8, page 165), there is no reason why this same resource should not be used also with students. At some point in the course of teaching the unit of work, perhaps before students engage with a task, teachers could discuss how other students tackled similar, though not necessarily identical tasks, and the strengths and weaknesses of their responses. For formative purposes it is important that the assessed work is annotated with comments identifying particular areas of weakness and diagnosis of problems, bringing in evidence from classroom observations if possible. There should also be some indication of the strategies that might be used to improve the work. This is a dimension that was lacking in SCAA's *Exemplification of Standards* materials and limited their usefulness. There is no reason, however, why teachers should not use these published materials with students and extend them by providing their own commentary on the diagnosis and remedying of weaknesses.

3 Student designed tasks

If students have helped to generate a set of criteria to assess achievement in a particular content area of the curriculum, they may be in a good position to devise relevant tasks that will enable them to meet these criteria. This may be familiar practice to teachers in upper secondary schools but it may be worth extending the practice to younger year groups on some occasions.

4 Self-assessment and peer assessment

The temptation with self-assessment is to provide the criteria and ask students simply to tick those that they have achieved (see Figure 9.1, page 175). This will reveal gaps but it may be of little help diagnostically. Students need to ask 'thoughtful' questions about their work. They will need to be trained to do this perhaps through simulation or role-play exercises. Since it is difficult for students to ask questions about their own work, peer assessment is a good idea. The most important thing for peers to remember is that it is not helpful to make *judgements* even if these are positive, e.g. 'I think you did this really well'. They simply inflate or deflate a student's self-esteem without helping them to learn anything about the task (see Chapter 5). More helpful would be questions that stimulate the student to think aloud, such as:

- Why did you do that?
- What do you mean here?
- What were you thinking?
- Could you do that differently?
- How could you get this to work?
- What will you do next?

Self-assessment should culminate in some sort of action plan for implementing strategies for improvement.

10 Doing justice to all the educational achievements of all students

Justice as fairness

In this chapter I consider two questions that schools need to ask about the assessment systems they establish:

- Do our assessments recognise the full range of educational achievements of our students?
- Do our assessments avoid biases that might unfairly disadvantage certain groups of students?

Both of these questions are about being fair to students by striving to make assessment systems sensitive to the need to recognise the full extent of their educational achievements. The aim is to prevent their life chances and the quality of their experience being diminished by decisions that are made on the basis of faulty or incomplete data. For this reason, these questions are also connected with questions about the validity of assessments (see Chapter 8 pages 151–6). No school can be expected to get everything right all of the time but their assessment systems will be enhanced if attention is paid to the practical implications of the answers to these two questions.

Beyond subjects: assessing the 'whole child'

In recent years assessment systems have come to focus almost exclusively on students' attainments in the subjects of the National Curriculum and the academic and vocational domains of GCSE, A–level and GNVQ. The National Curriculum 'core subjects' of English, mathematics and science and the related post–16 'key skills' of communication, application of number and use of information technology, receive special attention because considerable resources, both national and local, have been devoted to developing assessments in these areas. The degree of prescription associated with these assessments has inevitably meant that schools have also had to commit a great deal of time and effort to their implementation.

Whilst not wishing to decry the need for the development of assessment in subject areas, and the key skills of literacy and numeracy in particular, I do want to reiterate the point that I made in Chapter 2, namely that assessment systems should be consistent with the more general educational aims of the school. If these aims embrace the need for the school to promote 'the spiritual, moral, cultural, mental and physical development of pupils', in line with the injunction in Section 1.2 of the 1988 Education Reform Act, it is inappropriate to assess academic achievement but ignore the rest. As Richard Pring has said (reference in Chapter 2 page 33), 'Any kind of development that is important enough to promote is important enough to be assessed in some broad sense of the term'. There is justification for this because, if it is true that we tend to value only what we assess, we should assess what we value.

If the broader aspects of the school's mission (see, for example, Swavesey Village College's mission statement on page 32) are to be taken seriously in curricular programmes, and not become empty rhetoric, then a school should consider:

- What aspects of a student's physical, spiritual, moral, emotional, social and cultural development ought to be assessed in some way?
- How might this be done?

What broader aspects of achievement should schools assess?

Apart from the general statement of aims in the 1988 Education Reform Act, other central government sources have indicated areas of learning beyond subjects that are to be valued. In 1991 the then National Curriculum Council published non-statutory guidance on the 'whole curriculum' and delineated a number of cross-curricular skills, dimensions and themes. The skills were communication, numeracy, study skills, problem-solving, personal and social skills and information technology; the dimensions were gender, race, disability and social class. The cross-curricular themes were environmental education, careers education and guidance, education for citizenship, economic and industrial understanding and health education.

Some schools felt that these themes would have provided a more imaginative framework for a whole curriculum for the twenty-first century than the traditional subjects, which had the flavour of mid-twentieth century grammar schools about them. This was not to be, and, as the statutory subject orders were issued, attention to cross-curricular themes was inevitably given less priority. However, most schools continued to incorporate consideration of these issues in their curricular programmes, either by integration with subject teaching or through the vehicle of personal and social education (PSE) and its variants.

Values education

More recently, SCAA set up a Values Forum and, after much debate, secured consensus on a statement of core values to promote and support values education in schools. At the time of writing this book – 1997 – it is now preparing guidance on students' spiritual, moral, social and cultural development. In its July 1997 White Paper, called *Excellence in Schools,* the DfEE stated that it had asked SCAA to ensure that this guidance covers work-related learning, education for parenthood and citizenship.

The Department has set up an advisory group to discuss citizenship and the teaching of democracy in school. It also intends to provide a new national framework to promote extended opportunities for young people to benefit from activities outside the classroom. The intention of the Labour government seems to be to lead development in these wider aspects of education in schools and the wider community. It will be interesting to see what emerges.

During the previous Conservative administration, government guidance on cross-curricular skills, dimensions and themes never amounted to a statement of entitlement. However, educators who are committed to expanding the view of the whole curriculum have been bolder. Chris Watkins, of the London Institute of Education, has offered the following list of statements for teachers' consideration[1].

This list is helpful because it combines many of the areas identified by government agencies, employers and education professionals as those in need of development. It therefore provides a concise checklist for curriculum development. Teachers and school managers could take each statement and ask how related curricular or extra-curricular provision could be built into the educational programme of their school. The list is also framed in such a way that the skills, understanding and knowledge expected of students is made reasonably explicit. This, then, could provide a helpful guide for the development of assessment processes. However, this is where the problems start!

---

[1] Watkins, C. (1995) 'Personal-social education and the whole curriculum'. In R. Best, P. Lang, C. Lodge and C. Watkins (eds) *Pastoral Care and Personal-Social Education: entitlement and provision.* London: Cassell.

Pupils' personal-social entitlement

Pupils are entitled to respect, dignity and promotion of self-reliance; and knowledge, skills and understanding which help them to:

1 *maximise their academic achievement in school:*
   - communication skills;
   - skills of learning in classrooms;
   - co-operative work;
   - skills of managing study;
   - reflection and review.

2 *maximise the use of their academic achievements after school:*
   - skills of understanding themselves, their opportunities and choices;
   - personal-social skills, including self-presentation;
   - interpersonal skills for their future work and non-work contexts.

3 *maximise their contribution to and satisfactions from adult life:*
   - maintain bodily health, psychological health and healthy lifestyle;
   - develop interpersonal relationships including intimate and sexual ones;
   - understand social relations in family, work and community;
   - promote positive relationships, identify and avoid negative relationships;
   - skills of making moral judgements and developing appropriate action;
   - understand democratic and political processes;
   - skills in communicating ideas and opinions to influence social change;
   - understand and respect the beliefs, faiths and cultures by which people interpret life and on which they base their behaviours;
   - cope with change;
   - combat prejudice.

How should the broader aspects of learning be assessed?

It is probably no accident that Chris Watkins decided to concentrate on students' entitlement and provision rather than on expected student outcomes. This has been a notoriously difficult area in which to find agreement. In the 1980s the Assessment of Performance Unit abandoned its attempt to devise assessments for personal and social development. Similarly, the records of achievement pilot schemes, which were committed to recording students' cross-curricular, extra-curricular and personal achievements, raised as many issues as they solved. I was involved in the national evaluation of these pilot schemes at this time[2] and the problematic nature of making judgements about students' achievements in these areas soon came to the fore. For example:

1. There was evidence that students spent a good deal of energy 'second-guessing' what teachers expected of them in order to produce the required performance without necessarily internalising deeper social and personal understandings and skills. This paralleled the kind of superficial 'learning for the test' that has characterised much learning in academic areas.

2. Some students had limited opportunities to develop certain skills and personal qualities. This was particularly evident when students were encouraged to record what they had learned from involvement in out-of-school activities. Learning depended very much on the opportunities available. Some students, such as those living in remote rural areas, were disadvantaged, either because of limited opportunities or because teachers did not always recognise the value of those activities that were available to them, such as agricultural work. Thus there was a danger that a form of social divisiveness would result from inequality of opportunity. Perhaps the policy outlined in the government's 1997 White Paper will tackle this issue.

3. Associated with this was a concern about unjustified intrusion into students' private lives. More sinister still was the possibility that attempts to delineate the social and personal qualities, attitudes and skills that were being sought in students could act as an invidious form of social control. Many schools in the records of achievement schemes had devised checklists of personal qualities as a basis for a record of personal and social development. The following were common examples:

[2]Broadfoot, P., James, M., McMeeking, S., Nuttall, D., and Stierer, B. (1998) *Records of Achievement: report of the national evaluation of pilot schemes*. London: HMSO.

Attendance	Relationships with peers	Leadership
Punctuality	Relationships with adults	Sociability
	Consideration	Sensitivity
	Co-operation	Reliability
	Courtesy	Self-discipline
	Working with those in authority	Assertiveness
		Self-awareness
		Flexibility
		Initiative
		Resourcefulness
		Enthusiasm
		Perseverance
		Appearance
		Health
		Honesty

The qualities in the column on the left were generally unproblematic because schools could expect to have some reasonably objective information about punctuality and attendance; the qualities in the middle column were also qualities that all schools would expect to engender if they were to function as effective learning environments. The qualities in the right-hand column posed more difficulties because it could be argued that they present normative descriptions of what people *ought* to be like. Some writers at the time expressed concerns that the evaluation of such qualities could become a form of surveillance in which *all* aspects of a person's life could be documented and therefore controlled. In this sense, there are some problems with the notion of assessing 'the whole child'. Teachers were particularly unhappy about evaluating such qualities as appearance and honesty, although they recognised that some employers – the armed forces, for example – ask for this kind of information.

4 Another related concern was that the qualities presented in such lists could be seen as representing predominantly white, male, middle-class values. For example, the lists above miss many of the qualities valued by, say, the Asian community with respect to girls. A notion of cultural deficit is therefore implied if certain groups fail to measure up to such normative descriptions.

These issues are likely to recur in any attempt to promote personal, social, spiritual, moral and cultural development and then to evaluate and record the outcomes. This is not to say that it should not be done but that schools should be aware of these dangers.

Some views about best practice

Within the records of achievement pilot schemes there emerged some views about best practice that are probably worth reiterating as a guide for practice today:

1 **Consensus on valued qualities**
   When deciding on valued qualities to foster and record, some effort must be made to achieve a consensus between different interest groups, such as students, parents, teachers, employers and representatives of community and religious groups. Given the difficulty that the SCAA Values Forum has experienced, it may be more fruitful to try to forge this consensus at the level of the school and the local community than at national level. The school could set up a working party of relevant stake-holders in its community to discuss these issues. This would enable policy to be more sensitive to the very different contexts of schools in a nation which lacks homogeneity.

2 **Avoidance of social divisiveness**
   Schools need to beware of the possibility of actually creating social divisiveness through social and personal education and assessment, and should audit their arrangements specifically with this in mind. Whilst not wishing to subscribe to the extreme relativist position for which educationalists have been castigated by commentators such as Melanie Phillips[3], I would say that it is important to avoid creating an image of the good student, worker, parent, citizen or person that represents the views of only one section of the population.

3 **Ensuring opportunity for social and personal learning**
   It offends natural justice to evaluate social and personal knowledge, skills and understandings that students have little opportunity to acquire. It is important therefore that schools review their curricular and extra-curricular provision to ensure that students have opportunities for such learning.

4 **Ensuring judgements are made in context**
   If schools choose to evaluate and record students' personal skills and qualities, they should avoid presenting these as immutable traits, e.g. 'Peter is self-reliant', 'Jayne is flexible'. In any life there will be times when individuals will not be these things. It is better that contextualised examples are given of specific instances when an individual has demonstrated particular skills and qualities. As in

---

[3] Phillips, M. (1996) *All Must have Prizes*. London: Little, Brown and Company.

other kinds of assessment, judgements need to be supported by evidence. This probably has to be done descriptively rather than through ticks on a checklist.

5 **Fostering social and personal skills through main educational programmes**
Rather than create special programmes to promote social, personal, spiritual, moral and cultural development, it is often better to foster these skills and qualities through the main educational programmes of the school. One of the most significant developments within the records of achievement pilot schemes of the 1980s was the erosion of the pastoral/academic divide in some schools. Subject lessons should be regarded as occasions to foster personal and social skills which in turn will enhance learning in subject domains – a reinforcing cycle.

Empirical evidence for the idea that personal and social development supports intellectual development can be found in the US best-selling book *Emotional Intelligence*, by Daniel Goleman, published by Bloomsbury in 1996. When 95 Harvard University students from the 1940s were followed up in middle age, the men with the highest intelligence test scores in college were not found to have been particularly successful in their careers. Nor did they have the greatest life satisfaction or find the greatest happiness with friendships, family or romantic relationships. In contrast, those people with what Goleman calls emotional intelligence, who were self-motivated, persistent in the face of frustration, able to control impulse and delay gratification, who regulated their moods and kept distress from swamping the ability to think, who could empathise and hope, were often more successful in their personal and working lives.

This form of emotional intelligence is not just 'God-given'; interpersonal and intrapersonal understandings and skills can be fostered in much the same way as academic skills and understandings and in many of the same contexts. In other words, PSE does not have to be confined to a PSE period on the timetable; it should permeate all lessons. The implication is that all teachers – subject teachers as well as form tutors – can, and probably should, make the cultivation of interpersonal and intrapersonal skills and understandings part of their everyday work with students. Similarly they could make observation, evaluation and recording of these skills and understandings part of their regular practice. For example, at a very practical level, assessment records associated with assessment tasks in subject areas might contain a space to note achievement in the personal and social domain (see the example of an annotation sheet in Chapter 11 page 216).

6 **Involving students in assessment procedures**
As in assessment of students' academic learning, the involvement of students in the process is vitally important for many of the same reasons (see Chapter 9 pages 173–9). Within the records of achievement schemes, self-assessment and peer assessment were used extensively and it was common practice for students to discuss their own accounts of their social and personal qualities, skills and understandings with teachers and peers in order to agree a record or targets for future development.

Although finding the time and space for one-to-one dialogue with students was always a difficulty, most teachers recognised its value for learning. At first, the assumption was that times for teacher–pupil discussion would need to be timetabled, but gradually, as the idea grew that personal and social development could be integrated with subject learning, the perception of teacher–pupil discussion as a special event gave way to the idea that this could be more low-key and part of regular classroom practice. More formal arrangements might be necessary for agreeing a summative statement for reports to parents or the National Record of Achievement, but for formative purposes dialogue in the course of learning could be more valuable. In this respect, developing knowledge, skills and understanding in personal-social and cross-curricular areas is little different from learning within the formal academic curriculum and can be supported in many of the ways described in Chapter 9.

Ensuring that assessments provide equality of opportunity

The previous section has already raised issues of equity and social justice. In this section, I look more closely at whether the assessments used in schools are equally fair to different groups of students and how they might be made more so. This is not motivated by a concern that all students should achieve equal outcomes – such uniformity would be impossible and probably undesirable – but that all students should have equal opportunities to achieve the best of which they are capable and have their achievements recognised.

There are always enormous differences in the needs of individuals within any population, but when considering equal opportunities it is usual to think especially of the characteristics and needs of sub-groups. Groups identified by gender, social class and ethnicity are particularly important.

Gender and assessment

I begin with issues of gender for two main reasons. First, the under-performance of boys in external tests and examinations has been a focus for much media attention in the 1990s. Secondly, we have better data relating to gender than we have, say, for race or social class because information about the gender of students is routinely collected for most kinds of assessment.

In 1996, OFSTED commissioned a review of recent research on *Gender and Educational Performance* (full reference on page 209). I was a member of the team who carried out this review and will draw on its findings in this section. I have summarised the report's main findings about the so-called 'gender gap' in performance on the next page, because claims made in the media are sometimes exaggerated. The findings are based on data from the results of National Curriculum tests, GCSE, A– and AS–level, vocational qualifications and international surveys, from 1988–96.

After describing the gender gaps in performance, the OFSTED review then looks at possible explanations. Two levels of explanation are considered: in-school explanations to do with school organisation and processes of teaching, learning and assessment; and possible deeper social, psychological, economic and cultural explanations. For the purposes of this book, explanations of the gender gap which relate to features of the assessment processes themselves are particularly important.

Much of the evidence from research suggests that we need to question whether the gender gaps in performance in different areas represent 'real' differences in boys' and girls' ability or attainment, or whether these gaps are, to some extent, 'constructed' by the assessment instruments themselves or by some other aspect of the assessment process, such as patterns of entry. Recent research on the impact of assessment processes on performance has focused on a number of features of assessments:

1 **Entry patterns**
   Gender differences in educational outcomes can be affected by the courses chosen. For example, whilst over a million candidates each year take GCSE combined science, small numbers still take the separate sciences. Substantially more boys than girls take physics although the girls who do take this subject actually perform slightly better than the boys. Conversely, boys perform better than girls in biology although numbers taking the subject are similar. The best explanation for this phenomenon seems to be that there is a highly selective entry of very able girls for physics, whilst girls who choose biology may simply be taking this as a token science in their GCSE portfolio.

> **The gender gap in educational performance**
>
> - Girls have made slightly greater academic progress than boys between the ages of seven and sixteen.
> - By 1995 girls were outperforming boys at GCSE in terms of the proportions obtaining five or more A*–C passes. This gender gap emerged at the end of the 1980s; it coincided with the introduction of GCSE.
> - Girls outperformed boys, markedly, in English; in science, boys maintained a small advantage; in mathematics, performance was similar.
> - Apart from the compulsory 'core' subjects, there are sizeable gender gaps in GCSE entries. Some subjects are male-dominated and others are female-dominated.
> - Girls' and boys' performance in A/AS–level examinations has been broadly equal, but more female students than male students study for A–levels (approximately 40:33).
> - Gender-related patterns of entry to A–level subjects have persisted.
> - Boys have made somewhat more academic progress between GCSE and A–level than girls.
> - There was strong gender-stereotyping of subjects studied by 16-19 year olds for vocational qualifications in the mid-1990s.
> - In international surveys, gender patterns of performance for English boys and girls are similar to those in comparable countries. Girls are ahead in language; boys and girls are more evenly matched in mathematics; in science, boys begin to pull ahead of girls from age eleven.

Similar explanations to do with selective entry for some subjects may also explain why there is a cross-over in performance patterns at post–16. For example, in the mid-1990s in English, more boys achieved the highest grade at A–level whereas girls were more successful at achieving the highest grades in GCSE. The best explanation is that the small number of boys who choose this traditionally 'female' subject are a very able and highly motivated group.

There is also evidence that systems of tiered papers in mathematics actually produce gendered patterns of performance. In 1994, for example, significantly more girls than boys were entered for the intermediate grade: a difference of 21,000 individuals. This suggests either that the performance of girls is underestimated in mathematics, or that teachers enter them for the 'safe' tier to protect them from anxiety. This will allow them to achieve the vital 'C' grade whilst avoiding the risks of being unclassified.

2 Modes of assessment

Boys and girls perform differently according to the mode of assessment. Boys do significantly better on multiple-choice tests. The authors of the Third International Mathematics and Science Study (TIMSS) reported that at a time when girls in England were producing science and mathematics results comparable to boys in National Curriculum tests and GCSE, boys in England were still performing considerably better than girls in TIMSS tests. Around 80 per cent of TIMSS items were presented in multiple-choice format which might contribute to the discrepancy in the results. There are suggestions that multiple-choice questions favour boys because they like the 'eyes down' approach; they can avoid having to express themselves in writing; and they have greater confidence in choosing a response as correct – even if it is not!

There is also some evidence that girls find traditional 'sudden death' examinations less congenial than boys and this may affect their performance. This also might be one factor in explaining the 'cross-over' in performance post–16 because timed, end-of-course and end-of-module examinations play a greater part in A–level than GCSE. However, the evidence is not conclusive. Teachers *perceive* girls to have more difficulty with traditional examinations because they *seem* to them to lack the confident, self-assured, risk-taking approach of boys, but it is not clear that this translates into significant differences in performance. We need to face the possibility that some teachers are still viewing students in stereotyped ways.

The question of whether coursework favours girls has been a subject of a good deal of speculation since the introduction of the GCSE. There is no straightforward answer to this. The evidence indicates that girls do have some advantage over boys on coursework elements of examinations. However, the restriction on the amount of coursework that can be submitted for examination, imposed in 1994, has not reduced the performance gap accordingly. Jannette Elwood, a researcher at the London Institute of Education, has argued that coursework plays only a minimal role in determining the eventual outcome because marks on coursework tend to be 'bunched' and it is the marks on the examination papers that allow more discrimination and therefore contribute more to rank order and final grades. Other factors also intervene and may be equally important. For example, schools may select syllabuses with different coursework proportions according to their estimation of their teaching strengths or their perception of the relative confidence and ability of their students.

3 **Item content, context and style of response**
A consideration of the nature of test items – the questions students are asked and how they are expected to respond – is also important in any discussion of gender and assessment. For example, there is evidence, largely from the Assessment of Performance surveys of the 1980s, that both boys and girls prefer, and perform better on, tasks involving content with which they are especially familiar through direct experience in the home or the school. Thus, in science, girls perform better on items about personal and domestic situations, whilst boys do better on items about cars, buildings and machinery.

Similarly, there is evidence that if an item is set in a context to give it authenticity, boys and girls value this context in different ways. Whereas boys are more inclined to abstract issues from their context, girls take account of context details in their responses. This can create difficulties for them if this was not what the assessor intended.

Boys and girls also appear to favour different styles of response to assessment items which reflect their reading and writing preferences. The APU English team found that girls prefer to communicate their feelings about things in extended, reflective composition, while boys provide episodic, factual, commentative detail. These differences may account in some measure for patterns of performance across subjects and phases of education. The style of girls' reading and writing is valued in English and in the early phases of education, whilst boys' style preferences are valued in domains like science and in the later phases of education.

4 **Marker bias**
For some time, and particularly in higher education, concerns have been expressed about the objectivity of teachers as assessors. Some studies appear to show that assessors tend to mark the work of boys more highly than girls or that they exhibit a 'centralist tendency' (bunch the marks in the middle grades) when marking the work of girls. However, a study from the Associated Examining Board shows no evidence of gender bias in A–level examiners, indicating perhaps that marker bias may have diminished or disappeared, at least in relation to A–level.

This research on the impact of assessment practices on the educational performance of boys and girls does not, of course, offer complete explanations of *why* boys and girls make course choices and item responses in the way they do, or why they prefer certain modes of assessment. For these questions a deeper level of explanation is needed. The OFSTED review attempts to do this in its later sections. However, some guidance for school policy and practice can be extrapolated from the research on the impact of assessment procedures themselves:

- Schools should monitor gender patterns in entry to courses, and to systems of tiered papers in subjects such as mathematics, and develop strategies to encourage broader access if there is an evident need.
- To be fair to both boys and girls it is likely that a variety of assessment modes should be used so that all students have opportunities to produce their best performance.
- Boys and girls should also be helped to understand the demands of all modes of assessment, including those they favour least, and be taught techniques for responding in ways that will do justice to their learning.
- More generally, teachers will need to ensure that students understand how the demands of different subjects and courses can affect performance and help them to develop a repertoire of strategies so that they can produce their best performance in different assessment contexts. Evidence suggests that helping students to reflect on their experience (to develop meta-cognitive skills) in order to 'learn how to learn' can pay off in terms of performance.
- Schools should monitor marking for evidence of gender bias in the range of different assessments they carry out. Such monitoring should become part of the school's quality assurance procedures (see Chapter 8 pages 163–6).

There is another implication also, not so much for individual schools as for the profession as a whole. In so far as we now have evidence about the differential impact of different kinds of assessment on students, which may produce differential performance, we should be wary of attempts to manipulate assessments to produce different results. It is possible to do this. For example, it might be possible to reverse the current gender gap in performance simply by assessing everything through multiple-choice tests. Some forms of change may be desirable if current arrangements are clearly unfair to certain groups of students, but these changes need to be monitored and evaluated according to criteria of educational value and social justice. The profession as whole will need to have a voice in this.

Ethnicity, social class and assessment

In this section, I link ethnicity and social class together because in reality they are often combined in discussions about differential achievement of groups of students. Indeed, gender is often brought in as well, as in the characteristically robust statement of Chris Woodhead, the Chief Inspector of Schools, who claimed in 1996 that the failure of 'white working-class boys is one of the most disturbing problems we face within the whole education system'.

During the same year, OFSTED published a review of recent research on the achievements of ethnic minority students in schools (full reference on page 209). Like the review of research on gender, it summarised the evidence about the educational performance of various groups. Unlike performance in relation to gender there are no up-to-date national statistics on examination performance broken down by race or class. This information is simply not collected by examinations boards. However, LEA data and other research has identified some common patterns, and those relevant to this chapter are listed on the next page.

It does not take a great deal of imagination to see from this list how closely associated ethnicity is to social class when it comes to educational performance. Although a concerted effort in Tower Hamlets has helped Bangladeshi students to 'buck the trend', it is generally the case that those students of higher social class backgrounds do better on average than others, whatever their gender or ethnic origin. Other factors that are likely to have an impact on the achievements of ethnic minority groups include the effects of racial harassment or violence, exclusions from school (African-Caribbean students are three to six times more likely to be excluded from school than whites), and the persistence of negative or patronising stereotypes.

The OFSTED review of research in this area covers these issues. What it does not do is look in any detail at ethnic bias in the assessment procedures themselves, as was attempted in the equivalent review of research on gender. The probable reason for this is that there has only been very limited research in this area.

Concerns about cultural or social bias in tests and assessments

Since the introduction of IQ tests in which African-Caribbeans perform significantly less well than whites, concerns have been expressed that standardised tests and some other examinations may be culturally and socially biased. It has been argued that the testing situation and the vocabulary, style and content of such tests generally reflect the experience, assumptions and expectations of the white, male middle-

Educational performance of ethnic minority students in secondary schools

- Indian students appear to achieve consistently more highly, on average, than students with Bangladeshi or Pakistani backgrounds.

- Indian students are more successful than their white counterparts in some urban areas.

- There is no single pattern of achievement for Pakistani students, although they achieve less well than whites in many areas.

- Bangladeshi students usually have less fluency in English, and experience greater levels of poverty, than either Indian or Pakistani groups. They tend to under-achieve in comparison with other ethnic groups, although in one London borough (Tower Hamlets), by 1994, Bangladeshis were the highest achieving of the major ethnic groups – the result of a targeted programme.

- In many LEAs the achievements of African-Caribbean students are significantly lower than other groups, with the achievements of African-Caribbean boys being a particular concern.

- In some areas there is a widening gap between the achievements of African-Caribbean students and their peers.

- Asian students make better progress than whites of the same social class background, but the performance of African-Caribbean students is less consistent.

- Despite the greater progress made by some ethnic minority groups, studies outside London tend to show white students leaving school with the highest average achievements.

- Participation in post-compulsory education is higher for all major ethnic minority groups than for the white group.

- The participation of Asian young people is especially high and by age eighteen Asians are the most highly academically qualified of all groups (including whites).

- African-Caribbean young people are more likely to follow vocational courses.

class. For example, working alone and in silence for long periods of time is an alien and emotionally disturbing experience for many ethnic minority students.

The content of test items may also be beyond their experience in ways that assessment designers do not anticipate because they have not been able to transcend their own ethnocentric assumptions. An amusing story is told of an aptitude test used by the British Army for choosing suitable recruits. Candidates for selection were asked to run in a straight line on a level playing field between two posts. In this instance the potential recruits were Nepalese applying for selection to the Gurkha Regiment. Unfortunately none passed the test; they all zigzagged from post to post. The explanation for their seemingly strange behaviour was that the Nepalese rarely, if ever, walked or ran on the flat but had to zigzag their way up mountains. Since it was known that the Gurkhas made excellent soldiers, it was decided that the army should change the test!

Most test constructors are now aware of the problems of ethic bias in test items and will attempt to screen out those with inappropriate content or vocabulary. Teachers should attempt to do the same when devising their own assessments. However, this 'screening out' does not really tackle the issue of how, positively, to make inclusive assessments that recognise and celebrate the diversity of the achievements of different groups, i.e. providing genuine equality of opportunity to succeed. Possibly the wider use of authentic assessment tasks (see Chapter 6), which allow 'differentiation by outcome', is a way forward. However, this will require teachers to 'learn to see' the value in different kinds of responses from different groups of students.

In the second edition of a book entitled *Social Linguistics and Literacies*, by James Paul Gee, published by Taylor and Francis in 1996, this American author gives an example of the different way in which a lower-class African-American seven year old girl (Leona) and a middle-class Anglo-American seven year old girl (Mindy) tell a story. He describes Leona's response to the task as poetic: she tries to involve the audience; she uses syntactic and semantic parallelism, repetition and sound devices to set up rhythmic and poetic patterning in a way similar to biblical poetry, the narratives of many oral cultures, and much 'free verse'. Mindy's approach, in contrast, is prosaic; with the help of the teacher, with whom she is 'in sync', she produces a lexically explicit, coherent and school-based account of a complex activity.

Mindy's account is judged by the teacher to be successful and appropriate, whilst Leona's story is seen as just another example of her 'rambling on'! James Paul Gee argues that equity in assessment will only be achieved if the extraordinary poetic qualities of stories such as Leona's are fully recognised and valued.

Expanding teachers' perspectives

The implications for school policy and practice are much the same as those extrapolated from the research on gender. However, it will also be important to expand teachers' perspectives on what counts as 'good work' in their subject areas so that they do not ignore quality of a different kind from that which they expect. This is a task for school-based staff development but, again, it has wider implications because teachers will want to know that a wider definition of quality is recognised in formal examinations before they commit themselves to it. Teachers will therefore need to add their voice to that of James Paul Gee and others (see Further reading below) who are arguing for more inclusive assessments within formal testing and examination systems.

Further reading

1 An important review of research in the area of assessment and equal opportunities is the 1994 book by Caroline Gipps and Patricia Murphy entitled *A Fair Test? Assessment, achievement and equity*. It is published in Buckingham by the Open University Press.

2 The two OFSTED reviews of research referred to in this chapter are: *Recent Research on the Achievements of Ethnic Minority Pupils* (1996), by David Gillborn and Caroline Gipps; and *Gender and Educational Performance: a review of recent research* (1998), by Madeleine Arnot, John Gray, Mary James, Jean Rudduck with Gerard Duveen. Both are published in London by HMSO.

3 A recent book from America, where standardised testing has reigned supreme, argues for alternative assessment methods to 'create a diverse community of learners'. This is *Assessment for Equity and Inclusion: embracing all our children* and is edited by A. Lin Goodwin. It was published in London and New York, in 1997, by Routledge.

ACTIVITIES

1 Assessing social and personal achievement

This activity is designed to help teachers think about ways in which social, personal, spiritual and moral understanding, knowledge and skills might be assessed and recorded. The discussion might begin at whole school level, in a cross-curriculum working party or professional development day, or it might be tackled in the first instance by the school's assessment co-ordinator. The further development of the initial framework could then be 'devolved' to departments or year teams.

(i) Taking Chris Watkins' list of statements of personal-social entitlement as a basic framework (see page 195), amend it as necessary in the light of any new guidance published by SCAA or QCA. Also take into account the school's aims and any input from discussion with governors and representatives of the local community. The school may wish to make the development of such a framework a focus for discussion with governors and community groups.

(ii) Carry out an audit of the educational programme of the school, including extra-curricular provision, to identify opportunities for students to acquire the knowledge, understanding and skills in the social and personal framework. Identify the individuals and groups who will be asked to develop aspects of the framework, e.g. the history department might take on teaching about democratic and political processes, whilst year group tutors might incorporate 'coping with change' into a PSE programme.

(iii) These individuals and groups would then need to develop their schemes of work to provide opportunities for students to develop these skills and understandings. They will also need to think about the kind of evidence of students' learning that they will hope to find. It may not be necessary for them to develop entirely new activities and assessments. The *extension* of their current work to take account of social and personal dimensions may be quite sufficient. For example, group investigations in science, geography field trips or participation in sports teams will provide opportunities for the development, assessment and recording of personal and social achievements. It will be important, however, that teachers take account of these dimensions in their assessment schemes; this is often neglected.

(iv) Schools will, of course, be doing much of this already. It may be useful, however, to plan provision and recording of cross-curricular achievements more systematically in relation to an explicit framework with practical guidance about recording personal and social achievements with evidence that puts achievement in context.

2 Monitoring assessments for bias

In the 1980s the Equal Opportunities Commission supported a project called 'Genderwatch!' which produced materials for teachers to use to monitor aspects of curriculum, teaching, assessment and recording. These materials included lists of questions that teachers could use to 'interrogate' materials and processes. On the basis of the research evidence given in this chapter, schools could construct similar lists of questions to monitor their current assessment procedures for possible sources of gender, ethnic or social class bias. The following are some of the major areas they might wish to tackle:

- patterns of *entry* to different courses post–14 and post–16;
- patterns in *setting* and selection for entry to *tiered papers* in subjects such as mathematics;
- the patterns and frequency with which different *modes of assessment* are used in routine in-school assessment and in formal tests and examinations, and whether a single mode dominates;
- the familiarity of the *content* of assessment and test items to different groups of students, especially 'stimulus materials' such as texts in English;
- the way in which different students *respond* to assessment tasks and whether their use of item context or the style of their responses disadvantages them in comparison with other groups;
- any evidence that *assessment criteria* overlook some students' achievements because they are unexpected;
- patterns in the way students' work is *marked* and whether there is any evidence of bias.

3 Developing inclusive assessments

If the school has begun to create a bank if assessment tasks, in the way suggested in the activity at the end of Chapter 6 (page 123), it will be important to look at these also for any potential sources of bias. Both the tasks themselves and the students' responses to them should be evaluated to see whether they allow all groups of students to produce their best performance. If not, they may need to be revised. Particular attention should be paid to the *content* of the task, including stimulus materials, and the context in which the task is set to give it authenticity. Similarly, the *criteria* for assessment require scrutiny to see whether they capture the range of achievements that students might demonstrate in doing the task, including wider social and personal achievements.

11 Manageable recording and meaningful reporting

▆ Process and product

I have used record*ing* and report*ing* in the title of this chapter to emphasise that activity and objects (verbs as well as nouns) are implied. Perhaps the single most important insight to emerge from the records of achievement schemes of the 1980s was recognition of the importance of the recording *process* itself for motivation and learning. Unfortunately the government of the time never fully understood this, despite devoting £10 million to pilot schemes and evaluation. At the dissemination stage it chose to focus on reporting *formats* for National Curriculum achievements and the National Record of Achievement (NRA) without giving the nation's schools much support for the development of the processes that should be associated with these.

With respect to recording and reporting formats, especially reports to parents, most schools have travelled a long way in their thinking since the time when reports were limited to a single or double sheet covered in unintelligible hieroglyphics giving marks, grades, percentages and rank orders, often without explanation, and very little space for narrative comment. Even the more useful 'cheque-book' style of report, familiar in the 1970s and 1980s, has in many schools given way to more substantial reports with a full A5 or A4 page devoted to each subject with equivalent space given to comments by the form tutor and year head, the student himself or herself, and the parent or carer.

Undoubtedly, this development has been influenced by many things: the increased pressure for accountability to parents; the advice and regulations on the content and format of reports from central government; and the legacy of the records of achievement movement in the 1980s, which, if it did not influence government to any great extent, nevertheless informed the *zeitgeist* more generally.

In this chapter, I do not want simply to rehearse what I know many schools to be doing anyway. Nor will I provide a catalogue of recording and reporting formats; these are available from other sources (such as SIMS and LEAs). As in previous chapters, I will focus upon issues and possibilities that schools may wish to consider. My assumption is that recording and reporting should be consistent with the principles and practices outlined earlier, especially the principle of 'fitness for purpose'. Manageability, of course, is an equally important consideration; the requirements for form-filling have increased exponentially in the last two decades, in all the public services, and have actually threatened the effective delivery of these services.

So, what are the range of recording and reporting processes and products that need to be considered? Five broad categories can be considered:

- teachers' everyday records;
- reports to parents, including meetings with parents;
- individual education plans for students with special educational needs;
- official school records;
- the National Record of Achievement.

I will deal with all of these categories in some detail except for official school records which have to be kept for accountability purposes and for legal reasons but, of themselves, contribute little to school improvement. Essentially they are repositories of information about individual students, such as attendance records, incident reports, psychologists' reports, court reports, letters from/to parents, results of tests and examinations, copies of annual reports etc. It is important that these are kept centrally and with adequate procedures and safeguards concerning updating, access and use. An efficient system contributes to a school's smooth running – especially its capacity to respond to requests for information from parents, receiving schools or other agencies concerned with the welfare of students and the community – but it will have very little part to play in strategies adopted to raise students' achievements. School records, although important, have little value for developmental purposes except as a source of information, so issues about their structure and form are really beyond the remit of this book.

However, all the other forms of recording and reporting listed above have important roles to play in the fulfilment of a school's goals for developing students' learning and achievement.

Teachers' everyday records

Teachers in secondary schools have traditionally recorded their assessments in mark books. These have mostly been commercially produced and designed for teachers to see 'at a glance' the attainments and progress, over a year, of all the individuals in a teaching group. A double-page format has been the norm, with space for names on the left-hand side and a grid of columns for marks to be entered, with space for dates at the top. Little or no room has been allowed for narrative comments or notes of evidence. This design has been based on an assumption that assessment judgements are usually given in the form of a numerical mark or literal grade and can therefore be recorded in a space approximately 5mm × 5mm! If, as I argued in Chapters 5 and 9, a high proportion of teachers' assessments are to serve a formative purpose, this assumption needs to be challenged.

Certainly there needs to be some record of:

- what each student has done;
- what achievements they have demonstrated;
- what weaknesses have been identified and analysed (diagnosed);
- what targets have been decided;
- what strategies for improvement will be tried in the future.

If all these things are to be recorded in a teachers' mark book then its format would have to change with much more space, possibly a whole page, for each student. Primary teachers, with only one class of children to deal with, might be happy with this arrangement, but secondary teachers would undoubtedly protest that this would make the recording task even more onerous than it is already. As someone who started her teaching career in the late 1960s as the only teacher of religious education in a secondary modern school of 1,200 students, teaching 800 of them each week (truly!), I would have great sympathy with this feeling. A more radical alternative, therefore, might be to dispense with the teacher's mark book altogether, or retain it only in a much reduced form.

This idea is not new. It was first suggested to me by a teacher of modern languages in one of the records of achievement pilot schemes in the mid-1980s. She was teaching her students to take more responsibility for self- and peer assessment; it was a logical next step therefore to encourage them to do their own recording, usually after some discussion with her. She had provided sheets with appropriate headings related to questions, such as those listed in the bullet points above, and students kept these at the front of their language folders as a record of work done, their achievements and their targets.

The teacher believed that if the students were to learn from assessment then there was more value in having the records where they could refer to them. She had not dispensed entirely with her own mark book but she hoped that she would have the confidence to do so one day.

Another teacher, of a vocational course in an FE college, had gone the step further and claimed not to hold any detailed assessment records himself; all the information was in the students' own files. In some senses, this teacher's practice foreshadowed the development of student-based recording in NVQ and GNVQ which now requires continuous assessment records to be built up in students' files.

On the basis of these examples, one could argue that teachers' routine (formative) marking of students' work (see Chapter 5 pages 94–103) is itself a form of recording. Provided that this work is retained for at least the duration of a year, or the course, and can be made available as evidence to be used in periodic reviews and reporting, the comments and marks made directly on students' work may be sufficient to serve many of the purposes and uses previously fulfilled by the teacher's mark book.

To be consistent with what I have said in Chapters 5 and 9, about the different character and requirements of formative and summative assessment, a reasonably manageable recording system might therefore have the following elements:

1 A *primary record* of students' achievements, identified weaknesses, targets and strategies for improvement in the form of *formative comments* on the student's work itself. In most cases these would be recorded in work books or files but an annotation sheet might be required for certain assessment tasks or for students' work that produces what is sometimes known as 'ephemeral evidence'. Ephemeral evidence of such things as speech, drama, musical performance, collaborative working, can often be captured on video-tape, audio-tape or in photographs, but a written record in the form of notes describing the student's performance may be adequate. A simple annotation sheet is given on the next page in Figure 11.1; the headings provide reminders that it is important to record the content and context of the task and the range of achievements that are demonstrated, including social and personal skills and understandings.

2 A *secondary* record can be kept in a teacher's mark book but rather than duplicating the information that is already available in 1, this might contain simply a record of work completed and marked. A tick in a column under a heading cross-referenced to the scheme of work may be sufficient. This record could also contain *summative judgements*

of students' attainments made at regular intervals, but perhaps not more than once a term, or at the end of each unit of work (see 3 below).

Figure 11.1 **Sample annotation sheet**

ASSESSMENT RECORD

Name: _____ Date: _____

Subject/Curriculum area: _____ Unit of work: _____

Task and context: _____

_____

		COMMENTS
1	**Achievements and evidence:** a knowledge and understanding b processes and skills c personal and social d motivation and effort	
2	**Evidence of NC attainment targets**	
3	**Weaknesses and possible reasons**	
4	**Targets**	
5	**Action plan**	

Signed: (student)   (teacher)

3 Periodically teachers will need to *review* the work accomplished to make a *summative* judgement about each student's progress at defined points. Ideally this will be done in *discussion with the student* and will draw on the same *evidence* in work books etc. that was previously the focus of formative assessment. In Chapter 9, I pointed out that summative judgements can be based on the evidence used for formative assessment but the process cannot work successfully the other way round. Specially designed assessment tasks or tests (including SCAA's published optional tests and tasks) might be used specifically for summative purposes but, in my view, it is not a good idea to rely on these solely and ignore the evidence that is already to hand. Evidence collected from different types of task gives a more complete view of students' achievements.

Whatever evidence a teacher decides to draw upon, the purpose of such reviews would be to come to some judgement about the overall progress the student has made over the period or in the unit of work. This would be in relation to his or her own previous performance, in relation to criteria, and/or in comparison with peers. Inevitably some of the peaks and troughs of achievement would be evened out but this is inevitable in summative assessment and is a main reason for keeping it separate from formative assessment. Bearing this in mind, both teachers and students will need to understand the different character of formative and summative assessment and recording processes if they are to benefit from both.

■ Involving students in reviews

It is not essential that students should be involved in reviewing the evidence for summative judgements; it is perfectly possible for teachers to do this alone providing they have access to the evidence. However, there is much to be gained if they are able to find the time to do this with students, who will then have a better understanding of how judgements are made and what they mean.

Arranging reviews that involve students is always difficult to organise, even if this is only once, twice or three times a year. It is almost impossible if you are the only RE teacher in a large secondary school, as I was, or if your regular 'classroom' is the playing field or gymnasium. The situation is sometimes more manageable if curriculum organisation in schools is built around interdisciplinary teams with some team-teaching.

Some large secondary schools (e.g. Stantonbury Campus in Milton Keynes) have been 'restructured' as federations of mini-schools in order to enable more flexibility in curriculum organisation and staffing. In schools that have adopted such systems the numbers of students each team works with is usually smaller than in schools with more traditional structures. Similarly, team-teaching can be used to free up some time for one-to-one reviewing. This issue illustrates the need for consideration of assessment alongside broader issues of curriculum organisation and school management. All are interlinked.

Whether or not teachers choose to involve students directly in reviewing for summative purposes, they will need to decide how to record summative judgements in their mark book or other form of secondary record. They will probably deliberate over whether they should use brief narrative descriptions, National Curriculum levels, or some form of grading system. Narrative descriptions are often the most explicit and useful but they take most space and time to record. National Curriculum levels are so broad in their scope that they do not easily provide for the recording of smaller steps in progress that will occur over relatively short periods of time. Thus, while teachers and students need to know how achievement is referenced to National Curriculum levels, many schools develop other systems for recording progress on a regular basis.

■ Understanding what grading systems mean

In secondary schools, grading systems are endemic. These can be a useful shorthand but teachers, students and parents need to know what grades *mean*. For example, A–E rating scales can be used to indicate some form of absolute judgement against a criterion such as excellent, good, satisfactory, poor, very poor; or they can be used to indicate relative performance in comparison with a reference group, e.g. well above average, above average, average, below average, well below average. Moreover, if teachers are making comparative judgements, they need to be clear about the reference group with which individual performance is being compared. Are they making comparisons with the class group, the year group or the national group? An 'A' for achievement in Set 1 may mean something very different from an 'A' for achievement in Set 6.

If grading systems are to be used at all, it is important therefore that what each grade means is expressed in words and shared with colleagues and students. This need for clarity is also a strong argument for a common grading system across the school, especially if it is used for reporting to parents.

Reports to parents

External requirements (see Chapter 3) now demand that written reports are produced annually and sent to parents with notice of arrangements for discussion. This has been normal practice in most secondary schools for many years and many schools exceed the statutory obligation by reporting more frequently. For example, some schools produce interim reports early in Year 7 to let parents know how their child has 'settled in'. Such reports are usually very brief but they communicate any cause for concern that needs to be dealt with promptly. Similarly, as indicated in Chapter 3, a report might be produced early in Year 9, prior to option choices, with another report at the end of the Key Stage 3 with results of the national tests. In Year 11 a report of 'mock' examination results may be sent to parents before the issue of the National Record of Achievement to students at the end of their compulsory schooling.

As mentioned earlier, reports to parents are generally much more detailed and informative than they were even a decade ago. However, a number of issues remain that still pose difficult decisions for many schools, for example:

1 **Whether to use grades, marks, levels or comments in reports to parents** The issues here are much the same as those described in the previous section, except that the need to communicate clearly to parents is even greater than in communications with colleagues who are more likely to share the same language and assumptions. Schools are not encouraged to report using National Curriculum levels except at the ends of Key Stages when it is mandated. To do so could, in any case, be profoundly discouraging for many pupils who are likely to stay on the same level for two years. Marks, such as percentages achieved in tests, look impressive but can be meaningless unless parents are also told the spread of marks, which they almost never are.

Grades can be equally problematic unless there is common use across subjects and a key is provided to explain what grades mean. Some schools, however, find it useful to provide a scale of judgements (e.g. excellent, good, satisfactory, poor, cause of concern) for a general summary of attainment in sub-areas of a subject, or for cross-curricular achievements, such as relationships with staff, relationships with peers, attitude to work, personal organisation etc. This can be useful in providing a quick overview, but in almost all circumstances it needs to be supplemented by more specific narrative comments on areas of special strength or weakness, with advice about strategies for improvement.

2 **Whether to include predicted GCSE or A-level grades** A number of schools choose to include predictions of examination results in their reports to parents. Pressure to do this is often strong from parents who are concerned to know how their children are doing in their courses and whether they are 'on track' to get certain grades. The current requirement for predicted A-level grades in applications for admission to universities also encourages schools to engage in this kind of speculation. In my view the extension of this practice to earlier stages can be both misleading and dangerous. It is one thing to offer a prediction of final A-level grades six months before completion of what are, increasingly, modular courses with continuous assessment; it is something quite other to predict GCSE grades in Year 10, or even in Year 9.

The word 'prediction' carries with it mathematical or scientific connotations, yet there is rarely anything very mathematical or scientific about these kinds of forecasts. They are professional judgements which amount to a teacher saying, 'If Alice continues to produce work of this quality up till the time of the examination, and if nothing about the examination is unexpected, then I would expect her to achieve a grade X'. A teacher may well be justified in saying this to a parent, with these provisos, but the 'ifs' have to be recognised as critical. Offering a predicted grade without this kind of explanation can create negative reactions of either complacency or despair.

For example, I know of one student who achieved nine A*–C grade GCSEs who, in Year 10, was given predicted grades of E, F and G. When his worried father rang the school he was told that the grades had been based on tests marked at GCSE standard although the student was only two terms into his course. Whilst there may be some point in marking work in this way to provide guidance to students about the standard eventually expected (a formative purpose), the use of the results in this summative way was simply destructive. Even at A-level there are recognised problems with the use of predicted grades and, at the time of writing, the university admissions procedures are being reviewed. The expected outcome is a new system that uses actual not predicted grades.

3 **Whether to use comment banks** With the increased use of computers in schools it seems logical to harness information technology to the service of reporting. The extension phase of pilot records of achievement schemes, from 1988 to 1990, was asked specifically to look at the possibilities. At the time a number of commercial and non-commercial organisations were working in this area and the development of comment banks using database

programs was a favourite activity. These did not prove as successful as had been hoped because statements generated from comment banks were often bland and uninformative about individuals. I recall one parents' evening when I observed the parents of two different students sitting down together to compare reports generated in this way. In many respects the reports were the same and the only things the parents found of real interest were the statements that appeared in the report of the student who was not their child. They then wanted to know why these statements were missing in their own child's case! In order to be meaningful to parents, reports need to focus on the key issues in learning for each individual and provide some concrete evidence of the basis of a teacher's judgements. Computerised comment banks cannot easily do this.

4 **How to provide contextual information to support judgements**
The problem here is how to provide sufficient information about the context in which a student's performance has been produced without having to write long descriptions. Some schools have tackled this issue by providing short descriptions of the content of the curriculum in a given area before reporting students' progress in relation to that curriculum. Sometimes these descriptions are provided in a separate box at the top of each subject report; sometimes they are more closely integrated with the judgements.

Again, such statements may suffer from being so general that they do not provide the kind of detail that individual parents are seeking. In any case there is an argument for providing general details of the curriculum at the *beginning* of the year so that parents can monitor their child's progress for themselves. To this end some schools provide separate curriculum booklets. If this kind of booklet has already been provided then the evidence given in reports can be in the form of a very limited number of short examples to illustrate something special or something characteristic about a student's performance which the teacher wishes to draw to the attention of parents.

5 **Whether to include negative comments about a student** During the development of records of achievement pilot schemes, there was much debate about whether comments in written reports should be wholly positive. The general conclusion was that whilst one might expect the National Record of Achievement, as a report that might be used with employers, to be expressed in positive terms in the same way as CVs generally are, reports to parents should inform them of weaknesses as well as strengths. However, in order to maintain a student's motivation, it was widely agreed that reports should be

worded in *constructive* ways offering advice about ways forward. Moreover, if criticism was to be made it should focus on the behaviour and not condemn the person. In other words, the kind of reports that Roald Dahl amused us with in *Matilda*, should appear no more. For those who do not know this source, I quote two of his examples:

It is a curious thing that grasshoppers have their hearing-organs in the sides of the abdomen. Your daughter Vanessa, judging by what she's learnt this term, has no hearing-organs at all.

Fiona has the same glacial beauty as an iceberg, but unlike the iceberg she has absolutely nothing below the surface.

These are fictitious examples, but I can think of similar comments made by real teachers about real students. One such was: 'Jason has elevated sloth and idleness into an art form'.

6 **Whether to include a contribution from students** Many schools now include a self-report by students with the report to parents. Often this is constructed during tutor group time or as part of the PSE curriculum and is in the nature of a general reflection and review of the whole period since the last report. Often students write targets for the future. Undoubtedly this can be a valuable exercise because it encourages students to review their own progress and identify broad areas where they need to focus their efforts for improvement. However, there is a danger that it can become a repetitive and rather boring ritual unless carefully built into pastoral or PSE programmes with adequate attention to stimulus activity. Moreover, targets can be so vague or generalised as to be virtually meaningless. 'I will work harder in mathematics', or 'I will improve my handwriting' are so general that it is difficult to determine when the target has been met and students may simply repeat the target in the next report. Personal targets, set by students, may be most productive when done in the context of learning something specific, i.e. as part of ongoing formative assessment processes, rather than as something done on a special occasion for inclusion in a general report (see however the section on IEPs on page 226).

In some schools, rather than students contributing a general review, they are involved in the production of each of their subject reports which enables them to formulate specific targets for improvement. This happened in some schools I visited in connection with the records of achievement evaluation in the 1980s. In these cases, reports to parents had the additional advantage that they presented no surprises to students because all the contents had been discussed with them in detail before they went home to parents.

Discussions with parents

Whilst written reports to parents may have changed in recent years, arrangements for discussions with parents are often depressingly familiar to those who have experienced them over two or three decades. Many parents' evenings are still reminiscent of prison visiting arrangements, with parents queuing up for five minutes across a table with each subject teacher. Often this takes place in a noisy hall with similar conversations going on all around.

In the worst scenarios ritual behaviour is well established: the parents announce the name of their child and, if this fails to stimulate recall of a face, the teacher opens his or her mark book and tries to say something sensible on the basis of the marks that are displayed there. A mark book in which a string of grades is entered is therefore a kind of security blanket. Middle-class parents, particularly those who are teachers themselves, may have brought their child's report with them, and have some prepared questions, but for many parents the expectation is simply that they will be told in general terms how their child is doing and whether she is behaving herself.

This description may be a caricature but there has been a good deal of continuity in my experience of parents' evenings: first as a school student, then as a teacher, and most recently as a researcher and parent. The greatest barrier to change has almost certainly been the need for discussions with parents to be manageable. Schools have been faced with the problem of creating a system which allows all parents access to all of those who teach their child without tying up too much of teachers' out-of-school time. The question therefore is whether there are better ways of organising discussions with parents which are equally economical of teachers' time but more purposeful and productive.

Devising a more meaningful dialogue with parents

This is an area in which secondary schools might usefully draw lessons from primary schools, although the different organisation of the two phases of education does not allow straightforward adoption of practices from earlier years. The writing of formal reports to parents has had a shorter history in many primary schools but their development has often been closely integrated with parents' meetings for various purposes.

It has been traditional in primary schools to display children's work in various ways and in many schools the development of portfolios of examples of students' work has become an extension of this practice. Thus, when parents visit primary schools, they are usually able to see evidence of the programmes of study that children are working on, a representative sample of the standards of work produced by the class or group (on walls and in class or subject portfolios), and evidence of their own child's work in workbooks, individual portfolios or displays. In this way they can compare, in a very direct way, the standard achieved by their child in relation to the standards achieved by others and in relation to the curriculum as taught. Often the children themselves are involved in explaining their work to their parents.

What, then, can secondary teachers take from this?

1 Parents may get a better sense of how their child is doing (the perennial question) if they can compare their child's work with the standards achieved by others in a similarly direct way. If departments have produced portfolios of assessed work for standardisation and formative purposes (see Chapters 8 and 9), these could also be made available to parents, who, if they are also given direct access to their own child's work, could compare the two. Most parents, even the least sophisticated, are capable of *seeing* differences in standards which will give them a better insight into the progress that their child is making, both in relation to others and in relation to criteria, than can be communicated by content-free judgements or grades.

2 This kind of opportunity to look at the evidence can be the basis of three-way discussion between teacher, student and parent. This will build on the experience of teacher/parent/student conferences that parents may already have experienced in their child's primary school. This discussion should have some clear purpose, which, in my view, should go beyond simply imparting information. In so far as these meetings are relatively infrequent occasions, the best possible use should be made of them. As a general principle, I would suggest that each meeting should conclude with an agreement between all parties to implement some kind of action to help the student achieve an identified target. This must be possible even if the student is progressing well. I recall one student of mine who was working so hard that I was concerned about his physical and mental well-being. We discussed this and his father agreed that at ten o'clock each night he would insist that they both took a short walk before bed.

Whether it is prudent to include students in discussions with parents has long been a subject for debate. If there are matters to discuss that need to be dealt with in private then I suggest that parents' evenings of this kind are not the best place to do so. We are dealing here with general educational progress and how to create a partnership between home and school to support learning. This will benefit if discussion is open and explicit between all parties. School managers have a responsibility, however, to ensure that parents are aware that they can approach the school at other times if they are concerned about other issues, or if a situation arises that cannot wait till the designated parents' evening.

3. A third area which is worth debating in the light of primary practice is the role of the form tutor in discussing educational progress with parents. In most primary schools the class teacher has responsibility for discussing with parents both general progress and particular, subject-specific issues. In secondary schools, discussions with subject teachers predominate on the grounds that parents are interested in progress in subjects and feel that subject teachers alone have the authority to pronounce on subject-specific matters.

This is, of course, a good reason for most current practice. However, the small amount of time that can be allocated to each discussion severely limits its usefulness. Many schools encourage parents to restrict the numbers of appointments they make but this rarely does much to lengthen the time available. It is worth asking, therefore, whether the form tutor, or equivalent, should have a more central role in discussions with parents. This would require that form tutors regard it as part of their job to have an overview of their students' *academic* progress and any specific problems that need to be dealt with in specific subject areas. It would also require them to discuss such matters with subject teachers prior to the parents' evenings. It would take them beyond the kind of pastoral role traditionally associated with form tutors and towards more comprehensive responsibility for oversight of the total educational experience of students.

This extension of the pastoral role, to embrace a role as 'director of studies', has been advocated for some time by writers in the field of pastoral care. It was also recommended by the national evaluation of pilot records of achievement schemes in 1988 (see reference in the footnote to Chapter 10, page 196):

. . . we could detect the beginnings of movement towards the erosion of the traditional divide between pastoral and academic aspects of the curriculum. (. . .) Thus some subject departments were beginning to accept the need to plan for personal aspects of achievement with academic curricula and, conversely, some tutorial staff were beginning to see their role as being concerned with oversight and support for the total educational experience of their tutees, including both academic and pastoral aspects. In our view this trend is to be encouraged because it holds the promise of a valid and coherent curricular basis for (reporting) systems.

A shift of responsibility on to the form tutor as the principal participant in discussions with parents would mean that no teacher would have to prepare for more than thirty meetings each year – although *preparation* would be of the utmost importance. The burden might also be lessened because meetings could be spread over a number of shorter evenings; after all, it would not be so important to co-ordinate attendance with other teachers which is a principal reason for the mass jamboree. It might even mean that teachers managed to meet the usually 'non-attending' parents, whom they often claim the greatest need to see.

If arrangements of this kind were to be adopted, there is no reason, in principle, why parents should not see specified subject teachers as well if there is any matter that the form tutor cannot deal with. Most schools now welcome contact with parents throughout the year, as an occasion arises, and will set up a meeting with any member of staff if a parent requests it. These *ad hoc* meetings are often the most productive because they usually have a very specific focus. The arrangements for such meetings might be a further responsibility of the form tutor.

These suggestions for restructuring of parents' meetings already have a precedent in most schools: in the way that reviews are carried out for students with special educational needs.

■ Lessons to be learned from SEN reviews and IEPs

It is perhaps no coincidence that OFSTED inspectors often find more positive things to say about recording and reporting in Learning Support Departments than in many other areas of schools (see Chapter 1 pages 10–12). The procedures laid down in the Special Educational Needs Code of Practice appear to have stimulated the development of systems that might serve as a model for the whole school. Indeed, I know of one large school, whose headteacher is a SEN specialist, that has instituted a system of reviews and Individual Education Plans (IEP) for *all* students in the school.

The rationale behind this is that all students have some special needs and these deserve much the same attention as the most extreme cases. One might argue that this would impose a huge load of work on a limited number of staff but if form tutors could be brought in to implement such a system as part of their role, the situation might be manageable. In any case the number of students on the special needs register is so large in some schools that extending the system to all students, provided that more staff can be directly involved, might not impose too great an additional burden.

Key features of SEN reviews that are worth considering for wider application are:

- One member of staff (SEN co-ordinator in the case of students on the SEN register but this could be the form tutor for others) collects information from parents, subject teachers and significant others about each student's strengths, weaknesses, difficulties and useful strategies.
- A draft Individual Education Plan is drawn up *at the beginning of the school year* which identifies concerns, targets and possible courses of action for the coming year or six months.
- This plan is discussed with parents (face-to-face at meetings with parents or in other ways – by 'phone or letter) and amended as necessary. Parental involvement in target setting has particular value.
- Subject staff are asked to implement strategies to enable students to make progress towards their targets and to say how they will evaluate the achievement of targets. It is important to make targets specific and clear, realistic and accomplishable within a limited time frame, and reasonably easy to verify.
- Progress is reviewed at least once, but preferably twice or three times a year, and ideally linked in with the school's main reporting systems.

With some adaptation, a report similar to an IEP, which focuses importantly on targets agreed by teachers, students and parents, might usefully combine with the more usual overview given in form tutors' comments to parents. This would make reports and discussions less a summing up at the end of a period of study and more forward looking (prospective) and formative.

The National Record of Achievement

The original format

From 1991 until 1998 all school leavers were issued with a National Record of Achievement (NRA), affectionately known as 'the wine list' in some quarters because of its size, shape, gold-embossed burgundy cover and brass corners. Inside there were clear plastic pockets in which to display sheets recording: personal details; school achievements related to the curriculum; qualifications and credits awarded; other achievements and experiences, in school, out of school and in relation to key skills; and a personal statement by the student. A further sheet to record employment history after leaving school was also included. In other words the NRA was a rather 'posh'-looking *curriculum vitae*.

Whilst there is no doubt that the preparation of such a CV is a useful thing for all students to engage in as part of their preparation for working life, the product became detached from many of the processes that had been developing in the pilot records of achievement schemes during the 1980s. This was not intentional because the guidance sent out with the NRA emphasised its role in assessment, recording and reporting and in action planning. Indeed, there was specific additional guidance on action planning which was defined as the process of negotiated target setting in education and training. This was regarded as having four elements, in which the NRA had a central part to play:

- **reviewing achievement** including existing achievements which would be recorded in the NRA;
- **setting personal goals** including completing qualifications or courses, making career moves etc.;
- **determining learning needs** such as the knowledge and skills required to meet goals;
- **arranging learning provision** such as identifying courses to take.

It was expected that these action plans would also be kept in the NRA.

In those schools that had imaginative programmes of support for recording and strong links with potential users, the production of the school leavers' NRA represented a culmination and celebration of a way of working. In others, however, it became just an additional chore that consumed a good deal of precious time in Years 11 and 13 without much evident 'pay-off'. In 1996, a review of the NRA was carried out on behalf of government. This found that, although there was an 80 per cent take-up of the NRA by schools, it was not used well by students afterwards. Similarly, although 50 per cent of employers knew about the NRA, few used it within their companies. Most worrying of all was the fact that, although many educational and training initiatives included recording and action planning, few made use of the existing NRA system. Perhaps this was inevitable given that government had chosen, against advice, to put resources into the production of a glossy artefact rather than into organisation and staff development to support the recording and reporting process.

Restructuring: the new PROFIL

In 1996 the Dearing Review of 16–19 Qualifications recommended that the NRA should be restructured and relaunched. In February 1997, the Steering Committee, appointed to carry this work forward, published its report. Key messages included the identification of needs for:

- clarity on purpose and ownership and a new name to reflect lifelong use;
- a major focus to be on the processes of reviewing and recording achievement, setting targets and planning personal development;
- improved design to assist greater flexibility and accessibility for the user;
- better guidance on use;
- coherence with other related developments and initiatives.

To this end the Steering Committee recommended:

- promotion of the new NRA in ways complementary to other initiatives, especially careers education and guidance programmes in which it would find a natural home;
- market testing of a new name (Progress File or PROFIL);
- development of high quality guidance materials to assist effective use;
- trials of new materials in 1997/8;
- provision of training to those who will give guidance to users;
- opportunities for all fourteen to nineteen year olds to develop and record achievements in key skills, especially personal and interpersonal skills.

In June 1997, ministerial approval was given to proceed with trials in 1997/8. During this time up to 70 schools and 20 colleges are expected to trial three versions of guidance to users, and assist with evaluation and development of a distance learning pack for teachers. Other versions will be developed for specific contexts, such as for students with special needs. Subject to these trials, the new PROFIL will be phased in between September 1998 and September 2000.

Guidance will be particularly targeted at students who are now regarded as the principal users. Emphasis will be given to personal responsibility for lifelong learning and to this end guidance materials will give advice on:

- checking progress;
- setting goals and targets;
- developing and recording key skills;
- recording qualifications, credits and awards;
- writing personal statements and CVs for particular purposes, e.g. reviews, option choices, careers interviews, jobs, university and college applications etc.;
- help with career planning.

Given the variety of uses for records, a single glossy format is no longer thought to be appropriate. Instead, the PROFIL is likely to be in the form of a loose-leaf file, with sections and dividers. There will be no specifically titled pages but a logo will be made available for use on the stationery of a school, company or individual. A detachable presentation folder will also be included for students to use when they wish to present summaries of their achievements, with evidence, to other people such as careers advisers or potential employers.

At the time of writing this book, it is too early to say what the outcome of the relaunch will be and whether the new-look PROFIL will be more successful than the old 'wine list'. A great deal will depend on whether students find it useful and whether it can be fully integrated into the work of the school, especially its programmes for careers education and guidance which it has the potential to enhance.

■ The use of information technology

Mention was made earlier about the use of computers and information technology in the production of reports to parents. In principle, recording and reporting of students' achievements should provide ideal opportunities for IT applications. However, as the evaluation of pilot records of achievement schemes showed, many schools appeared to go up a blind alley in the 1980s by adopting mechanistic comment bank systems. Unhappy with them, some schools reverted to more conventional hand-written or word-processed reports that could be more easily personalised.

This is not to say that there is little potential for the use of computers in this area. Indeed, it is still very great, especially as the access of students to computers has increased. The most productive use of computers will probably depend, however, on every student possessing their own computer file or disk and having the encouragement and facilities to update their personal records on a regular basis. This is one suggestion that has been made in connection with the relaunched National Record of Achievement, which will include pockets for computer disks. The principle could be extended, however, to recording and reporting in a wide range of contexts.

As early as 1986, in an FE college, I saw evidence of how well IT-supported student-centred recording and reporting could work, despite the rather primitive hardware available at that time. A software program had been developed 'in house' which encouraged students to write their own records and reports, in free prose, using headings, brief course outlines and assessment criteria. The computer program required subject teachers to set up student disks with headings of curriculum units and a brief description of content. A simple, non-expert user guide was produced to enable them to do this and co-ordinators conducted induction sessions. When disks had been prepared, students then entered their self-assessments under these headings using the assessment criteria. There was a limit of five or six lines per entry so the computer overwrote previous text rather than adding to it. This had the advantage of forcing students to reconsider and summarise their assessments as they went along.

The resulting self-reports were used as the focus for discussion with the relevant teachers in short review sessions. The students' accounts could be easily amended, if necessary, after the teacher's assessment had been considered alongside the self-assessment. The software program also enabled different types of print-out for different purposes, e.g. working document, 'pukka' print-out for parents, or Record of Achievement. Students were at the heart of this process. They held the passwords to their files and ownership, both literally and symbolically, rested with them. This increased their interest and motivation but it also put self-assessment and dialogue between teacher and student at the centre of the process. Potentially, such uses of IT could assist formative assessment as described in Chapter 9.

In the time that has elapsed since 1986, software programs have been produced by commercial and non-commercial organisations and may be used in similar ways. SIMS (Schools Information Management Systems) has been particularly active and provides training as well as software for recording and reporting. There is evidence, however, that many of the available IT resources are still under-used.

From 1993 to 1995, the National Council for Educational Technology (NCET) carried out a small-scale survey of the use of IT in assessment, followed by support for nineteen development projects across primary and secondary education, FE and HE. These projects divided into two main groups: those in which IT was used by staff for record-keeping and/or reporting; and those in which students themselves used IT to record their own progress and activities, or those of their peers. The NCET identified twelve categories of use: recording progress; self-assessment; peer assessment; reports to parents; reports for internal review; reports to external agencies; records of achievement; use of comment banks; use of Optical Mark Reader (OMR); special needs; diagnostic/ initial assessment; analysis of aggregated data. There was no evidence that more than six of these possible uses were operational in any one project and two or three was the norm.

On the basis of the evidence collected across the nineteen projects, the NCET team came to the following conclusions:

The use of IT in assessment: NCET conclusions

- Using IT for assessment can enhance the assessment process by making it possible to assess different aspects of achievement.

- Assessment information can become more accessible; using computers can enable the presentation of information in different ways for different audiences.

- Using IT can improve the quality of reports: both in terms of presentation and in the range and scope of what is reported on.

- Using IT can promote a consistent approach to assessment within and across institutions.

- Using IT encourages rethinking of existing processes, including the relationship between assessment and curriculum and teaching.

- Using IT, especially to produce a high quality record of achievement, can improve student self-esteem, skills and motivation.

- Using IT for assessment can improve IT competence and confidence among staff because they are involved in a 'real' task.

- IT can reduce the burden of administration, although in the short term the gains do not outweigh the training and development time.

▶

- It is essential that software for assessment is not considered in isolation from the software used for management and administration. Difficulties were experienced with software which was incompatible with existing systems and especially with importing and exporting data.
- Technical support must be adequate.
- Adequate time must be allocated for training, for both staff and students, which may need to be repeated.
- Access to both hardware and software must be adequate.
- Senior management support is essential.

Adapted from *Using IT for Assessment: key issues*, published by NCET in 1995.

The last finding in the list above is particularly important. Indeed, in its summary of its findings, the NCET project placed greatest emphasis on management support for the effective use of IT in assessment:

Any implementation of new IT systems requires a significant investment, particularly in terms of staff time, expertise and enthusiasm. This will only be possible if senior managers give active commitment and a positive lead. These projects clearly show that IT can provide real benefits in the processes of recording and reporting, but the benefits will only be realised if appropriate investment is made at an early stage.

ACTIVITIES

1 Developing principled recording and reporting systems

This is an opportunity to revisit the Activities associated with Chapter 2, especially Activity 2 (see page 41). It can be carried out as a whole school activity by the school assessment co-ordinator or working group, or within departments.

(i) To begin with, compile a list of all the forms of recording and reporting that are currently in use in the school or department; include such things as everyday records, reports to parents, discussions with parents, school records, IEPs, the NRA/PROFIL.

(ii) Create a large matrix with these listed down one axis and the school's principles for assessment, recording and reporting listed along the other.

(iii) Discuss the possible contents of each cell with a view to specifying a procedure that will allow the principle to be fulfilled in the context of each form of recording and reporting. It will not be possible to fill in the cell in all cases; for example, it is unlikely that official school records could be integrated into teaching and learning. However, this exercise should ensure that the possibilities are systematically considered and good reasons are given for creating specific procedures. It will probably be sufficient if all principles are met by one or more procedures and that they are not actually contradicted by others.

(iv) An additional activity might then be to take a range of records and reports and discuss, in small groups, the extent to which they, and the processes that led up to their production, fulfil the principles. If they do not, the groups need to consider how they might be reconstructed so that they do.

2 Developing the use of IT for recording and reporting

(i) Begin with an audit of the existing position so that the school knows where it is starting from. Two things need to be known: the existing level of IT use in the school and the existing level of IT skills amongst teaching staff, support staff and students. It may be helpful to record these two things against the twelve categories of use identified by the NCET IT in Assessment project:

- recording progress;
- self-assessment;
- peer assessment;
- reports to parents;
- reports for internal review;
- reports to external agencies;
- records of achievement;
- use of comment banks;
- use of OMR;
- special needs;
- diagnostic/initial assessment;
- analysis of aggregated data.

(ii) Next, it may be important to do some research into what more might be possible. The NCET IT in Assessment project would be one source of information. This publishes case study material and a directory of software for assessment. The address of the NCET is Milburn Hill Road, Science Park, Coventry CV4 7JJ. The Employment Department also publishes a directory of computer-assisted assessment products and producers. The address is Employment Department, Moorfoot, Sheffield S1 4PQ.

(iii) On the basis of these two sources of information, the next task would be for an IT in Assessment working group to consider expanding the school's current systems. Important questions to ask would be:

- What additional training would be required for students, teachers and support staff?
- What additional hardware and software would be required and how it would relate to existing systems?
- What specialist technical support would be necessary, and how it would be found?
- How would IT systems be co-ordinated?
- What might be the impact on curriculum, teaching and learning and would this represent improvement?
- Would long term benefits be likely to outweigh initial costs?

(iv) If a decision is taken to go ahead with development then senior management will have an important role to play in resourcing and supporting development through provision of finance, training, personnel and a structure for co-ordination.

12 Using assessment data for monitoring and target setting

▇▇ Archery across the curriculum

Among metaphors in education that are enjoying current popularity, a number are drawn from an analogy between education and archery. 'Target setting' is particularly ubiquitous. I used this analogy in Chapter 8 and have referred to targets and target setting on a number of occasions. Whilst I was writing this book, the government, through SCAA, released its September 1997 consultation paper on *Target Setting and Benchmarking in Schools* (by mixing metaphors surveyors were also called in to aid the task of raising standards!). Sir Winston Churchill once said, 'How infinite is the debt owed to metaphors by politicians who want to speak strongly but are not sure what they are going to say'. So perhaps that explains it!

In the previous chapters, when I referred to target setting, I had in mind the very specific targets that might be set by students and their teachers concerning next steps in learning. These would have reference to students' current achievements and provide substantive guidance on what needed to be done next. They might refer, for example, to a need to achieve greater clarity about the dominant themes in the novels of Thomas Hardy by reading more of his work, or ensuring that multiplication tables are thoroughly memorised.

This is target setting with particular reference to the content of learning, which is very important. But government uses target setting in another sense which usually refers to the achievement of goals measured in terms of test results and examination passes. Thus the government's 'drive to raise standards' is usually conceived in terms of increasing the proportion of students who succeed in gaining qualifications of one kind or another.

National targets

The previous Conservative government established National Targets for Education and Training for 2000. There were three targets for Foundation Learning:

- By age 19, 85 per cent of young people to achieve five GCSEs at Grade C or above, an Intermediate GNVQ or an NVQ Level 2.
- By age 19, 75 per cent of young people to achieve Level 2 competence in communication, numeracy and IT competence; by age 21, 35 per cent to achieve Level 3 in these key skills.
- By age 21, 60 per cent of young people to achieve two GCE A–levels, an advanced GNVQ or an NVQ level 3.

In addition, Advisory National School Targets, relevant to secondary schools, were set out in advance to the government from SCAA and the National Advisory Council for Education and Training Targets (NACETT) in 1996:

- 80 per cent of 14 year olds to achieve Level 5 and 50 per cent Level 6 in National Curriculum tests.
- 55 per cent of 16 year olds to achieve five GCSEs at A*–C or equivalent.

At first there was consistent progress towards the Foundation Learning targets but in 1994 and 1995 the rate of progress slowed (especially on the first target), making them more challenging. At the time of writing, they are under review.

Part of the problem for the government may be that individual schools do not identify closely with the drive to raise standards nationally. In one sense this is perceived as not their problem. Their more immediate concern is with institutional performance and particularly their position in the performance tables, because this influences their success in recruiting students and ultimately their financial viability. An awareness of this is probably a major reason why the government has launched its schools' target setting and benchmarking initiative at this time. By setting benchmarks for individual school improvement it will be able to link school targets to national targets.

Schools are not, however, concerned only with global results, such as the proportion of A*–C grades obtained at GCSE, although these are important. Most secondary schools are also interested in whether different departments are equally effective and whether the school is effective for different groups of students and individuals. They are therefore likely to be interested in promoting school improvement by setting targets at several levels: whole school targets; departmental targets; targets for sub-groups, such as boys and girls or ethnic minorities; targets for individual students.

It is possible to 'pull targets out of the air' but realistic targets should be based on expectations of performance drawn from analysis of assessment data. The more differentiated the targets, the more detailed the analysis of assessment data will need to be. Before I deal with target setting as a means to promote school improvement, I will describe the different kinds of analysis of assessment data that have been used in recent years.

Measures of school effectiveness

School effectiveness research was perhaps the biggest growth area in educational research during the 1990s. A number of prestigious institutions and eminent researchers are active in a field which has produced both new theory about the measurement of performance and practical ways of helping schools to analyse their own results. These groups do not always agree about the best way of going about these tasks and the arguments are somewhat academic, if not esoteric, and difficult for the non-statistician (like myself) to understand. It is probably not necessary to understand the finer points of the debate although it is important to be aware of the broad issues.

Performance indicators

One thing that all school effectiveness research has in common is the collection and analysis of performance indicators (PIs). The differences arise from the choice of performance indicators and the way they are treated.

Output measures

Most indicator systems start with measures of *output*. In the current climate the outputs that have the greatest public currency are achievements measured by performance in National Curriculum tests and external examinations. In consequence, they are a basic component in all school effectiveness research. There are, however, other outcomes that might be considered: for example, 'staying on' rates, truancy rates and student destinations post–18, or less tangible outcomes such as aspirations, attitudes and quality of life.

For schools that put great emphasis on 'promoting the spiritual, moral, cultural, mental and physical development' of students and preparing them 'for the opportunities, responsibilities and experiences of adult life', it is often disturbing to have their effectiveness as a school reduced to a single measure such as the proportion of students achieving higher grade GCSE passes.

Moreover, the emphasis on a single indicator is worrying for other reasons. In an interesting article in the *Times Educational Supplement* on 19 September 1997, the political commentator Peter Kellner argued that too great a burden was being placed on a single sequence of tests and examinations. They are now required to fulfil four functions:

- assessing the achievements of individual students;
- generating value-added information about schools;
- measuring the progress of schools towards institutional targets,
- measuring the progress of the educational system towards national targets.

Kellner argues that, just as the Thatcher government plunged the country into economic recession by making money supply the main economic policy target, and thus changing the relationship between money supply and the rest of the economy, making examination and test results the sole policy target is likely to change the relationship between assessment and the rest of education.

There is already evidence of this happening. In their report to SCAA on value-added measures, Carol Fitz-Gibbon and Peter Tymms[1] described some strange things already happening in schools:

- **tunnel vision** stressing the achievement of targets at the expense of other educational functions;
- **sub-optimism** entering students for 'easier' subjects and directing resources to those who could yield the highest value-added scores rather than spreading the resource equitably;
- **myopia** giving precedence to achieving immediate goals in terms of high scores rather than promoting skills and knowledge of lasting benefit in adult life;

[1] Fitz-Gibbon, C. and Tymms, P. (1997) *The Value-added National Project: final report*. London: SCAA.

- **measure-fixation** skewing resources to those students expected to gain Ds in the hope of pushing them into the A*– C category, the key measure;
- **misinterpretation** reducing complex value-added analyses to a single number or cause-and-effect conclusion;
- **misrepresentation** cutting corners in the way that examinations are conducted and marked;
- **gaming** seeking to ensure that the intake measure is as low as possible in order to depress the baseline on which value-added is calculated;
- **ossification** rigid systems producing increasingly distorted data as time goes by.

The authors recommended that 'profiles' of schools, based on a number of indicators, should be published; in the short and medium term this is unlikely to happen because of the undoubted political attractions of the single indicator system. Profile information systems would also be a great deal more expensive, although Carol Fitz-Gibbon has set up systems of this kind (PIPS, MidYIS, YELLIS and ALIS), based at Durham University, and many schools have 'bought into' them.

Input measures

The problem with taking outputs alone as indicators of school effectiveness, even when more than one measure is considered, is that comparisons made on this basis rarely compare like-with-like. This is the familiar argument against the publication of league tables of 'raw results' that take no account of the different contexts and intakes of schools. Whilst the actual grade a student achieves will be of vital importance to him or her, aggregated results which take no account of background factors may be a crude and unfair measure of the relative effectiveness of the school as a whole. This is the argument for value-added measures.

It is important, therefore, to collect information about *inputs* as well as outputs so that the two sets of information can be considered together in any judgement of school effectiveness. The intake characteristics usually considered are:

- prior attainment as measured in earlier tests and examinations;
- ability as measured on standardised tests;
- prior attitudes to school;

- gender;
- ethnicity;
- English as an Additional Language;
- special educational needs;
- socio-economic status and aspects of home background such as single parent families.

There is some debate among school effectiveness researchers about which of these indicators is/are most important. Educational performance is linked to social class and the DfEE's 1996 annual report, *Statistics in Education*, provides evidence of the links between GCSE performance and the proportions of students taking free school meals (FSM), the only measure of socio-economic status that is routinely collected. The 'Top 10' LEAs on the performance tables had average FSM levels of 12 per cent, whilst the 'Bottom 10' LEAs had average FSM levels of 36 per cent.

It is known that some schools achieve great things in disadvantaged circumstances but, since they start from a lower base, the socio-economic status of their intake should be taken into account when measuring their effectiveness or setting targets. It is interesting therefore that in its proposals for target setting and benchmarking, the government has indicated that benchmarks for individual secondary schools will be constructed on the basis of data on free school meals. Free school meals are, however, a crude measure of socio-economic status, especially if, as has been indicated, numbers of students *taking* meals free school meals is to be used rather than numbers of students *entitled* to free school meals. Either because of pride or because of ignorance of procedures for claiming, there will be numbers of students who do not take up their entitlement. Thus the figures are likely to be distorted.

The fact that performance is so closely related to social class has led many school effectiveness researchers to argue that the best input measure is prior attainment. This itself will be influenced by social class, and other intake variables such as gender, ethnicity, and special needs, so can be taken to subsume them. Moreover, measures of prior attainment are one of the more useful of the input indicators because they are usually finely differentiated but relatively easy to obtain.

There is, however, a further question about *which kind* of measures of prior attainment are best for judging value-added. The 1997 consultation paper on *Value-added Indicators for Schools,* also published by SCAA, makes it clear that 'national curriculum tests provide, in principle, the best basis for value added measures'. In so far as the National

Curriculum assessment system was set up with evaluation of performance across the system as one of its four purposes, one could respond, 'Well they would say that, wouldn't they!'

The results of national tests do provide a uniform measure for all schools and analysis of large samples of results have revealed a high correlation (0.8) between Key Stage 3 results and GCSE. It is almost certain therefore that any future national system for providing value-added feedback to schools and value-added league tables, will relate outcome measures, such as GCSE grades, to input measures in the form of national test results at the earlier stage.

There are likely to remain some problems with this. If high stakes are attached to the measures of prior attainment as well as the output measures – as they certainly are at Key Stage 2 because of the publication of primary school league tables – then prior attainment measures are liable to distortion in some of the ways described by Carol Fitz-Gibbon and Peter Tymms (see pages 239–40).

Some researchers argue that this would not be the case if other tests, such as standardised tests (e.g. CATs, NFER-Nelson tests, Richmond tests, and reading tests), with known predictive validity, were to be used. Whether these are actually tests of prior attainment, or tests of ability or potential, is a moot point (see Chapter 7), but they may be a more reliable input indicator if no high stakes are attached to them. A number of value-added systems and services to schools have used such tests as baseline data for some time with some success[2]. Moreover, teachers tend to have confidence in them because the tests have been properly standardised. The national evaluation of Key Stage 3 assessment carried out by Exeter University in 1996 revealed that many teachers felt that national tests were still subject to change and some random fluctuation in results from year to year. Thus, despite assurances to the contrary, Heads of English are unlikely to be convinced that the 1997 dip in students' performance nationally was the result of poorer students rather than a more difficult test paper. One would expect, however, that confidence in national tests will continue to rise gradually as the system 'beds down'.

Process measures

If output measures are analysed in relation to inputs (methods of analysis are discussed on page 244–52,) we would still expect to find some variability in results. In other words, some schools will perform relatively better or relatively worse than others with similar intakes. In

---

[2] A review of standardised tests, correlating test scores with GCSE outcomes, is given in Schagen, I. (1996) *QUASE: Quantitative Analysis for Self-Evaluation: Technical Report 1996*. Slough: NFER.

order to find out what makes the difference one has to open the 'black box' between input and output to investigate school processes. These process variables are likely to provide some of the answers.

There is no intention on the part of government to collect process variables as part of a national system of value-added or for benchmarking purposes. This would be impossible to do on a national scale. However, there is an expectation that schools will collect this kind of data themselves in order to explain their own results and to identify areas for improvement. In July 1997 the DfEE invited tenders for the production of case studies of how schools self-evaluate using target setting in a developmental cycle (see page 252). It is intended that these will be the basis of further guidance to schools. It will be up to schools therefore to identify those process variables that are likely to be most relevant. Two kinds of processes need to be considered:

- classroom processes;
- school management processes.

We already know a good deal about the kind of things that need to be looked at because school effectiveness research has made a study of the characteristics of effective schools, i.e. those schools whose results exceed expectations given their intakes.

In a review of research in this area, for OFSTED[3], Pam Sammons and colleagues at the London Institute of Education identified eleven characteristics of effective schools:

1. Participatory leadership
2. Shared vision and goals
3. Teamwork
4. A learning environment
5. Emphasis on teaching and learning
6. High expectations
7. Positive reinforcement
8. Monitoring and enquiry
9. Students' rights and responsibilities
10. Learning for all
11. Partnerships and support

These characteristics provide a source of process indicators that schools might profitably investigate in order to explain their own results. It is notable, however, that these indicators tend to stress management processes and are less specific about classroom processes. This is an

[3] Sammons, P., Hillman, J. and Mortimore, P. (1995) *Key Characteristics of Effective Schools: a review of school effectiveness research.* London: OFSTED.

obvious gap in school effectiveness research although researchers are currently working on it. It explains why speculation about the effectiveness of different classroom strategies, such as whole class teaching, is often just that — speculation. There is little incontrovertible evidence that certain methods produce better results in all contexts, although, as I pointed out in Chapters 5 and 9 with reference to the work of Paul Black and Dylan Wiliam (see page 96), formative assessment as part of teaching could hold an important key. It is one area in which the evidence in support of a particular approach is very strong.

Those schools that have 'bought into' the indicator systems from the Curriculum, Evaluation and Management Centre at Durham University (see page 240) have some information on classroom processes collected for them by means of questionnaires to students. For example, the A–Level Indicator System (ALIS) collects information on such things as teacher's presentation of topics, exercises, preparing essays, class discussions, audio-visual materials, use of IT, receiving help from another student etc.

Although it may be convenient to have this kind of information collected for you, there are few reasons why schools should not do this for themselves. In an earlier book, written with Robert McCormick, I looked at ways of conducting school self-evaluations and collecting data about processes[4]. The collection and analysis of evidence about processes will be an important part of any school self-evaluation because the analysis of performance statistics alone cannot tell schools *why* things are as they are or what they need to do.

Ways of analysing assessment data

In this section I will attempt to explain briefly and in simple terms the kind of analyses performed on input and outcome data to render measures of school effectiveness, especially 'value-added'. These procedures vary tremendously in their statistical complexity. Schools can carry out some procedures for themselves; others require expert help. There are four main ways of carrying out such analysis:

- simple subtraction;
- simple linear regression;
- multiple regression;
- multilevel modelling.

[4] McCormick, R. and James, M. (1988, 2nd edition) *Curriculum Evaluation in Schools*. London: Routledge.

■ Simple subtraction

This method takes account of only one measure such as GCSE passes. It is not appropriate for measuring value-added at individual student level because few students can compare past GCSE performance with current GCSE performance. However, it is commonly used for comparing past and present performance of the school as a whole. If a school gained 55 per cent A*–C grade GCSE passes in 1996 but 59.5 per cent passes in 1997, the school can be described as having improved by 4.5 per cent in one year. This kind of analysis is within the arithmetical capabilities of most people and performance tables are published on the assumption that this kind of calculation will be carried out by schools, parents and journalists.

One common source of (deliberate or inadvertant) confusion is worth remarking on, however. The league tables that the media commonly produce immediately after the publication of GCSE results can be misleading in the sense that they use the numbers of candidates *entered* for GCSEs as the basis of their calculations. They do this because these statistics are readily available from examinations boards at this time.

However, these figures can produce a distorted picture if a school has chosen not to enter a sizeable proportion of the age cohort for these examinations. The league tables produced at a later date by the DfEE can be substantially different because proportions of, say, five A*–C passes are calculated on the basis of the Schools Census (Form 7) returns made in January, which should account for *all* students in the age cohort including those not expected to sit GCSE examinations. It is important therefore to scrutinise the evidence of the basis on which these calculations are made before any firm conclusions are drawn.

■ Simple linear regression

This method is now widely used and is within the capabilities of most secondary schools provided they have access to a statistics software package and some staff with knowledge of simple statistics and IT skills. This is where the mathematics departments are most often co-opted!

The method usually requires that for each student there are two measures: an output measure, such as GCSE results, and an input measure such as prior attainment in the form of results on National Curriculum tests or standardised tests. These two sets of data are entered into the computer which then relates them using a statistical formula and produces an estimation of what 'might reasonably have been expected' in line with the results of similar students in the total population.

Depending on how many students are entered and where they come from, comparisons can be made with other students in the school (or subgroups of them, such as boys and girls), or with students in similar schools, or with students in the LEA or the nation as a whole.

The results of this analysis can be presented in a scattergram which has input scores on the horizontal axis and output scores on the vertical axis (see Figures 12.1, 12.2 and 12.3). Each dot on the scattergram correlates the performance of a student with his or her prior attainment. The line that slopes from the bottom left to the top right of the graph represents the regression line or 'line of best fit'. The regression line represents the average output of all students whose data is entered in relation to each level of input. In most cases the line would be ragged so it is smoothed out to make it straight. In statistical packages this regression line is worked out for you but it is possible to draw an approximate 'line of best fit' manually.

Students whose dots fall on the regression line can be said to have performed as predicted because their performances are in line with the average of those with similar input characteristics. Those above the line have performed better than predicted and those below the line have performed worse than predicted. These graphs can be particularly useful to schools in monitoring performance because, by plotting individual scores, they stimulate questions about reasons for the performance of particular individuals or groups. The following is an example of the way in which one school analysed and interpreted GCSE results in 1996.

An example of valued-added analysis

The John Warner GM School in Hoddesdon, Hertfordshire, had 565 students in 1996/7 and serves a catchment of two housing estates. The majority of parents belong to the Registrar General's social classes IV and V (semi-skilled and unskilled). Ten per cent of the intake is of Italian (Sicilian) descent and all of these students are bilingual. An additional five per cent of students are Travellers who only attend school for about half of the year; few of these sit public examinations so their statistics were not included in the calculations.

Matthew Baxter, the Deputy Head, carried out a regression analysis of his school's GCSE results in 1996. (I am grateful to him for letting me draw on his work here.) He used CAT scores as input data to compare with GCSE results. He gave each GCSE grade a points score (A=8, B=7, C=6 etc.) and then averaged the grade scores for each student to provide a single statistic. (He did this in preference to aggregating them because students were entered for different numbers of GCSEs.) Using a computer package he then plotted the results of all students on a scattergram (Figure 12.1).

Figure 12.1 Year 9 CAT scores plotted against average GCSE score 1996

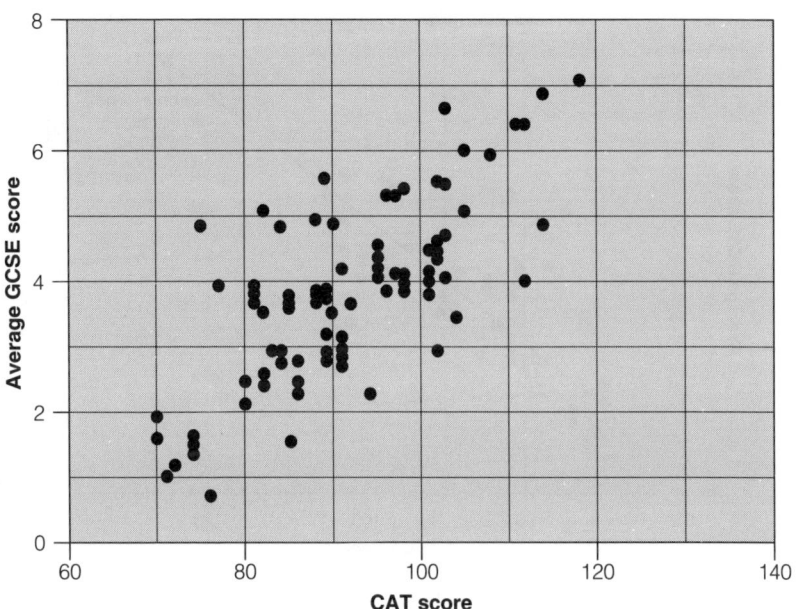

The immediate impression was that there was a high correlation between input and output scores because results 'looked as if' they bunched around an imaginary line of best fit. However, a proper regression analysis revealed a correlation of only 0.54 – well below the 0.7, or preferably 0.77, usually required to allow meaningful statements to be made about relationships between prior and present performance. It was necessary, therefore, to think about why the correlation was so poor.

The graphs had been printed out in colour with sub-groups within the population identified by different colours. This enabled the data to be re-analysed and interpreted in different ways. Nothing much could be said about social class variables because the school caters for a fairly homogenous client group, however some interesting patterns were noted with respect to gender and ethnicity.

Parents and governors of the school had been concerned for some time with the poor performance of girls, which appeared to go against the national trend. Matthew Baxter therefore decided to disaggregate boys' results from girls' results and present them in two scattergrams whilst retaining the regression line for the total mixed cohort on each graph (see Figures 12.2 and 12.3 on the next page). These scattergrams

248 Using assessment data for monitoring and target setting

Figure 12.2 **Performance of girls against school average**

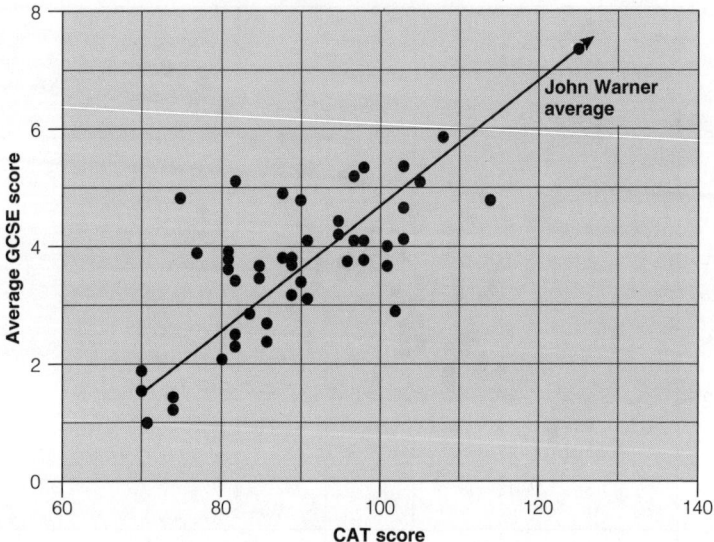

Figure 12.4 **Performance of boys against school average**

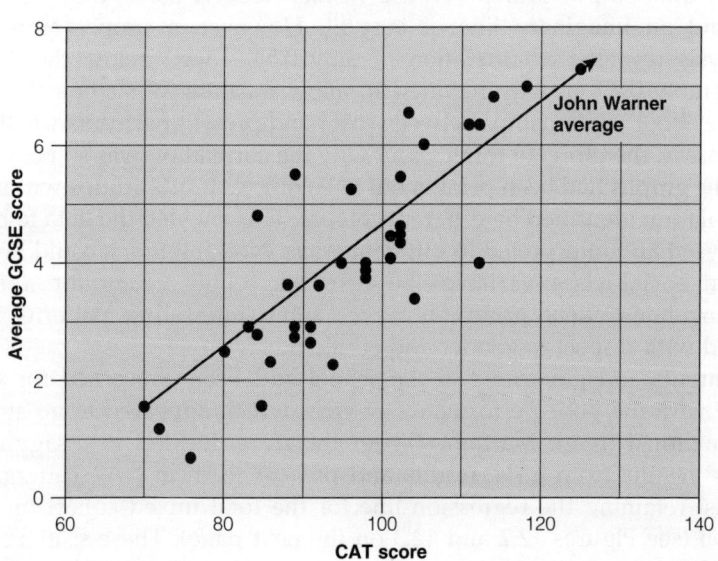

then revealed that although boys' GCSE scores were often higher than girls' GCSE scores, more boys' scores fell below the regression line than did girls' scores. Therefore girls actually made *more progress* at the school than did boys, despite appearances to the contrary. The 'poor' performance of girls in terms of GCSE scores could therefore be attributed to intake factors. Why the school recruits girls with lower prior attainments than boys would need further investigation; the proximity of single sex schools sometimes has an effect even if they are not formally selective.

The original scattergram was interpreted further by isolating those students whose scores fell furthest from the regression line – the 'outliers' who performed significantly differently from the others. Fourteen students were identified: seven furthest above the line and seven furthest below the line. In the former group of seven, four were Italian; there were also two Italians in the latter group of seven. Thus six of the group of fourteen who performed significantly differently from the others were of Italian descent, representing over half of the group of eleven Italians in the cohort.

It was not easy to explain this pattern but Matthew Baxter, the Deputy Head, thought that both English as an Additional Language and social norms in the close-knit Italian community could have had an effect. Poor early performance on the CATs because of language difficulties, combined with relative freedom from negative peer-group pressures, might have helped some Italian students to perform significantly better than expected at GCSE if their language skills had improved.

Statistical analyses can show the existence of relationships between factors but, unlike experimental studies, they cannot explain for certain why the relationship occurs. In other words, a study of the data allows explanations to be hypothesised but these need to be tested further. There are ethical objections to conducting experiments in schools, and in the above case it would be difficult to imagine what kind of experiment might be mounted to test Matthew Baxter's hypotheses. However, reasons can be explored further in more qualitative ways by observing and asking questions.

Whatever the explanation for the atypical performance of the Italian group, when the outliers were deleted from the sample and a new regression line drawn on the basis of the remaining students, the input and output data achieved a much higher correlation of 0.798 (see Figure 12.4 on the next page). It was concluded that the original regression line was useful for *value-added* analysis, but that the revised regression line would be more useful for *target setting* because, by taking out unexplained performances, it gave a clearer picture of how the average student at each intake level could be expected to perform.

Figure 12.4 **John Warner School and national lines of regression**

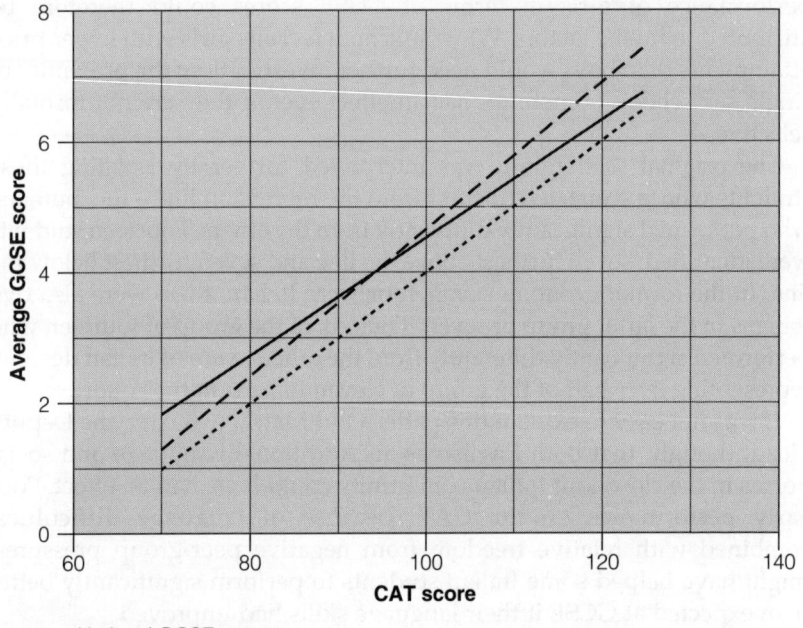

- - - - - National GCSE scores
———— J.W. GCSE scores
– – – J.W. GCSE scores (adjusted)

Multiple regression

In the above example, Matthew Baxter produced graphs taking only one intake variable into account initially but then he looked at the different patterns for different groups and also created different regression lines by adjusting the composition of the population. For most purposes in schools this is sufficient although, by using computer software, it is possible to enter more intake variables into the equation and produce multiple regression.

The ALIS project, for example, will produce tables based on both simple and multiple regression. In order to do this it will enter data about average GCSE score, prior attainment, gender, and parent's occupational status. However, Carol Fitz-Gibbon (for reference see page 260), the originator of the system, cautions that other factors 'frequently add only a small amount to the accuracy of the prediction equations'. Indeed, it is 'dangerous to include too many predictors' and 'on the whole, the answer obtained from taking account of prior achievement is sufficient'.

Multi-level modelling

This method is beyond the technical resources of most schools and challenges the statistical understanding of most teachers (and many academics!). However, there are agencies who will provide multi-level modelling as a service to schools.

Multi-level modelling is based on the idea that, whilst there are undoubted effects attributable to background factors associated with the *individual student*, such as social class and prior achievement, there are also effects due to the *composition of the group* in which the individual finds himself or herself – the classroom, the department, the school, the LEA etc. For example, the *proportion* of students in a class whose parents belong to a certain social class will have an effect. Multi-level modelling allows for these 'compositional effects' by taking account of measurements (average occupational status of parents, the proportion of boys or girls) at several levels, e.g. student, classroom, department, school, ward, LEA. It therefore 'adjusts' for the *interactions* among a number of variables and the *cumulative effects* of the peer group on the student.

Teachers will have a commonsense understanding of the relevance of this kind of analysis because they will have noticed differences between year groups and classes with ostensibly similar characteristics in terms of spread of ability. The 'rogue' forms or year groups often pass into the mythology of schools! However, the techniques of multi-level modelling require a very high level of statistical sophistication. Harvey Goldstein and colleagues at the London Institute of Education have designed multi-level modelling software for use on IBM PC compatible computers and regular workshops are held in London to help people to use it. Whether it is cost effective to employ multi-level modelling techniques *at the level of the single school* is, however, debatable.

On the one hand, this kind of analysis is able to detect differences that other forms of analysis may miss, and may be particularly useful for analysing departmental differences. On the other hand, the kind of analyses carried out by Matthew Baxter, in the example on pages 246–50, may be quite adequate for most in-school purposes and will rarely require the 'buying-in' of external expertise.

Multi-level modelling is therefore probably more valuable, and perhaps vital, for providing rigorous analyses of data involving comparisons across numbers of schools: for research purposes, for the national analysis of OFSTED inspection data and for the creation of benchmarks at national and LEA level.

Target setting in schools

Section 19 of the 1997 Education Act makes provision for legislation to require targets to be set and published by the governing bodies of maintained schools. From 1 September 1998 this requirement will come into effect. At the time of writing, the government, through SCAA/QCA, is consulting on its proposals for legislation so readers will need to check that the summary which follows accords with the regulations published early in 1998.

A five-stage cycle for school improvement

Target setting is intended to be an integral part of a five-stage cycle of development for school improvement that the DfEE is seeking to promote. The five elements are based on questions that the school should be asking themselves:

1 **How well are we doing?** This requires the school to analyse student performance and audit its teaching and management. It will therefore need to analyse data about student outcomes. As explained above, the most useful kinds of analysis will relate outcomes to intake variables to give value-added measures. However, in order to explain patterns in performance and to identify areas for action, it will also be necessary to collect data about processes, such as teaching and management. Thus the statistical analysis of results will need to be supplemented by observational data (perhaps on the lines of the OFSTED Framework for Inspection) to provide evidence in relation to input, output and process indicators.

2 **How well should we be doing?** This requires the school to compare its own results with the results of similar schools in order to identify strengths and diagnose weaknesses as a basis for establishing priorities for improvement. The benchmarking information to be supplied by the DfEE and LEAs is intended to help with this task.

3 **What more should we aim to achieve this year?** This requires the school to set clear, specific and measurable targets which focus in particular on raising standards of attainment in national tests and examinations.

4 **What must we do to make it happen?** This requires the school to integrate improvement targets into the school development plan through focused action planning.

5 **How successful have we been?** This requires the school to take action to implement the action plan and to monitor and evaluate the impact of the action against the success criteria.

In essence this will be a familiar cycle to most schools and not unlike the school development planning cycle – or even the action research cycle – which they may have been working with for some years. The difference lies in its very specific focus on raising attainments in terms of test and examination results in line with national benchmarks. Schools need to realise, however, that this national agenda does not preclude them from setting other goals and targets as well. This will be important if they regard education as having wider functions, such as promoting human flourishing and participatory citizenship.

■ Target setting requirements

The initial proposals from government indicate that regulations are likely to require schools to set targets in the following terms:

- a single target to be set for each of the three core subjects at the end of each key stage;
- these targets to be measured by National Curriculum tests in English, mathematics and science at age fourteen and GCSE examination results or equivalent at age sixteen;
- at the end of Key Stage 3, targets to be expressed, subject by subject, in terms of the proportions of students reaching Level 5 and above;
- at Key Stage 4, targets to be expressed in terms of the proportion of students achieving a grade C or better in GCSE English, mathematics and science (either single or double award, or in an individual science subject);
- an additional indicator, at Key Stage 4, is likely to be the proportion of students attaining a number of A*–C and A*–G grades in GCSE.

It is also proposed that schools and LEAs should agree targets covering a three-year period. This will involve reviewing results of the previous year in the autumn term and setting targets for the following academic year by January. This will allow five terms to achieve them. On a rolling three-year cycle, this will involve schools in reviewing their performance against the previous year's targets, reviewing targets already set for the current year and setting new targets for the following year. The government's 1997 consultation paper on target setting presents this in the form of a diagram which is reproduced below.

Timetable for the introduction of school target setting

Autumn term 1998	Autumn term 1999	Autumn term 2000
Review 1998 results	Review 1999 results	Review 2000 results
Review targets for 1999*	Review targets for 2000	Review targets for 2001
Set targets for 2000	Set targets for 2001	Set targets for 2002

* where schools have taken part in the pilot year

Schools will be expected to publish their targets in their governing body's annual report, and possibly also in their prospectus. Thus in June each year they would be required to publish both the results of the previous year and the targets for that year and the next. They would also produce contextual information that will help parents to make sense of these data, such as numbers of students on the special educational needs register. It has long been argued that it is impossible to say anything meaningful about trends based on one year's results. Therefore, government is also consulting on the possibility of requiring schools to report results for the previous three years to illustrate trends to set alongside targets.

■ Benchmarks

In order to set appropriate targets, government, through QCA, now publishes benchmarking information. This is intended to enable schools to evaluate their own standard of performance by measuring it against standards achieved by other schools with broadly similar characteristics. Benchmark data do not set targets but, by showing what the best schools with similar intake characteristics achieve, benchmarks are expected to set challenges for less successful schools.

Although there are strong arguments for grouping schools according to a variety of background factors such as those used in multi-level modelling, which takes account of student-level, school-level and ward-level factors, the government has opted for a benchmarking system based on existing national data sets such as the Schools Census (Form 7). This avoids the expense of additional data collection but may render the groupings somewhat problematic. Secondary schools are grouped on the basis of prior attainment (as measured by national test results), gender balance, the proportion of students taking free school meals (a very rough measure of socio-economic status) and whether the school selects by ability.

Although all schools will be placed in a group for the purposes of drawing up the benchmarks, they will not be told which group they belong to. Thus, when they receive the benchmark information from QCA they have to decide themselves which group best represents their characteristics. They will be helped to do this by flow charts which ask just two questions: Is the school selective? What percentage of students in the school take free school meals? According to their answers, schools will then be directed to one of eight benchmark tables.

Benchmark tables, to be published annually, indicate the range of performance found within each group. Performance is represented according to the proportion of students achieving Level 5 and above at Key Stage 3, and the proportion of students achieving five or more A*–C grades, five or more A*–G grades, and one or more A*–G grades at Key Stage 4.

Information is presented in tables giving the standards achieved by schools at the mid-point (the median), the 25th percentile (the lower quartile), the 75th percentile (the upper quartile) and the 95th percentile (the top 5 per cent). The upper quartile figures will therefore be the benchmark for the whole group – what they should aim for. The standard of the top 5 per cent of schools will be the benchmark for those already achieving the standard of the upper quartile.

Given this level of guidance it is hard to resist the inference that schools will in reality have very little freedom to vary their targets from the benchmarks. Some schools will undoubtedly feel that QCA should 'go the whole hog' and just tell them what their targets should be! However, the consultation paper makes the important point that:

> Many LEAs and schools have access to more data than the national benchmark information can provide. Some LEAs and schools might therefore wish to carry out their own benchmarking exercise, using factors available locally but not nationally.

From February 1998 schools also have access to more detailed information via OFSTED's Performance and Assessment reports (Pandas). These are constructed on the basis of school inspection data and show how schools compare with others in similar circumstances. Pandas include more details on the background factors, taken from electoral ward statistics, such as the number of children in overcrowded households, single parent families and the proportion of adults in higher education.

Procedures for setting targets

The government's 1997 White Paper *Excellence in Schools* made it clear that setting school targets was the responsibility of each school's governing body, working with the senior management team. However, targets will need to be agreed with the LEA. The White Paper sets out how the government, LEAs and schools are expected to work together. The relevant section of the Paper (Chapter 3 paragraph 13) also provides a sequence of events:

- The government sets national targets and publishes national performance and benchmark data.
- Each LEA provides benchmarking data and guidance to all its schools to help them set targets.
- Each school sets draft targets, taking account of the comparative data and their own previous best performance, for discussion with its LEA.
- Schools and LEAs agree targets, covering a three-year period and subject to annual review.
- Where, exceptionally, an LEA cannot reach agreement with a school on its targets, the LEA may invoke the early warning system.
- The individual school targets are included within each LEA's Education Development Plan.
- The DfEE and OFSTED monitor and contribute to the process to ensure targets are high and ambitious enough.

This process will be a major innovation at all levels of the education service and schools in particular will need support and training. It is proposed therefore that monitoring and target setting should become an integral part of the activities supported through the Grants for Education

Support and Training (GEST) for school effectiveness, with an additional amount allocated to LEAs for pump-priming.

From the 'What' to the 'How'

It is one thing to set targets for school improvement; it is quite another to put in place the kinds of processes that will lead to their achievement. The danger is that, having expended a great deal of the available human and material resource on analysing data and setting targets, schools will have very little time or energy left for actually doing anything about improvement, although this is of paramount importance.

There is also another danger, of which schools need to be aware, that targets framed in terms of specific kinds and proportions of test and GCSE passes may skew their improvement efforts in inequitable ways. In a paper on *Literacy, Numeracy and Economic Performance,* produced for the Centre for Economic Performance in September 1997, Peter Robinson points out that current and proposed targets could be reached without doing anything for the bottom ten to fifteen per cent of the attainment range. By emphasising proportions of passes at higher grade levels, targets focus on raising attainment at the top and middle of the range. He argues that, 'Schools need to be given incentives through the setting of National Targets which oblige them to focus on the lower end of the attainment range' because this is the group for whom lower levels of education are 'associated with a significantly higher risk of unemployment'.

Bearing this in mind, schools should exercise caution in putting all their resources into the familiar tactic of mentoring potential grade D GCSE candidates (or even going to the expense of having all grade D passes re-marked in the hope that some will be upgraded!). This is dubious practice if it leads to the neglect of those towards the top or bottom end of the range. The political pressures to concentrate on the 'borderliners' are, however, likely to be as strong under the new target setting arrangements as they have been since the first publication of league tables of raw results.

Presumably the research on school self-evaluation which has been commissioned by SCAA/QCA will reveal examples of a wider range of strategies adopted by schools. There is already some evidence of strategies used by schools to improve progress towards national targets in an evaluation for NACETT carried out by Ian Schagen and Penelope Weston at the NFER[5]. The evaluation team made visits to nine

---

[5] Schagen, I. and Weston, P. with Hewitt, D. and Sims, D. (1997) *Hitting the Targets: evaluation of progress towards foundation targets 1 and 3 by English region.* Slough: NFER.

secondary schools and interviewed a range of staff in each, including senior and middle managers. In a number of these there was a 'raising attainment programme' of some sort. Most of these focused in some way on changing the culture of the school to one that celebrated achievement.

Specific strategies used included the following. I have extracted them from the report and grouped them loosely into two categories.

Strategies directly involving students and classroom processes

- introducing new commendation and certificate systems to reward achievement and increase motivation and self-esteem;
- introducing academic mentoring for borderline C/D GCSE candidates;
- reducing the number of GCSE subjects taken per student to encourage quality instead of quantity in performance;
- introducing paired reading or literacy tutoring schemes (older with younger students) to improve reading and writing skills;
- adopting a 'Pacific Rim' approach by assuming that all can succeed if they are prepared to make great efforts;
- instituting a 'cardinal rule' that students should not interfere with the learning of others;
- giving special attention to the least motivated groups (of boys especially) by introducing a ten-hour weekly homework contract in Year 11;
- introducing one-to-one review on a regular basis;
- providing a two-day residential, run by teachers and employers, for potential Year 11 under-achievers with the aim of improving motivation through a series of challenges;
- providing students with templates to help them structure their written work;
- providing an enrichment programme of generic skills, especially study skills, group work and exam technique;
- target setting for effort and attainment with individual students followed up with one-to-one review with allocated tutors.

Strategies focused on management and staff development:

- making staff take responsibility for student performance and emphasising this in staff appraisal and training;
- introducing programmes of action research on specific areas such as language development;
- recruiting outstanding teachers;
- creating various types of 'alert' systems;
- providing training for teachers in how to structure lessons more effectively;
- providing INSET to help teachers identify and utilise different teaching and learning styles;
- providing training and support to teachers to encourage peer observation of lessons, generally, and the different ways that boys and girls learn, in particular;
- OFSTED-style reviews of teaching and learning methods in departments, carried out by senior managers.

Interestingly, formative assessment integrated into teaching, which I have advocated at various points throughout this book, was hardly mentioned in the NFER report, except obliquely. However, the one example where improvement as a result of a particular initiative is actually quantified includes a description of a strategy with a strong element of formative assessment.

> Five years ago, the new head of science in an 11–16 school assembled a new team of five staff and introduced a modular GCSE (Salters' science) with a strong practical focus. Students are expected to make presentations and prepare visual displays which reinforce learning. There is a key words policy to enhance scientific vocabulary and concepts. Year 9 and 11 students go through a revision programme, in addition to the feedback after each module. Underachievement is spotted and support offered. Over the last seven years the 5+ A*–C attainment in science has increased from 38 per cent to 50 per cent.

This example perhaps serves to illustrate that schools and departments which improve their assessment *results* are those that have developed assessment *processes* to serve truly diagnostic and developmental functions. This, I have argued, is an essential part of all good teaching.

Further reading

There are now many books available on school effectiveness and school improvement. The two I give here are from perhaps the best known 'stables' of monitoring and school effectiveness research: *Monitoring Education: indicators, quality and effectiveness* by Carol Taylor Fitz-Gibbon, published by Cassell in 1996; and *Forging Links: effective schools and effective departments*, by Pam Sammons, Sally Thomas and Peter Mortimore, published in 1997 by Paul Chapman Publishing. Both give some attention to performance at department level as well as whole school level, which makes them of special interest to secondary schools.

ACTIVITIES

1 Value-added analysis of school assessment data

This activity will need to be carried out by the school assessment co-ordinator or working group but the help of someone with skills in IT and simple statistics may need to be co-opted.

(i) Take two sets of data for a given cohort, perhaps last year's GCSE cohort or last year's Year 9. One set of data should be output measures such as GCSE results; the other should be input data such as prior attainment on national tests or standardised tests such as CATs. If necessary, convert scores into a single statistic such as average GCSE score.

(ii) Enter them into a computer statistics package and create a scattergram and regression line for the whole cohort. Software such as *Excel, Lotus* and *SPSS* will do this.

(iii) Then disaggregate the cohort and create separate scattergrams for sub-groups according to subject, gender, ethnicity, social class, special educational needs or any other dimension that you think might be important.

(iv) Plot the whole cohort's regression line on each scattergram and interpret the patterns. Are there some groups that are achieving consistently above or below average? Is there anything that outliers share in common? How might these patterns be explained and what kind of evidence would you need to collect to be sure?

(v) These findings could then be discussed with staff as a whole group, or individually, or by department, as appropriate, with a view to identifying targets and strategies for improvement at several levels: whole school, department, class and student.

2 Deciding strategies for improvement

This activity should be a whole school activity, perhaps the focus of a professional development session, but discussion could be in sub-groups, such as departments, before preferences for action are brought to a whole staff meeting.

(i) Take the list of strategies identified from the NFER report and listed in the last section of this chapter (pages 258–9). Add any further strategies that are known at the time (take account of QCA guidance if available) or those that staff have suggested. Type each one on to a card and leave some blank cards for further suggestions.

(ii) In groups (probably departments plus the senior management team) ask staff to carry out a diamond ranking exercise. Start by going through the whole pack of cards and select nine that each group wishes to consider seriously. Then split each group into sub-groups of three or four, or pairs, and ask them to rank the strategies on the cards in order of preference, with 1 × 1st choice, 2 × 2nd choices, 3 × 3rd choices, 2 × 4th choices, and 1 × 5th choice. These can be laid out in the following way:

$$
\begin{array}{c}
1 \\
2 \quad 2 \\
3 \quad 3 \quad 3 \\
4 \quad 4 \\
5
\end{array}
$$

Next ask the small groups to show their choices to the other sub-groups and to explain the reasons for their rank order. They should revise their rank order in the light of discussion with others. Ideally, each department, should come up with a single selection of strategies in an agreed rank order.

(iii) The diamond rankings of departments and the SMT can then be taken to a whole staff meeting and discussed in a similar way. It will be important to consider whether certain strategies need to be implemented across the school as a whole, or whether a certain amount of flexibility should be allowed within and across departments. The principal consideration should be that whatever strategies are chosen, they fit with the aims and principles of whole school policy.

Index

accountability 24, 25, 67, 95, 107, 167, 212, 213
accreditation 165
Accreditation of Prior Learning (APL) 80
achievement tests 126–8, 129
action plans, action planning 11, 13, 83, 191, 216, 228, 253
age equivalent scores 136, 142
aggregation 131, 232, 234, 240
A–level, AS–level 76, 77, 81, 111, 143, 145, 146, 148, 192, 201, 202, 203, 204, 219, 237
appeals (procedure) 164
aptitude tests 128–9, 208
aspects of achievement 119
assessment tasks 86, 106, 123, 142, 155, 168, 172, 177, 182, 215, 217
attainment target 11, 52, 55, 56, 74, 79, 113, 115, 123, 124, 174, 187, 215
audio-recording 90, 104, 105
authentic assessment 115–18, 122, 135, 208

'backwash effect' 156, 162
bank of assessment tasks 211
baseline date 12, 153, 240, 242
benchmarks 236, 237, 243, 252, 253, 254–6

Capey Report 1996 80, 81, 84
certification 24, 25, 27, 78, 143, 258
'clean slate' approach 51
cognitive ability tests 129–32, 137, 153
comments 11, 61, 95, 96, 98, 100, 101, 102, 107, 113, 190, 212, 214, 215, 219, 221
comment banks 220–1, 230, 232, 234
comparison of students 8, 15, 60, 61, 64, 109, 133, 135, 142, 146, 217, 218, 224, 246
competence 80, 81, 84, 114, 116, 147, 148
consistency of judgements/standards 11, 15, 35, 39, 59, 62, 91, 123, 145, 157, 162–7, 176, 188, 190, 232
continuous assessment 15, 57, 80, 107
co-ordinator(s) 20, 21, 33, 38, 40, 41, 42, 49, 58, 63, 64, 65, 68, 84, 85, 104, 105, 114, 150, 210, 231, 233, 260
coursework 75, 79, 115, 142, 163, 176, 203
criterion-referencing 34, 84, 126, 128, 142, 143, 145, 146–49, 172, 184, 185, 187

Dearing Review of the National Curriculum and Assessment 1993 59, 70–1
Dearing Review of 16–19 qualifications 1996 71, 76, 77
departments 10, 22, 33, 38, 55, 57, 58, 59, 60, 63, 85, 101, 104, 123, 168, 190, 233, 237, 245, 260, 261
departmental guidelines 38–9, 41, 42
diagnosis 15, 25, 26, 27, 29, 33, 65, 142, 171, 184, 186, 190, 214, 232, 252, 259
diagnostic tests 58, 127, 171, 234
differentiation 118, 208, 241

disaggregation 247, 260
discrimination 127, 152, 203

educational change 17, 18–19
end-of-key-stage descriptions/
  statements 58, 61
entry patterns 201–2, 211
equal opportunities 32, 196, 200–9
essay tests 111–13
ethnicity 206–9, 211, 241, 247, 250, 260
evidence 14, 22, 27, 32, 34, 37, 41, 44, 56, 66, 67, 75, 79, 81, 83, 87, 89, 90, 91–3, 104, 107, 118, 122, 169, 185–6, 187, 188, 199, 210, 214, 215, 216, 217, 221, 230, 244
examination(s) 75, 78, 79, 86, 107–8, 126, 142–6, 153, 155, 163, 168, 201, 209, 219, 236, 238, 246, 252
exemplars 11, 15, 79, 100, 112, 124, 165, 166, 167, 169–70, 172, 174, 176, 189, 190
Exemplification of Standards material 58, 67, 165, 187, 190
Exhibitions 120–1

feedback 22, 25, 54, 67, 95–100, 107, 161, 172, 173, 180, 185, 259
fitness for purpose 24, 76, 85, 106, 109, 151, 213
formative assessment 11, 12, 15, 24, 26, 27, 28, 29, 55, 67, 96, 101, 102, 107, 128, 171–85, 186–9, 200, 215, 217, 220, 227, 231
form tutor 225, 226

GCSE 8, 11, 43, 54, 58, 61, 67, 74, 76, 79, 113, 118, 131, 143, 145, 148, 163, 176, 192, 201, 202, 220, 237, 245, 249, 250, 253, 255, 257, 258, 259
gender 200–6, 209, 211, 241, 247, 250, 260
GNVQ 8, 43, 74, 75, 76, 77, 79, 81, 84, 143, 146–9, 176, 190, 192, 215, 237
grades/grading 5, 6, 7, 8, 11, 23, 25, 27, 35, 38, 75, 78, 95, 96, 97, 98, 100–2, 107, 113, 143, 145, 173, 202, 203, 212, 214, 218, 219, 223, 224, 246, 255

indicator systems 244
Individual Education Plans (IEPs) 15, 65, 127, 142, 213, 226–7, 233
inference(s) 87, 89, 91, 92, 94, 104, 155, 171
information technology 230–3
intelligence tests 130, 199, 206
interim reports 65, 219
International Baccalaureate (IB) 77
ipsative/self-referenced assessment 126, 184

judgements 26, 33, 34, 41, 43, 57, 66–7, 87, 88, 89, 92, 108, 122, 148, 186, 187, 189, 214, 215, 218, 220, 221, 224

key skills 79, 81, 114, 183, 192, 228, 229, 230, 237
Key Stage 2 48, 49, 51–2, 72, 242
Key Stage 3 11, 44, 48, 49, 54, 57, 61, 63, 67, 72–6, 106, 108, 116, 161, 176, 187, 219, 242, 253, 255
Key Stage 4 11, 48, 70, 76–80, 83, 253

learned helplessness 97
learning theories 179–83
level descriptions 30, 55, 56–8, 101, 108, 172, 187, 188, 190

marks/marking 5, 6, 7, 10, 14, 15, 22, 35, 54, 55, 67, 78, 79, 86, 94–102, 112, 168, 173, 176, 204, 205, 215
marker bias 204–5, 211
mark books 102, 214, 215, 223
measurement 55, 238, 240
meta-cognition, meta-cognitive skills 112, 121, 173, 176–7, 205
moderation 11, 15, 30, 75, 79, 80, 94, 162–70
modes of assessment 203–5, 211
monitoring 15, 17, 20, 25, 27, 52, 65, 127, 131, 132, 205, 246, 253, 256, 260

multi-level modelling 255
multiple-choice 109, 110–11, 113, 203, 205
multiple intelligences 130

National Curriculum assessment 2, 10, 12, 13, 26, 29, 30, 43, 44, 51, 54–6, 60, 61, 62, 68, 106, 148, 149, 154, 156, 162, 164, 166, 167, 180, 242
national data collection 58, 60, 62
National Record of Achievement 8, 15, 66, 73, 83, 200, 212, 213, 227–30, 233
national tests 29, 54, 116, 161, 219, 221, 242, 252, 260
'next steps' in teaching and learning 26, 27, 49, 105, 171, 182, 189, 236
non-statutory guidance 47, 59
normal distribution 5, 8, 98, 132, 137, 138, 143
norming 126, 134, 135, 150
norm-referencing 11, 125, 126, 132–3, 142, 143, 145, 146, 149, 184
NVQs 8, 43, 79, 84, 90, 146–9, 164, 165, 180, 215, 237

observation schedules 90, 104
OFSTED inspections 2, 3, 8, 10, 12, 13, 17, 21, 30, 38, 49, 145, 201, 205, 206, 226, 252, 259
optical mark reader (OMR) 232, 234
optional tests and tasks 59, 63, 116, 123, 217

Pandas 256
parents' consultation meetings 15, 223–6
peer assessment 94, 173, 176–7, 191, 200, 214
pencil-and-paper tests 109, 111, 154
percentile ranks 125, 136, 137, 142
performance indicators 238–44
performance tables 25, 237, 241, 245
policy document 3, 10, 17, 38
portfolios 11, 12, 15, 44, 52, 78, 81, 108, 138, 143, 164, 165, 166, 169–70, 176, 190, 223, 224
praise 97, 180
prediction 24, 128, 131, 152, 153, 220, 246
prior attainment 240, 241, 242, 246, 249, 250, 251, 255, 260
PROFIL 66, 83, 229–30, 233
progress/progression 10, 11, 37, 48, 49, 50–1, 60, 66, 72, 81–2, 83, 87, 90, 99, 102, 104, 107, 126, 184, 185, 186, 188, 202, 217, 221, 222, 227, 232, 234, 239, 249
psychometric tests 132, 155, 171
publication of results 15, 62, 143, 240, 254, 257
punishments 97

rating scale 91
recording systems 8, 14, 16, 44, 65, 90, 102, 187, 210, 215, 232
records of achievement 8, 11, 12, 165, 174, 178–9, 196, 197, 198, 199, 200, 212, 214, 220, 222, 225, 230, 231, 232, 234
reflective practitioner 88, 103, 183
regression analysis 245–51, 260
reliability 114, 134, 135, 138, 147, 151, 157–9, 185, 186, 242
reports to parents 12, 15, 22, 52, 60–2, 64, 65–6, 183, 200, 212, 213, 218, 219–26, 230, 232, 233, 234
response mode/style 112, 204, 211
reviews/reviewing 107, 108, 122, 187, 215, 217–8, 222, 227, 228, 229, 231, 234, 254, 258, 259
rewards 97, 180, 258

sample/sampling 79, 80, 89, 102, 110, 133
school development plan/programme 190, 253
school effectiveness research 238, 240, 243, 244, 260
school prospectus 31, 254
Scottish Highers 78

Index

selection 25, 27, 68, 143, 153
self-assessment 11, 15, 173–9, 189, 191, 200, 214
self concept 97
self-esteem 97, 99–100, 107, 177, 191, 232, 258
SEN Code of Practice 8, 65, 226
sizing up 87
social class/socio-economic status 206–9, 211, 241, 246, 247, 251, 255, 260
staff/professional development 3, 19, 20, 32, 69, 104, 166, 178, 183, 209, 210, 228, 259
standard age scores 131, 135–6, 137
standard deviation 98
standardisation 78, 79, 131, 168, 224
standardised tests 28, 29, 85, 86, 115, 126–42, 149, 152, 163, 171, 240, 245, 260
standards 11, 16, 50–1, 55, 61, 74, 75, 96, 98, 99, 105, 107, 112, 124, 146, 148, 157, 166, 168, 169, 172, 173, 174, 176, 178, 220, 224
stanines 136, 137
statutory/legal requirements 43, 45, 47, 51, 54–68
summative assessment 26, 27, 28, 30, 34, 55, 67, 96, 107, 108, 114, 122, 123, 143, 183–4, 186–8, 215, 217
syllabus 74, 75, 78, 112, 125, 145, 204

target 81, 123, 200, 215, 216, 222, 224, 229, 239

target setting 15, 24, 25, 34, 37, 90, 214, 228, 230, 236, 249, 252–7, 258
teacher assessment (TA) 29, 30, 44, 52, 53, 54, 56–62, 64, 73, 74, 116, 126, 157, 163, 164, 165, 172
test-wise 110
tiered papers 54, 63, 118, 202, 204, 205, 211
TGAT 26, 29, 154, 167
transfer/transition 15, 25, 48–57, 72–3, 83
triangulation 94

validity 51, 56, 59, 76, 86, 106, 110, 113–14, 116, 126, 127, 131, 132, 135, 138, 143, 147, 150, 151–7, 158–62, 168, 171, 185, 186, 192, 242
value-added analysis 12, 28, 127, 239, 240, 241, 242, 243, 244, 245, 246–9, 252
verifiers/verification 78, 80, 81, 147, 164, 165
video-recording 90, 104

whole child/person 32
working group(s) 12, 17, 20, 21, 38, 41, 42, 46, 105, 150, 198, 210, 233, 260
written policies 7, 16, 28, 38, 42